A "Christian America" Restored

A Christian America Restored

The Rise of the Evangelical Christian School
Movement in America, 1920–1952

Robert Glenn Slater

PICKWICK *Publications* · Eugene, Oregon

A CHRISTIAN AMERICA RESTORED
The Rise of the Evangelical Christian School Movement in America, 1920–1952

Pickwick Publications
An Imprint of Wipf and Stock Publishers
199 W. 8th Ave., Suite 3
Eugene, OR 97401

www.wipfandstock.com

PAPERBACK ISBN: 978-1-5326-3377-5
HARDCOVER ISBN: 978-1-5326-3379-9
EBOOK ISBN: 978-1-5326-3378-2

Cataloguing-in-Publication data:

Names: Slater, Robert Glenn, author.

Title: A Christian America restored : the rise of the Evangelical Christian School Movement in America, 1920–1952 / by Robert Glenn Slater.

Description: Eugene, OR: Pickwick Publications, 2019 | Includes bibliographical references.

Identifiers: ISBN 978-1-5326-3377-5 (paperback) | ISBN 978-1-5326-3379-9 (hardcover) | ISBN 978-1-5326-3378-2 (ebook)

Subjects: LCSH: Christian education—United States. | Church schools—United States—History.

Classification: LCC LC621 S5 2019 (print) | LCC LC621 (ebook)

Manufactured in the U.S.A.   08/21/19

Contents

Acknowledgments

Dietrich Bonhoeffer wrote from prison, "In normal life we hardly realize how much more we receive than we give, and life cannot be rich without such gratitude. It is so easy to overestimate the importance of our own achievements compared with what we owe to the help of others." Echoing Bonhoeffer's words, I want to express my sincere gratitude to so many individuals who have helped me in this work that began as my doctoral dissertation for the University of Tennessee.

First, let my express my gratitude to Ernest Freeberg, my advisor, counselor, and friend over the creation of this work. He worked with me tirelessly and held me to a high standard while always encouraging me to never give up. My respect for him as a scholar and teacher is immense. I considered it a real honor to work with Dr. Freeberg and will be eternally appreciative of his constructive criticism, time, and patience.

In addition, individuals such as Lynn Sacco, Kurt Piehler, and Barbara Thayer-Bacon each provided their own input into this work serving as members of my dissertation committee at the University of Tennessee. During the writing of this work, my employer, Maryville Christian School is to be thanked for giving me so much flexibility in undertaking such a task.

Finally, this book is dedicated to "my girls," my wife Gail Slater and daughter Kate. Both of them have shown unwavering support of my work as I went through four college degrees and this particular work. They remain my greatest supporters and critics who bolster my academic study relentlessly. My love for them is beyond words.

Introduction

In 1946, the National Association of Evangelicals held its fourth annual convention in Minneapolis, Minnesota. In the aftermath of World War II, this association of conservative Protestants met to discuss issues facing their Christian faith and the nation. The President of the Association, Bishop Leslie R. Marston, opened the convention with a message entitled, "Evangelical Christianity in a Pagan Age." At a time when many Americans felt a sense of relief and jubilation with the end of the war, Bishop Marston bemoaned the sad state of American society, claiming it had surrendered to paganism.[1] He noted several areas of concern, including education. Specifically, Marston decried "modern education which made the child and his immediate desires the center of the universe." He also cited examples of public high schools portraying great American heroes in a negative light and their propagation of Freudian psychology. Marston concluded his bleak feelings about education by stating, "These instances, admittedly extreme, nevertheless indicate the direction of powerful currents in modern education which seek to swerve youth from the charted channel of Christian virtues into the whirlpool of paganism."[2]

A few days later, Stephen W. Paine of Houghton College submitted a report from a subcommittee of the convention, the Commission on Christian Educational Institutions. Departing from reports of prior years which focused almost exclusively on the need for Christian values in higher education, Paine stated, "Believing that the field of distinctively Christian training at the elementary and secondary level has been comparatively neglected and yet is of vital importance to the future of evangelicalism, we recommend

1. Marston, "Evangelical Christianity," 20.
2. Marston, "Evangelical Christianity," 22.

1

that time be given in the 1947 annual meeting of the N.A.E. for a public presentation of the merits of this area of evangelical education."[3]

Mark Fakkema and Frank Gaebelein, already significant figures in the world of Christian education, worked alongside Paine on this commission. At that time Fakkema served with the National Union of Christian Schools and Gaebelein held the position of headmaster of the Stony Brook School of New York.[4] Over the next few years, these two men would take their places as leaders of a small association of Christian schools which, by the end of the century, emerged as an important component of the religious right and the nation's private educational system.

A year later, in April 1947, Mark Fakkema arrived at the next meeting of the National Association of Evangelicals to suggest sponsorship of a national organization that would consolidate the many Christian schools that already existed. This proposal, entitled, "The Christian Day School, Its Place in Our Christian Program," not only sought to define Christian Day schools, but also made an urgent plea to the evangelical leaders present for their support of these institutions. Fakkema made many bold statements that revealed his uncompromising attitude toward Christian education. He made it clear that Christian schools should not be confused with Sunday school, Vacation Bible School, or released-time instruction. Fakkema acknowledged the worth of these programs but also explained that, "they imply a minor Christian educational influence that can never make right the major anti-Christian influence of the average public school of today." He concluded that the nation needed Christian day schools to be a substitute for the public school system.[5] The general assembly of the National Association of Evangelicals (NAE) enthusiastically approved this proposal establishing the National Association of Christian Schools (NACS). As the fifth annual NAE convention drew to a close in Omaha, the Resolutions Committee made a specific resolution stating, "We recommend that this convention go on record as favoring all movements which seek to bring the impact of Christian teaching to bear upon our national life."[6]

Although not even noticed by the larger educational community, for the first time, a nationwide non-sectarian Protestant Christian school organization had been founded. Specific numbers do not exist, but historian James Carper has speculated that between 1920 and 1960 some 150 of these

---

3. Paine, "Report of the Commission," 56.

4. Paine, "Report of the Commission," 57.

5. Fakkema, "Christian Day School," 36–37.

6. "Report of the Resolutions Committee," 12.

schools were established.[7] At the time of the establishment of the NACS, approximately 11.5 percent of all American students attended non-public schools.[8] Government statistics in the 1947–48 school year note that of that 11.5 percent, 81 percent of these nonpublic schools possessed a religious affiliation dominated almost exclusively by Roman Catholic institutions.[9] Hence, at its inception, the NACS schools appeared numerically insignificant when compared to the public schools and the major non-public school groups such as the Catholic, Episcopal, or Seventh Day Adventists.

Despite this very inauspicious beginning, today's Protestant Christian schools have bloomed into a worldwide movement and the fastest growing element of America's private educational institutions. Statistics reveal that these Protestant Christian schools have arisen during the last century to become a significant component of America's private school sector. While the U. S. educational establishment has struggled for most of the twentieth century with such issues as funding, test scores, competing in a global market, school shootings, teacher retention, and religious issues such as school prayer, a multitude of private Christian schools have quietly popped up all over the landscape. This segment of private education has grown very fast, with thousands of these schools being established since the 1960s.[10] In the 1980s, Christian school advocates claimed that the establishment of these schools stood at a rate of two per day.[11] Today's largest Christian school organization, the Association of Christian Schools International, currently boasts having twenty-two thousand schools worldwide serving approximately 2.5 million students.[12] In 2015, Catholic schools remained the largest private school segment in America at 38.8 percent, but that number has dropped from 54.5 percent in 1989. At the same time, Christian schools have gone from 10.9 percent of the private school population in 1989 to 13.5 percent in 2015.[13] Clearly, America's Christian school movement is no longer just a small contingent of tiny classrooms working out of church basements.

The term "Christian school" needs an appropriate definition before continuing. Generally speaking, it could be argued that most schools in early America possessed a predominant Christian orientation. For most of the

7. Carper, "Christian Day School," 111.

8. National Association of Christian Schools, "Evangelical Christian School Movement," 4.

9. "Statistics on Non-public Secondary Schools," 3.

10. Provenzo, *Religious Fundamentalism*, 81.

11. Carper, "Christian Day School," 111.

12. Simmons, *Worth It*, xii.

13. Council for American Private Education, "Private School Statistics," 1.

nineteenth and some of the twentieth century, America's public schools allowed the teaching of non-sectarian Christian principles that included studies
of the Bible. In addition, sectarian schools such as those run by Catholics,
Lutherans, and Seventh Day Adventists also claim to be "Christian" schools.
So, for clarity, the Christian schools discussed in this work refer specifically to
private, non-denominational Protestant schools formed primarily by conservative evangelical Christians in the mid-twentieth century.

Historian James Carper goes further in this definition by pointing out
the great deal of diversity that exists today among these schools. Some of
them contain no specific affiliation with a church in their respective community and hence can be classified as independent. Others enjoy direct
connections with a specific church which provides subsidies and facilities.
Speaking of facilities, today's Christian schools range from modern multi-
building campuses to poorly equipped classrooms in small churches. The
average number of children in these schools stands at approximately 150
students, ranging from enrollments as low as ten pupils and as large as two
thousand. In terms of programs of study, the majority follow traditional
teaching methods while a few, for economic or pedagogic reasons, offer
only individualized self-paced courses. The schools also vary widely in their
ethnic makeup. A final characteristic centers on their relationship to the
overall educational community with some being fiercely separationist, re-
jecting any form of state regulation or licensing while others cooperate and
collaborate with state and local public education authorities.[14]

However, despite this diversity, these Protestant schools retain a common philosophy of Christian education. All of these institutions maintain
a strict profession of the centrality of Jesus Christ and the Bible in their
educational program. They strive to use a conservative Christian perspective throughout the school and integrate biblical truth into all disciplines of
study. Likewise, moral values, explicitly tied to biblical teaching, can also
be found in all these institutions.[15] Perhaps this distinction is best summed
up by Dr. Paul Keinel, the former executive director of the Association of
Christian Schools International, "Christian schools are Christian institutions where Jesus Christ and the Bible are central in the school curriculum
and in the lives of teachers and administrators. This distinction removes us
from direct competition with public schools. Although we often compare
ourselves academically, we are educational institutions operating on separate philosophical tracks. Ours is a Christ-centered education presented
in the Christian context. Theirs is man-centered within the context of the

14. Carper, "Christian Day School," 113.
15. Carper, "Christian Day School," 114.

supremacy of man as opposed to the supremacy of God."[16] Simply put, Christian education attempts to organize all instruction in ways that support the beliefs of the Christian faith, aiming to instill in all its students a Christian based worldview.

The origin of this largely unnoticed educational and religious movement is the topic of this book. Uncovering the beginnings of these schools will be analyzed from two angles. First, this study will attempt to pinpoint the origins of this movement in a particular era in the twentieth century. Second, this study will examine the reasons and impulses behind the rise of these religious organizations. Focusing on the interrelationship between time frame and causes will ultimately provide a vivid snapshot of the foundation of this movement that claims to be not only an integral part of twenty-first century American education, but also an overlooked, critical component of the contemporary religious right in the United States.

Several historians and sociologists have sought to identify the historical beginnings of this educational movement. David Nevin and Robert Bills, who authored *The Schools That Fear Built: Segregationist Academies in the South,* focused on the racial aspects of these so-called "Christian schools" that arose in the deep South as a result of school integration.[17] Nevin and Bills imply that Christian schools emerged from racial issues in the 1960s, and give no consideration to the possibility that such schools existed prior to this time. Others, such as James Carper, have focused more on the explosive growth of the movement in the 1960s–1980s while giving only scant attention to its exact period of birth. The most definitive study of America's private schools, Otto Kraushaar's, *American Non-Public Schools: Patterns of Diversity,* written in 1972, provides more information on the history of why private schools have been established, but only briefly mentions Christian schools, probably due to their extremely small numbers at the time.[18] James Reed and Ronnie Prevost discuss the origins of Christian education in America from a philosophical standpoint focusing specifically on the Puritans of early America all the way to the reaction of Christians to the liberal thought of John Dewey in the twentieth century. However, specific mention of the efforts of conservative Christians to start their own schools during this era does not appear.[19]

Scholars within the Christian school movement have also attempted to discover the historical beginnings of these institutions. Paul Keinel, who

16. Keinel, "Forces Behind the Christian School," 1.

17. Nevin and Bills, *Schools That Fear Built.*

18. Kraushaar, *American Non-Public Schools,* 36.

19. Reed and Prevost, *History of Christian Education.*

served as the executive director of the Association of Christian Schools International from 1985 to 1999, wrote *A History of Christian Education*. Keinel sees Christian education as having deep roots going back to the early Christian church of the Roman Empire. He traces this theme up through the Medieval Age all the way up to the Puritans in colonial America.[20] Curiously, his work stops there and does not address the Christian schools in the twentieth century. Keinel draws broad conclusions, arguing for the presence of Christian schools as a continuation of a long history of religious schooling in America. However, Keinel neglects to explicitly explain the twentieth-century phenomenon of Protestant Christian Schools. Kenneth O. Gangel and Warren S. Benson, who have both authored numerous books on Christian education, collaborated on *Christian Education: Its History and Philosophy*. In a similar fashion to Keinel, they spend much time trying to highlight the ancient and medieval roots of Christian education. They focus much more time on the nineteenth-century Industrial Revolution and its impact upon education in America. The authors also examine Horace Mann in detail as someone who attempted to instill some semblance of Christian values into the newly formed "common schools." These historians from within the movement provide a great deal of information about this institution from the long range view, but, like Keinel, fail to discuss in depth the actual beginnings of these schools in the twentieth century.

Two unpublished dissertations, written on the 1947 founding of the National Association of Christian Schools, provide more specifics. "A History of the National Association of Christian Schools During the Period of 1947–1972" written in 1972 by Warren Sten Benson and "The Development of the National Association of Christian Schools" written in 1955 by Frances Simpson both relate details of how the movement began on a national level. Simpson's work even contains interviews of some of the key leaders in the 1940s. Both dissertations provide important details about the beginning of the national organization, however neither really seeks to address the issues going on in the nation and from within the Christian community that prompted the push for these schools in this particular era.

The second component of this work on Christian schools involves the more complex question as to the reasons why these institutions emerged. On the surface, many today might see these schools as being based upon reactionary fears of religious extremists. Much evidence does indeed point to many events over several decades in the nineteenth and early twentieth centuries that pushed conservative Protestant Christians to abandon their support for public education and to start their own schools. Historians,

20. Keinel, *History of Christian Education*.

educators, and sociologists frequently commented on this phenomenon during the 1970s and 80s at a time when Christian school enrollments mushroomed. In 1987 Paul Parsons conducted a study of Christian schools in thirty states and concluded that these schools arose from the desire of Christian parents to flee the "pagan" public school system. At the same time, Parsons also surmised that Christian schools reflected the commitment of evangelical parents to train their young in their own way and thereby create a grassroots movement capable of resisting the secularizing trend of American society.[21] Kraushaar, in his earlier mentioned work on private schools, explained the rise of private religious schools in the twentieth century in this way, "The newly emerging evangelical Protestant sects, brimming with renewed vigor and holy vitality, charged that the watered down religion purveyed by the public school was 'godless.' And so, the unsolvable issue of religion in the public schools became an added incentive for Protestants, Catholics, and later, for Jews to build their own schools in which the true faith could be transmitted."[22] Susan Rose produced an in-depth study of two specific Christian schools in the 1980s and also noted the reaction against rising secularism. In addition, she pointed to a very complicated set of dynamics at work in the establishment of Christian schools which included "a backlash against feminism, social protest movements, fears of disintegration of the family and the increasingly hard world of economic uncertainty."[23] Neal Devins makes a stronger statement by using the word "rebellion" in describing the Christian schools. He stated, "Though this movement was concentrated in the South and may have benefitted somewhat from resistance to public school integration, it was undeniably connected with a larger pattern of fundamentalist or conservative rebellion at the trends in public education."[24] The contemporary perceptions of these schools as an extremist reaction all come from the studies of the 1970s and 80s. More recently, familiar themes abound in James Carper and Thomas Hunt's chapter on Christian schools in their book *The Dissenting Tradition in American Education*. These historians describe the "dissent" of these schools as being tied to their response to "higher criticism of the Bible, Darwinism, growing cultural and religious pluralism, and the fundamentalist-modernist controversy that fractured many Protestant denominations."[25] Therefore, while the twentieth-century reactionary element of the origin of this movement will be clearly

21. Parsons, *Inside America's Christian Schools*, 24.
22. Kraushaar, *American Non-Public Schools*, 21.
23. Rose, *Keeping Them Out*, x–xi.
24. Devins, *Public Values, Private Schools*, 144.
25. Carper and Hunt, *Dissenting Tradition*, 201.

acknowledged, this study will also pursue answers from the earlier decades tied to the history of education and Christianity in America.

This book will focus on the first half of the twentieth century; in particular the three decades from 1920 to 1950. Taking into account all of the long range history of Christianity and education in America, the point will be made that a series of forces and events during these thirty years converged in 1947 with the founding of the nation's first non-sectarian Protestant Christian school organization, the National Association of Christian Schools. The civil rights movement of the 1950s and the secularization of American education in the 1960s and 70s no doubt led to an explosion of Christian schools. However, it will be argued that the actual beginning of the Christian school movement predates these years reflecting the deeper historical impulse of American Protestantism toward establishing a Christian nation going back to the Puritan ideal of establishing a "City on a Hill." In addition, this movement also illustrates the reaction of conservative Christian leaders to changes in the United States brought about by immigration, liberal theology, expanding governmental power, and secular philosophies which all threatened their power and their dreams for a nation based upon Christian values.

Chapter 1

"A Christian America"

To understand the origins and causes of the Christian school movement, it must be understood that America's schools have always carried the burden of the very high expectations, hopes, dreams, and demands of its citizenry. The American public has developed a deep faith in education over the last two centuries. The result has been that the schools have taken a greater role in society and in many cases supplanted the church and the home.[1] Nothing short of the future of the republic has been laid at the feet of our educational institutions.

Numerous examples in our history point to this fact. The founding fathers of our nation made it clear that the survival of the republic rested upon an educated citizenry. Thomas Jefferson saw public schools as key democratic institutions that could teach correct political concepts.[2] In the aftermath of the American Revolution, many leaders expressed concerns about the balance between order in the new nation and the unbounded freedom that seemed to come from principles of the struggle with Britain and thus emphasized the importance of educating citizens to be virtuous so as to exercise their freedom in a correct manner.[3]

Horace Mann's leadership of the common school movement also reflected his convictions about the critical role of education in the future of the American republic. Historian William Hayes described it this way, "Mann felt that no political structure, however artfully devised, can inherently guarantee the rights and liberties of citizens, for freedom can be secure only as knowledge is widely distributed among the populous. Hence,

1. Beggs and McQuigg, *America's Schools and Churches*, 49.
2. Mondale and Patton, *School*, 2.
3. Spring, *American School*, 48–49.

universal popular education is the only foundation on which republican government can securely rest."[4] As America became more ethnically diverse in the 1800s, the task of "Americanization" fell to the schools which meant an added responsibility to instill universal American values and the English language into the children of newly arrived immigrants. Again, the future of the nation seemed to be at stake as the schools were society's primary tool for assimilating the foreigners.[5]

In the first decades of the twentieth century, many Americans continued to be concerned about the growth of urban problems, including high crime rates and juvenile delinquency, an anxiety that was only amplified by the economic uncertainty of the 1930s. Robert Church and Michael Sedlak noted that once again schools faced the challenge of dealing with the issues of the day. They stated, "During the twenties and thirties, the schools were constantly called upon to redress the failures of the family, culture, and economy areas over which the schools exercised no significant control. The educational establishment was continually asked to protect and guard American youth from forces far stronger and more influential than the schools could realistically hope to be."[6] Diane Ravitch summed up the overall role of schools in our nation's history this way, "Probably no other idea has seemed more typically American than the belief that schooling could cure society's ills. Whether in the early nineteenth century or the twentieth century, Americans have argued for more schooling on the grounds that it would preserve democracy, eliminate poverty, lower the crime rate, enrich the common culture, reduce unemployment, ease the assimilation of immigrants to the nation, overcome differences between

ethnic groups, advance scientific and technological progress, prevent traffic accidents, raise health standards, refine moral character, and guide young people into useful occupations."[7]

Beyond dealing with societal issues, schools also serve as a conduit of ideas seen by some as "America's Civil Religion." Conclusion have been drawn depicting public school educators as seeking to shape their students as participants in an idealized version of American society. Promoting a unified belief in American exceptionalism has also served as a key responsibility of public education.[8] This can be traced this idea from colonial times, when education had a strong religious foundation, up to through the twentieth

---

4. Hayes, *Horace Mann's Vision*, 20.

5. Cremin, *Transformation of the School*, 66–67.

6. Church and Sedlak, *Education in the United States*, 374.

7. Ravitch, *Troubled Crusade*, xii.

8. Bankston and Caldas, *Public Education*, 2.

century, as society wrestled with the controversies over the Cold War and the drive for racial equality. Historians Carl Bankston and Stephen J. Caldas have emphasized how public education has created a "cult of the state." To sum it up, "Schooling has been a part of the civic faith of many nations. In the United States, though, it was linked to the long-standing image of Americans as moving toward a special destiny, and the peculiarly American version of the faith in education was shaped by the nation's history."[9]

Educational historian Joel Spring also provides insight into the distinct purpose education has played in the history of our nation by emphasizing ideas and power. Tracing its role from colonial days to the present, Spring cogently argues that public education has always been a tool of the Anglo Protestant majority to establish and maintain their place of prominence in American society. He argues that the establishment of "common schools" reflected more than just a desire to have an educated citizenry. The creation of public schools provided a means to make everyone conform to the values of Anglo Protestant America, whether it be through promoting an ideology, religion, or maintaining a social hierarchy. As pluralism became more prevalent over the decades, Anglo Protestants have had to work with greater intensity to keep a grip on their power.[10]

To support this thesis, Spring draws upon several broad historical themes in the overall story of public education in America. First, he makes the point that schools have been used in the overall culture wars that have developed in our nation. Spring explains it this way, "One reason for the nineteenth century development of public schools was to ensure the dominance of Anglo-American values that were being challenged by Irish immigration, Native Americans and African Americans."[11] Religion also became a part of this culture war in the nineteenth century since the immigrants challenged traditional American Protestantism. Hence, Spring concludes that schools in the United States played the role of what he calls "ideological management." While this ideology has evolved over the centuries, the question regarding the propagation of a particular set of beliefs has always been present in American education and remains so to the present day.[12]

Therefore, in describing the role of education in American history, Joel Spring sheds light on the long held national faith in education to accomplish goals of vital importance to the future of the republic. In addition, Spring makes it clear that using schools to accomplish national goals also serves

---

9. Bankston and Caldas, *Public Education*, 167.

10. Spring, *American School*, 4.

11. Spring, *American School*, 4.

12. Spring, *American School*, 4–5.

the dual purpose of imposing Anglo Protestant power. To achieve these ends, he uses a term that will be central to this book. In his discussion of the first public schools, Spring states, "Common school reformers believed that education could be used to assure the dominance of Anglo-American culture, reduce tensions between social classes, eliminate crime and poverty, stabilize the political system, and form patriotic citizens. For common school advocates, education would be key to creating the good society."[13] Creating "the good society" stands in a broad sense as the goal all Americans share in regard to their educational institutions, while at the same time being a source of controversy reflecting the changing profile of the nation.

By in large, the creation of a "good society" has consistently centered on teaching good citizenship and patriotism. The previously cited work by Bankston and Caldas clearly illustrates their idea that schools served as a tool to promote America's civil religion and thereby propagate a common set of values. Thomas Jefferson believed that a "good society" would result from creating virtuous citizens capable of making sound political decisions. Horace Mann felt that an educated populace with a clear moral compass to be imperative to the future of the republic. Attempts at Americanization of immigrants in the nineteenth century would ensure a more homogeneous culture for the growing United States. Indoctrinating loyalty in American children during the Cold War seemed crucial to the future of the nation during the nuclear age. In the twenty-first century, with the emphasis on multiculturalism, inclusion, and creating a competitive work force in the global economy, our nation's schools have continued to be tasked to create a "good society" for the sake of preserving the future of our nation while at the same time upholding existing power structures. Therefore, if the goals of public education have been fairly consistent, the first question, regarding the specific origins of an alternative form of Christian-based education, must be examined.

Returning to the second question of this work dealing with the causes for the birth of this movement in 1947, the reactionary element will certainly be acknowledged. However, it will also be argued that Christian schools came about for the same reason as public schools, in essence, to establish and maintain Joel Spring's idea of the "good society" which centers on Anglo Protestant dominance. For decades, the nation's schools stood as a bastion of this power, but by the mid-twentieth century, a small minority of conserva-tive evangelical Christians gave up on public schools and sought to resurrect their version of a "good society" and re-establish their power in the wider culture through the creation of private Christian schools.

13. Spring, *American School*, 78.

So, conservative Christians sought to define their version of the "good society" in American history and specifically address the unique challenges of the twentieth century. Simply put, to these individuals the "good society" meant the establishment of a "Christian America." Many historians have probed into this long held belief and dream of evangelical Protestants. Historian Patrick Allitt pointed to a deep tradition of American Christians going back to the days of the Protestant Reformation that led to the belief that "our republic would only prosper if it was inhabited by virtuous Christian citizens."[14] Richard Hughes explains the idea of a Christian America this way, "From the colonial period to the present, many American Christians have made the claim that God anointed America—first the colonies and then the nation—as his chosen people."[15] Hughes sees this concept deeply embedded in the mindset of twenty-first-century Christians while pointing out how their actions often do not always reflect consistency.[16]

As expressed by Robert Handy, "From the very beginning, American Protestants have entertained a lively hope that someday the civilization of the country would become fully Christian."[17] He argues that, while an established church never materialized for the faithful, they sought to create a Christian America using other means. Seeking to cross denominational lines, the Protestants in the nineteenth century employed a variety of strategies to usher in their dream which included specific actions toward making Christianity a chief characteristic of the nation's newly formed public schools.[18]

The goal of a Christian America continued into the early twentieth century. Many Christians viewed the year 1900 with great optimism and a belief that this was to be a "Christian Century."[19] George Marsden describes fundamentalist Christians in the 1900s as having a strong sense of "trusteeship" for American culture. Hence, they often promoted the idea of the nation returning to the early years of a country committed to Christian principles. Joel Carpenter's work on fundamentalism in the United States during the years between the world wars further illustrates the desire of these Christians to bring revival back to the nation and a return to biblical values. Carpenter explains that despite feelings of rejection from American

14. Allitt, *Religion in America*, 6.

15. Hughes, *Christian America and the Kingdom*, 18.

16. Hughes, *Christian America and the Kingdom*, 4.

17. Handy, *Christian America*, viii.

18. Handy, *Christian America*, 101.

19. Handy, *Christian America*, 117.

society, conservative fundamentalists in the 1920s and 30s still clung to a belief in a Christian America.[20]

In sum, numerous historians have all suggested the long held belief in the idea of a "Christian America." Going back to the tradition of the Reformation and the Puritans, Protestants have come to see America as a nation chosen by God to be a beacon of Christianity to the rest of the world. This dream did not include a particular established church, but rather consisted of a society and culture thoroughly guided by the teachings of the Bible and Christian leaders. In this version of the good society faithful Protestant followers of Christ would not necessarily be oppressive toward other religions, but would see their way of life as so expansive and influential that other belief systems would be insignificant. Then, America would truly be a "New Jerusalem."[21]

To be more specific, defining the term "Christian America" involves several characteristics. Early Christian school leaders spoke of it frequently and implied numerous attributes of their form of the good society. In an extensive 2000 study, several hundred individuals across the nation were asked to define this evangelical concept. Of the sixty percent of the respondents who acknowledged the validity of this idea, six key characteristics of a "Christian America" surfaced. These would include: a commitment to religious freedom, a populace consisting of a majority of faithful Christians, a U.S. government embodying Christian principles, a belief in godly theistic founding fathers, a permeation of Christian principles and values throughout the culture, and acceptance of a public expression of Christian symbols and customs. Opinions varied considerably in this study, but they all acknowledged that the United States had strayed from a Christian past and needed to re-emphasize one or more of these characteristics.[22]

From the perspective of evangelical Christians, from the colonial days up to the twentieth century, this dream of building a "good society" faced numerous attacks from such foes as immigrants of different faiths, "godless" philosophies such as Darwinism and liberal theology, and the changes in society brought on by industrialization and modernity. By the 1920s and 30s, conservative Christianity had suffered a number of defeats in the eyes of the American public and these Protestants began to see their dominance waning. Yet, the followers of the more conservative brand of the faith, labeled fundamentalists, retreated and reorganized in the years between the wars with goals of warning the nation about its spiritual decline

20. Carpenter, *Revive Us Again*, 6.

21. Bankston and Caldas, *Public Education*, 17.

22. Smith, *Christian America?*, 22–37.

and consequently bringing the Christian faith back to prominence. They developed their own subculture, barely noticed by mainstream society, and created a network of like-minded believers through publications, radio, conferences, and higher education. Joel Carpenter put it this way, "Ironically, they were freed by their defeats in the anti-modernist controversies to concentrate on these more positive tasks. While they were predicting the world's imminent demise and building a subculture to protect themselves from worldly society, fundamentalists were also retooling their evangelistic techniques and seizing upon inviting cultural trends to mount a renewed public presence. Their goals were time honored evangelical ones: to bring revival to America and the gospel to the world."[23]

The 1940s saw an upsurge in church attendance and a new approach by the conservative Christian community. In 1942, two evangelical ministers, J. Elwin Wright and Harold Ockenga, trying to create a more upbeat and harmonious image for their brand of Protestantism, founded the National Association of Evangelicals which aimed to renew the image of their branch of Christianity in the eyes of the general public. As the nation experienced resurgence in Protestantism in the 1940s, the goal of a Christian America resurfaced.

However, now the approach had changed. In the nineteenth century, the Protestant attempt to make America into a godly republic looked forward. Protestants on the frontier of the New World saw the idea of a Christian America as a vision for the future. However, by the early twentieth century, their version of the "good society" became a goal to be reached by looking fondly backward toward a vision of the past colonial days and the era of the early republic, times that they perceived as a distinctly Christian. Instead of establishing a Christian nation, these religious leaders now sought to "re-establish" a Christian nation that had faded over the decades. This became the hallmark strategy for evangelical Christian leaders from the 1920s to the present time to create their version of a "good society" and revive their influence and power in the culture.

For a small group of conservative believers, this could best be achieved through private Christian education. For decades, Christian colleges existed as the chief means of propagating Anglo-Protestant values and power. However in the early twentieth century, we see for the first time the emergence of non-denominational Christian elementary and secondary schools. Abandoning public education as a lost cause, a small cadre of conservative Christians all over the nation began to form their own schools much akin to what their Catholic enemies had done in the nineteenth century. While in a very basic

23. Carpenter, *Revive Us Again*, xii.

sense, these Christian schools shared common goals with public education in terms of providing sound academics coupled with a commitment to growing good citizens, the gradual exclusion of spiritual education, most notably Protestant Christianity, alarmed these Christians. Believing that they had an obligation to teach religion while at the same time returning the nation to its perceived Christian foundation, these educators took the step of starting entirely new schools. One of the first, the Stony Brook School of New York, established in 1922, fit right in line with the goal of re-establishing the Christian heritage of America. As one historian has written, "Stony Brook represented a return to what had been the first tradition of American education—training young men in Christian principles for Christian service."[24]

In the first meeting of the NAE in 1942, keynote speaker Harold Ockenga lamented the decline of Christianity in many aspects of American life. Dr. Ockenga expressed fears about a lack of unity among evangelicals, the rising power of Roman Catholicism, liberal theology, the dearth of radio exposure for conservative Christianity, and the faults of American education. "Unless we can have a true revival of evangelical Christianity, able to change the character of men and build up a new moral fibre," Ockenga warned, "we believe that Christianity, capitalism, and democracy, likewise, to be imperiled."[25] In this setting, the rise of the Christian school movement, albeit quite small, took root. The evangelical Christian School movement of today originated from the universal American faith in schools' ability and obligation to create the "good society" and for Protestants in the United States, this meant that America needed to return to being a Christian nation. With the decline of Protestant power in the twentieth century, the Christian school movement emerged in the 1940s as a means for evangelicals to regain their power and continue to pursue their dream of a "Christian America."

24. Lockerbie, *Way They Should Go*, 47.
25. Ockenga, "Unvoiced Multitudes," 19–39.

Chapter 2

"Education in 'Christian America'"

In early days of the National Association of Christian Schools, Mark Fakkema, serving as its executive director, wrote extensively about the need for this new organization. Typical of his audacious approach, in 1948 he wrote a short pamphlet entitled, "Christian Schools or a Pagan Nation—What Shall it Be?" In this publication, Fakkema stated boldly that Americans needed "Christian Schools for a Christian America."[1] Over many years, he argued, the biblical foundation of the United States had been destroyed by a secular public school system and the time had come to establish Christian schools to return to the beliefs of the founders. He pleaded with a sense of desperation, "What we sow, we reap. When the State that knows no religion takes charge of the preparation of the American youth, then we must surrender the future life of America to a life which knows no religion. What step could be more momentous for a nation founded upon the principles of the Christian religion?" Fakkema went on to describe the inextricable link between religion and education and announced that the founders never intended for youth to be deprived of religious training. He also lamented the irreligion of the public schools by saying that in the early days of the country, the Bible served as the principle textbook, whereas now it was prohibited.[2] Fakkema concluded his polemic by laying down the challenge for all Christian parents to make the sacrifices necessary to start up schools founded upon the Bible. He proclaimed, "Do it for the sake of our beloved country . . . that you may help check the downward trend toward secularism—totalitarianism—atheism. Do it for the sake of your church—your children—your children's children. DO IT FOR THE SAKE OF YOUR

1. Fakkema, *Christian Schools or a Pagan Nation*, 10.
2. Fakkema, *Christian Schools or a Pagan Nation*, 3–4.

GOD." He concluded by saying it plainly, "We invite you to join the Back-to-God movement in education."[3]

Fakkema's goal of getting "back to God" illustrates the fact that some conservative evangelicals in the 1940s felt that the only way to save America from a disastrous future lay in a return to its so-called Christian heritage. One of the critical steps toward this end was the creation of Christian day schools. Achieving the "good society" of a "Christian America" would come through an education that individuals, such as Mark Fakkema, believed would be similar to that advocated by the forefathers which was based upon Bible and the Protestant faith. The founders of the Christian school movement in the early to mid-twentieth century repeatedly placed this claim at the heart of their arguments for an alternative educational system.

However, in analyzing the claims of individuals such as Mark Fakkema, the history of education and religion reveals a more complicated picture, a story of conflicts that undermined his image of a bygone era when the nation was supported by Christian schools. In a general sense, however, most historians agree that religion did indeed form the basis of most of the earliest schools in America. Joel Spring states that education in colonial New England served an important social function in that it sought to maintain the authority of the government and the church. Citizens needed to be literate so they could better obey the laws of God and the state. Hence, from the beginning, education served as a societal panacea, albeit based upon Christian principles.[4] For ministers such as Cotton Mather, the main objective of education involved obtaining knowledge of the scriptures in order to prepare children for a saving knowledge of Jesus and a life of battling Satan.[5] In 1642, the Massachusetts legislature passed a law which placed educational responsibilities on each town in the colony and required educational instruction for youth. However, educational historian John L. Rury makes an important point about the role of schooling in colonial New England by saying "it was intended to supplement, not supplant the central role of the family in transmitting religious values and basic literary and computational skills."[6] In this early form of public education, the General Court of the colony also assessed taxes to employ "Protestant teachers of piety, religion, and morality."[7]

3. Fakkema, *Christian Schools or a Pagan Nation,* 14–15.

4. Eck, *New Religious America,* 14; Spring, *American School,* 11.

5. Rury, *Education and Social Change,* 29; Elias, *History of Christian Education,* 121.

6. Greenawalt, *Does God Belong in Public Schools?,* 13; Elias, *History of Christian Education,* 32; Reed and Prevost, *History of Christian Education,* 294.

7. Dierenfield, *Battle Over School Prayer,* 6; Hartman, *Education and the Cold War,* 7.

Beyond the King James Bible, in colonial New England three books provided the basic curriculum for children. The first primer, known as the *Hornbook,* actually consisted of a single piece of parchment that contained the alphabet, the Lord's Prayer, and other religious doctrines. A simple verse found in the *Hornbook* would be, "In Adam's fall, we sinned all."[8] By 1690, the first edition of the *New England Primer* appeared and eventually replaced the *Hornbook.* This became a staple for all New England children and contained the names of the Old and New Testament books arranged alphabetically, the Lord's Prayer, the Ten Commandments and "An Alphabet of Lessons for Youth" which illustrated each letter containing a rhyming couplet with a moral lesson. In addition, Massachusetts produced in 1640 the first book written and printed in the colonies, *The Bay Psalm Book.* Utilized as a reader, it consisted of a collection of psalms selected by several ministers. Over the course of twenty-seven editions, this book received widespread usage throughout the colonies and in Britain.[9]

Beyond teaching literacy and instilling biblical precepts, these early New England schools also prepared young men for professions in law or the ministry thereby complementing the work of the church. The citizenry supported this education fully since they were almost all Protestants.[10] Puritan leaders established an educational system designed to craft their version of a good society which meant a well-ordered religious state that would be a model for the rest of the world.[11] However, this model also included a lack of tolerance for such groups clearly deemed a threat such as Roman Catholics and Quakers.[12]

The Puritans exemplified two concepts that would later be among the major beliefs and goals of twentieth-century evangelicals and Christian school leaders. First, the notion of freedom of religion came from the fact that the Puritans did indeed flee persecution in England and came to the New World in order to worship freely. Second, the belief in a Christian nation arose from the attempt of these settlers to establish a commonwealth based on the precepts of the Bible.[13] The good society of a "Christian America," began in New England and grew to a mythic state.

---

8. McClellan, *Moral Education in America,* 3; Rury, *Education and Social Change,* 31.

9. Reed and Prevost, *History of Christian Education,* 294–95.

10. Rury, *Education and Social Change,* 36; Dierenfield, *Battle Over School Prayer,* 6.

11. Spring, *American School,* 13.

12. Beggs and McQuigg, *America's Schools and Churches,* 39.

13. Lambert, *Founding Fathers,* 1.

Even though the Puritans possessed an extensive educational system based on their religious beliefs, a closer look at other American colonies reveals some degree of educational diversity spread across the seaboard. According to E. Vance Randall, "Schools were established by village towns, trading companies, religious orders such as Jesuits, a variety of religious denominations, and individuals such as ministers, women, and town schoolmasters."[14] Lawrence Cremin stated, "virtually anyone could teach and virtually anyone could learn, at least among whites, and the market rather than the church or the legislature governed through multifarious contractual relationships."[15] The Middle Colonies extensive cultural diversity shaped the educational system there, including such groups as Lutherans, Presbyterians, Quakers, Roman Catholics, Jews, and Dutch Calvinists each created their own parochial schools. In New Netherland, for example, the schools enjoyed close ties to the church and community, much like New England. Religious instruction sat at the heart of the curriculum and the teachers often served as assistants to the local pastor. Beyond the classroom, teachers would perform such duties as ringing the bell for Sunday services, reading aloud the Ten Commandments, teaching catechism and assisting with baptisms.[16] Quaker schools in Pennsylvania also stressed their own unique moral, social and religious ideas. Early on this sect promoted abolitionist ideas and by 1700, provided instruction in integrated schools. The "African School" started by the Quaker Anthony Benezet went a step further by exclusively educating African-American boys and girls.[17] Philosophically, Quaker schools contrasted sharply with the Puritans in that they did not stress depravity but rather the basic innocence of the child. Believing in the Inner Light, they felt that their students were inherently neither good nor evil and would follow their natural propensities.[18] In the Southern colonies, private tutors dominated education, which was limited to the children of wealthy plantation owners or apprenticeship schools for the poor. Classical studies from tutors included religion, but not as an integral part of the curriculum.[19] Hence, religious and educational differences did exist in

14. Randall, "Religious Schools in America," 84.

15. Cremin, *American Education*, 559.

16. Anthony and Benson, *Exploring the History*, 297.

17. Button and Provenzo, *History of Education and Culture*, 45.

18. Elias, *History of Christian Education*, 122–23.

19. Reed and Prevost, *History of Christian Education*, 295; Pulliam and Patten, *History of Education*, 85–90.

early America even though it could be argued that the differences were only differing strands of Protestantism.[20]

In the years of the Revolution and early republic, Enlightenment thought emerged as a major philosophy and in some ways appeared contrary to orthodox Christianity. The Enlightenment stressed the essential goodness of man and the value of science and reason which conflicted with the Christian view of man's depravity and need for a supernatural savior. Some historians see this as a major threat to the nation's religious orientation by saying, "Many of the Enlightenment thinkers were highly critical of the philosophical assumptions of Christian theology and education. In proposing that knowledge comes from sense, experience, reason, and feelings rather than from authority, history, and tradition, Enlightenment thinkers or philosophes tended to undermine the traditional basis of Christian theology and education."[21] Christian school leaders of the twentieth century would later see this as one of the first cracks that threatened this notion of a "Christian America."

However, once again the picture is more complicated as most educational and political leaders of this era had no difficulty wedding the two philosophies. The founders pinned their hopes for the future of the nation upon the notion of a republic which provided its citizens with liberty while also maintaining order. Central to this hope would be an educated citizenry and a vital component of this education would be moral training based upon the Protestant Bible that would produce virtuous, well-behaved citizens.[22] Not surprisingly, the need for education can be seen in many statutes of the early years such as the Northwest Ordinance of 1787 which stated that, "since religion, morality, and knowledge were essential to good government and the happiness of mankind, schools and the means of education should forever be encouraged."[23]

The views of founders such as Benjamin Rush, Noah Webster, and Thomas Jefferson illustrate the way many leaders during the Revolutionary period integrated their Enlightenment ideas with a support for Protestant religion, and applied this in their approach to education in the early republic. Benjamin Rush, the notable Philadelphia physician who lived from 1746–1813, campaigned for educational reform in the new nation. He believed that schools train young Americans in the civic virtues, imparting to them a unified culture devoid of sectarian strife. Rush felt strongly

20. McClellan, *Moral Education in America*, 7; Eck, *New Religious America*, 37.

21. Elias, *History of Christian Education*, 127.

22. Kaestle, *Pillars of the Republic*, 5; Rury, *Education and Social Change*, 49.

23. Michaelsen, *Piety in the Public School*, 47.

that education needed to include Christian religious principles or the new republic could not succeed. He favored teaching the Bible, which he believed supported the revolutionary ideals of equality. To accomplish this goal, Rush called for state support of denominational schools as he felt they could work together to unite the nation.[24]

Noah Webster (1758–1843), the Connecticut lexicographer, suggested the teaching of religion as a means of instilling a patriotic, nationalistic spirit. He favored religious instruction in schools, but felt that the Bible should only be used specifically in particular courses to provide moral lessons.[25] Known as the "Schoolmaster of America," Webster, like Rush, believed that education could serve as an essential tool for creating a unified culture, and he opposed any schooling that might instead preserve and perpetuate aspects of European culture.[26]

Thomas Jefferson, a strong advocate for public schools, felt the chief end of education to be the raising of moral men who would be attuned to the workings of nature and nature's God, devoted to the principles of liberty, and ready to assume their role as educated and responsible citizens.[27] An education would not only make them more aware of their individual rights but would also instill in the students a shrewd vigilance against tyranny.[28] As a deist, Jefferson, like most Enlightenment thinkers, embraced the existence of God and placed it in the context of his overall philosophy.[29] He did not support teaching the Bible to children, feeling that they did not possess the maturity to understand it. Opposing the imposition of a specific religious belief as a form of mental tyranny, Jefferson felt that moral lessons should be taught in generic terms based upon reason and history. Morality based upon the precepts of the Bible had a vital role in education, but religion, to Jefferson, thrived best if left to be taught in the confines of the church and home.[30]

Hence, the founders of the United States viewed Enlightenment principles and traditional religious beliefs of the colonial period as compatible and they considered belief in God and respect for biblical authority to be essential parts of a proper curriculum for schools in the new nation. However,

24. Kaestle, *Pillars of the Republic*, 5–6.

25. Urban and Wagoner Jr., *American Education*, 90.

26. Spring, *American School*, 48; Greenawalt, *Does God Belong in Public Schools?*, 13–14.

27. Michaelsen, *Piety in the Public School*, 80.

28. Pangle and Prangle, *Learning of Liberty*, 108.

29. May, "Enlightenment and America," 166.

30. Randall, "Religious Schools in America," 85–86.

as historian Frank Lambert suggests, the founders never intended to establish a church-state framework, but rather supported an emerging "free marketplace of religion." "By their actions, the Founding Fathers made it clear that their primary concern was religious freedom," explains Lambert, "not the advancement of a state religion." Later, in writing the Constitution, no mention of God existed. While the founders understood Christianity to be the basis of a moral society, they worried about religion's place having seen its abuses in Europe. Religion would flourish better and meet the needs of diverse populace when placed in a marketplace setting rather than impose it through government coercion.[31]

Christianity and Enlightenment thought agreed on two important points although they differed in their approaches. First, both philosophies emphasized the importance of individual choice in the search for truth. Christians could find truth in seeking God through the study of the Scriptures. Enlightenment men would question the role of God and conduct their own investigations for truth based upon observation and reason.[32] Likewise, both belief systems shared great optimism for the future. With the establishment of the United States, Christians held out hope for Christ's millennial reign, while Enlightenment thinkers similarly foresaw a golden age of peace and justice based upon a rational and moderate revolution.[33]

Secularizing tendencies might have existed in the Enlightenment beliefs of individuals such as Jefferson, but nevertheless, by 1790, the population of the new nation contained a 75 percent white Protestant majority.[34] Therefore, most of the schools still contained a distinctive Protestant flavor and continued under their control. While the term Protestant would include Puritans, Quakers, Presbyterians, and Anglicans, the fact remained that their schools did more than teach students to read and write; assimilation and indoctrination into church life occurred. Some of these schools even received public financing.[35] Individuals such as Rush, Webster, and Jefferson argued in vain for public schools, but this belief would not catch on until well into the nineteenth century.[36]

Great changes came in the nineteenth century and perhaps none more notable than the soaring population resulting from massive immigration. Starting in 1830, the population of the country grew at a steady rate of about

31. Lambert, *Founding Fathers*, 8–11, 205–6.
32. Lambert, *Founding Fathers*, 10.
33. May, "Enlightenment and America," 169; Bloch, *Visionary Republic*.
34. Spring, *American School*, 47.
35. Elias, *History of Christian Education*, 150, 154.
36. Kaestle, *Pillars of the Republic*, 61.

35 percent per decade until the start of the Civil War. The number of immigrants during this era increased 240 percent. From 1840 to 1870 the population doubled, and doubled again by 1900. With this, America became more urbanized as foreign workers provided cheap labor for the growing, industrialized economy.[37] Due to population shifts and rapid diversification of the economy, it became apparent that many institutions of earlier generations, such as schools, would either change or perish.[38]

Beyond the economic impact, other changes, most notably in religion, surfaced during the first decades of the nineteenth century. Statistics reveal these dramatic changes. In 1800, the United States could claim to be almost 95 percent white Protestant and with that 85 percent could claim to be English speaking Calvinists. By 1860, this number would drop to 60 percent. This suggests that the upheaval caused by massive immigration marked the beginning in the decline of American Protestantism.[39] Hence, the United States in the nineteenth century would become more diverse and the resulting changes would not only impact education, but would also challenge the distinctively Protestant nature of the schools.

Education in the antebellum period continued to stress the traditional goals of citizenship, industry, upright behavior, and reflected Protestant confidence about the future. However, rising ethnic diversity, poverty, cultural alienation, the growth of cities, and the presence of new belief systems caused a greater sense of urgency about education and hence, more interest by state leaders about schooling.[40] As a result, crusading social reformers began to push for a government system of "common schools." Concerned about America's social changes, they feared the possibility of social conflict in the absence of universally held values and a shared identity. Consequently, reformers proclaimed the need for public education.[41]

Governor William Marcy of New York illustrated this changing attitude. In the 1830s, Marcy, a Democrat, garnered a reputation for limited government by withholding state funds for internal improvements. However, in 1834 and 1835, he pressed the legislature to appropriate monies for public education not only for individual schools but also for teacher training. Even in 1837, when the state and nation felt the effects of an economic panic, Marcy continued to press for these same measures saying, "education

---

37. Marty, *Righteous Empire*, 124; Kaestle, *Pillars of the Republic*, 63–64; Rury, *Education and Social Change*, 55.

38. Welter, *Popular Education and Democratic Thought*, 30.

39. Hutchison, *Religious Pluralism in America*, 19–20; Hutchison, "Diversity and the Pluralist Ideal," 36.

40. Kaestle, *Pillars of the Republic*, 64.

41. Rury, *Education and Social Change*, 74, 76.

in all its branches, but particularly that which includes the common schools, is the highest object of public concern."[42] The common school movement marked the beginning of active participation of the state in education and a noticeable shift in power and direction away from the family and the church in terms of control of the schools.[43]

Horace Mann (1796–1859), a social reformer who eventually became the secretary of education for the state of Massachusetts, led the common school movement. In evaluating the schools of Massachusetts in the early part of the nineteenth century, Mann found severe inequities. With no state supervision, schools varied widely from town to town. Some received support from local taxes while others charged parents fees. Wealthy children could stay in school longer, while the very poor did not attend at all. Visiting almost a thousand schools over six years, Mann found deplorable facilities, inadequate and inconsistent curriculum, overcrowded classrooms, and poor instruction. Over the course of the 1830s and 40s, through numerous meetings and annual reports, Mann proposed a publicly funded system of education, which eventually became the model for the rest of the nation.[44]

Mann had three distinct goals for this new system of public education. First, he felt it was imperative that there be state agencies to control the public schools. Seeing the gross inequities that existed in schools run by churches and small towns, he could see no better solution than to let the state guide the schools for the sake of fairness and uniformity. Second, Mann believed that a unique feature of public schools would be their ability to be used as an instrument of government policy. Based on his concerns as a social reformer, Mann felt that the schools could lessen the conflicts between economic classes and racial groups. In essence, schools could become the "central institution for control and maintenance of the social order."[45] Mann's establishment of a public system of education would become a critical means for "Americanizing" the immigrants and providing the ongoing maintenance of American values at a time of rapid social change.

The third goal of Horace Mann's vision for education revolved around the issue of religion. He strongly felt that schools should be a "moral compass" for children. But, the issue of the role of Christianity in his public schools would prove to be one of the most difficult issues he faced. In New England, tradition dictated that the Bible be used as a textbook as well as a basis of

42. Welter, *Popular Education and Democratic Thought*, 62.

43. Tyack and James, "State Government," 39–69; Randall, "Religious Schools in America," 86.

44. Michaelsen, *Piety in the Public School*, 70–74; Mondale and Patton, *School*, 25–31.

45. Hayes, *Horace Mann's Vision*, 22–23.

moral and religious education. In his first educational tour in 1837, Mann found some sectarian teaching in the schools, but in the nine eastern counties of the state which contained more than 60 percent of the population, the practice had largely disappeared.[46] Mann had personally long since rejected the rigid Calvinist teachings of his youth, in favor of a more liberal Christian faith as a Unitarian. Motivated by a belief in non-doctrinal religion, he supported what he considered to be the fundamental precepts of the Bible, but he did not support sectarianism in the public schools. He wanted the schools to promote moral virtue, but not the teachings of a specific church.[47] In Mann's oft quoted 1848 *Twelfth Report to the Massachusetts Board of Education,* he devoted a major portion to the subject of religious education. He made clear his ardent admiration for the moral teachings of Christianity as related in the Bible. He explicitly stated that he would never seek to exclude the Bible or religious instruction from the schools. He specifically listed qualities of true Christian virtues that included piety, justice, a commitment to truth, love of country, humanity, universal benevolence, sobriety, industry, frugality, chastity, moderation, and temperance.[48]

At the same time, Mann had to be very cautious in recommending any reduction in the role of Christian teachings in the common schools. He found himself in a dilemma in that if he did not advance a moral education with a religious foundation, he risked being labeled irreligious and his common schools condemned as secular. On the other side, if he did make religion a foundation of his approach to moral education, he had to make a choice about which religious tenets to choose.[49] In negotiating this conflict, Mann leaned heavily upon legislation already in place. The Massachusetts School Law of 1827 prohibited sectarian religious instruction in public school classrooms in the state. The law specifically ordered teachers to "impress upon the minds of children the principles of piety, justice, and sacred regard to truth, but forbade them to use any book which was calculated to favor any particular religious sect or tenet."[50] Because he envisioned the new state supported common school system as an institution that would benefit children and youth of diverse backgrounds, he felt that there had to be certain limits placed upon religious teaching. So, as a compromise, he suggested that the King James Bible be read without comment by either teacher

46. Culver, *Horace Mann and Religion*, 271.

47. Gutek, *Historical and Philosophical Foundations*, 193–95; Gangel and Benson, *Christian Education*, 269.

48. Hayes, *Horace Mann's Vision*, 65–66.

49. Hayes, *Horace Mann's Vision*, 25–26.

50. Dierenfield, *Battle Over School Prayer*, 14; Culver, *Horace Mann and Religion*, 218.

or pupil. Mann described it this way, "Our system earnestly inculcates all Christian morals; in receiving the Bible it allows it to do what is allowed in no other system—to speak for itself. But here it stops."[51]

Pragmatic reasons also existed for bringing religion into the newly formed public schools. Mann realized that while he wanted the citizens of Massachusetts to accept the notion of tax supported schools, the majority of the schools in the state had an affiliation with a Christian denomination and hence, the community leaders of the various churches might see the new public schools as a threat to their beliefs.[52] By promoting Christian principles within the schools at least in a nominal way, Mann hoped to gain their support and allay their fears that he was promoting godlessness. Horace Mann sought a pan-Protestant religious curriculum in the Massachusetts public schools. He hoped that the sectarian Protestant tenets, whether found in orthodox Congregationalist, Baptist, or liberal Unitarian churches, would be propagated within the confines of their own church buildings.

However, as with many of his reforms, the issue of religion proved to be a source of great conflict in which Mann faced constant criticism. Mann's sensitivity to keeping the schools non-sectarian exacerbated the situation. One of the best examples of this occurred in 1838, when Reverend Frederick Packard of the American Sunday School Union, sent a letter to Mann asking if a book, *Child at Home,* would be a suitable addition to a common school library list currently being assembled. Mann responded in an irritable manner, revealing his dislike of the Calvinist doctrine of his youth. He declared the book unacceptable and stated that it would not be tolerated in Massachusetts because it taught eternal perdition for the most minor of offenses. Mann harshly critiqued the book page by page, and at the end of his letter, he lectured Packard on the dangers of sectarianism. Packard, an ambitious book promoter, responded back by emphasizing the importance of the principles of piety and stated that they should be impressed upon the minds of children whether it bordered on sectarianism or not. This brought another harsh response by Mann denouncing Packard's belief that piety could only be taught by teaching the existence of a God who meted out punishment to evildoers. As the conflict became more public, Packard addressed a group of Congregational ministers and criticized Mann and the state board of education for being anti-evangelical. A few months later, Packard took his case to the newspapers and eventually one of the members of the state board resigned out of a concern that the common schools

51. Culver, *Horace Mann and Religion*, 252; Greenawalt, *Does God Belong in Public Schools?*, 15.

52. Hayes, *Horace Mann's Vision*, 65.

promoted a godless secularism. Eventually, Mann's Unitarian friends rallied to his cause, charging Packard with stirring controversy simply because he wanted to peddle his inferior books. Packard continued to argue the value of doctrinal beliefs like the Trinity, baptism, and original sin as crucial factors in a child's education. Mann responded by saying that while basic Christian values should be taught, doctrinal differences should be left to the home and particular church. The controversy eventually quelled, but nevertheless, charges of godlessness in the common schools still echoed in the more conservative churches.[53]

To the frequent charges he faced over the alleged irreligion of the common schools of Massachusetts Mann replied, "Everyone knows that I am in favor of religious instruction in our schools, to the extremist verge to which it can be carried without invading the rights of conscience which are established by the laws of God and guaranteed to us by the Constitution of the State."[54] Going further, he stated, "I have felt bound to show, that so far from its being an irreligious, an anti-Christian, or an un-Christian system, it is a system which recognizes religious obligations in their fullest extent; that it is a system which involved a religious spirit, and can never be fully administered without such a spirit; that it inculcates the great commands upon which hang all the law and the prophets; that it welcomes the Bible, and therefore welcomes all doctrines which the Bible really contains."[55] The President of Amherst College, Heman Humphrey, agreed with Mann in an 1843 lecture when he commented on the value of universally accepted biblical precepts such as the Ten Commandments and the Golden Rule. He felt that the common school should focus on these Christian truths without involving itself in doctrinal disputes. "Let the grown people be Trinitarians and Unitarians," he explained, and "be content to let the children be Christians."[56]

Beyond specific uses of the Bible in classrooms, broad Christian principles also existed in other places in the curriculum of the public schools. William McGuffey's *Eclectic Reader*, an enormously popular set of textbooks that stressed patriotism and moral values, stands out as the best example. First published in 1836, these books taught children to read through the use of moral tales. Historian Joel Spring explained their use this way, "The idea was that while the students learned to read, they also learned the morality

---

53. Messerli, *Horace Mann*, 309–15; Culver, *Horace Mann and Religion*, 55–110.

54. Culver, *Horace Mann and Religion*, 235; Dierenfield, *Battle Over School Prayer*, 15.

55. Gangel and Benson, *Christian Education*, 273.

56. Humphrey, "Bible in Common Schools," 10.

that would be this common morality of society. And that is the idea that if you should work hard and acquire wealth then you are blessed by God." An example found in an 1879 reader said, "Lesson 40: Charlie and Rob. 'Don't you hate splitting wood?' asked Charlie. 'No, I rather like it,' said Rob, 'It's a tough job and it's nicer to conquer it.' Now which of these boys do you think grew up to be a rich and useful man and which of them joined a party of tramps before he was thirty years old?" Another example from an earlier edition told the story of a chimney sweep, who alone in the house of a rich woman, became tempted to steal her watch. He said to himself, "If I take it, I shall be a thief. Yet nobody sees me. Does not God see me? Could I ever, in all my life, be happy again? Would God ever hear my prayers again? And what should I do when I come to die?"[57] McGuffey, a Presbyterian minister and frontier schoolteacher, explained his reasons for the religious concepts in his readers by saying, "The Christian religion is the religion of our country. From it are derived our notions on the character of God, on the great moral Governor of the universe. On its doctrines are founded the peculiarities of our free institutions. From no other source has the author drawn more conspicuously than from the sacred Scriptures. For all these extracts from the Bible I make no apology."[58]

Common schools did have a negative effect upon the many private religious schools that existed since colonial days. Some closed due to the fact that families could not afford both private tuition and the new school taxes. Many others, especially those sponsored by various Protestant denominations, simply got absorbed into the public school system. For example, New York City in 1829 contained 430 private schools. By 1850, only 138 remained. In Massachusetts, the private academies dwindled from a number of 1308 in 1840 to 350 by 1880.[59]

Mann's work illustrates the attempt of the new nation to overcome the dilemma of establishing a neutral governmental structure out of a society made up of a people deeply attached to their various religious faiths. These early public schools reflected the informal establishment of a sort of mainstream Protestantism in the nation. The schools came to be used to transmit the dominant Protestant culture and ethic. The specific use of the King James Bible and the McGuffey reader created a clear connection between these schools and the support of a basic nondenominational set of Protestant values. In addition, in many regions of the country, church affiliated schools remained designated as the local public schools and continued to

---

57. Minnich, *Old Favorites*, 18–19, 27.

58. Dierenfield, *Battle Over School Prayer*, 14.

59. Nasaw, *Schooled to Order*, 109.

receive government financial support well through the nineteenth century.[60] However, Mann's work also shows the great challenge of trying to instill a set of generic religious values upon a nation becoming more diverse in its faiths. Despite later criticism by the leaders of the Christian school movement, Protestants in the nineteenth century now had a bond with public education that would endure for decades, a loyalty to this institution which aimed to instill in children a common set of values based upon the teachings of their faith. But, while the nineteenth century saw the birth of a close bond between education and the Christian faith, the century also produced the first significant threats to this partnership.

As the nineteenth century progressed, the growth of the Roman Catholic Church quickly emerged as the most serious threat to the Protestant goal of a Christian America. Between 1830 and 1870, the number of Roman Catholics in the United States more than quadrupled to four million. Because of their poverty, these immigrants from Ireland and Germany took the cheapest trip to America and wound up in the northeast, the region in which Bible reading was most central to the common school curriculum.[61] When foreigners arrived in the industrializing cities, school officials and city leaders saw the schools as the best means to transmit Anglo-American Protestant values. In 1840, foreign born residents made up nearly half of New York City causing a state assemblyman to proclaim, "We must decompose and cleanse the impurities which rush into our midst."[62] Conflict soon developed over the question of religion in parts of the country where large numbers of Roman Catholic immigrant children attended these schools. They found New York public schools free and open, but also very Protestant. Hence, Irish Catholic children in New York attended schools that exposed them to the reading of the King James Bible, the singing of Protestant hymns, and pro-Protestant teaching.[63]

Beyond these daily classroom issues, the newly formed public schools reflected the overall national feeling of distrust that Protestants had toward Catholic immigrants, who were seen by many as a threat to U.S. institutions and values. Some viewed the Catholic Church as a subversive organization set up to do the bidding of the Pope in Rome. The top-down nature of the church, in which the faithful followed the teachings of the Vatican, conflicted with American ideals of independent minds, freedom,

---

60. Davis, "Public Policy," 160–61.

61. Hamburger, *Separation of Church and State*, 202–4; Dierenfield, *Battle Over School Prayer*, 16.

62. Kaestle, *Pillars of the Republic*, 161–63.

63. Perko, "Catholics and Their Schools," 124–26; Mondale and Patton, *School*, 33

and democracy.[64] Horace Mann established the common schools not only to educate the masses, but also to stand as a bastion against the Catholic faith. "When Protestantism arose," he wrote," freedom of opinion for each, and tolerance for all were the elements which gave it vitality and strength. The avowed doctrine of Catholicism was that men could not think for themselves."[65] Theodore Parker, a Boston Unitarian minister stated bluntly, "The Catholic Church opposes everything which favors democracy and the natural rights of man. It hates our free churches, free press, and above all, our free schools."[66]

For Catholics and any other religious minorities, the public educational system spreading across the nation offered few comfortable options. These parents could enroll their children in the Protestant public schools, start their own parochial system, which was costly, or try to fight what they perceived as clear sectarianism in the schools. Ultimately, Catholics utilized all three options to varying degrees, but the creation of their own schools emerged, to the Protestant majority, as the most noticeable and threatening choice. Pulling away from the public schools proved to be no easy task, and attendance languished for years, but nevertheless, the offensive and blatant Protestant slant in these institutions fueled this response.[67]

Beyond the prayers and daily King James Bible reading, parents of Catholic children resented offensive textbooks. One of them for example, warned that if Irish immigration continued, the United States would become "the common sewer of Ireland." Additional passages called the pope the "anti-Christ" and claimed the church to be in league with Satan to diminish scriptural truth.[68] In the 1830s, Bishop John Hughes of New York emerged as one of the first to call for a parochial Catholic school system. A fierce opponent of the Protestant bias in the city schools of New York, Hughes once proclaimed, "We are unwilling to pay taxes for the purpose of destroying our religion in the minds of our children. That such books should be put into the hands of our children is unjust, unnatural and intolerable." Father Richard Shaw, a church historian, went further to say, "This situation would lead to some twenty thousand children running around the

---

64. McGreevy, *Catholicism and American Freedom*, 23; Marty, *Righteous Empire*, 128.

65. McGreevy, *Catholicism and American Freedom*, 12, 18, 39.

66. Parker, "Sermon of the Dangers," 242–43; McGreevy, *Catholicism and American Freedom*, 39.

67. Lazerson, "Understanding," 304; Mondale and Patton, *School*, 33–34.

68. Rury, *Education and Social Change*, 94; Kaestle, *Pillars of the Republic*, 88.

streets of New York without the benefit of education because they refused to be part of a system biased against themselves."[69]

As the Catholics created their own parochial system, a number of issues arose which would linger well into the twentieth century. The issue of funding surfaced immediately as Catholic leaders asked for state support for their schools. Bishop Hughes led the first battle over this issue in New York City in the 1830s. The fiery, uncompromising Hughes challenged the Free School Society of New York, a private organization responsible for allocating tax monies to the city's schools. This exclusive Protestant society had already denied funding requests from Baptists and Presbyterian schools on the basis of their sectarianism. Hughes, however, saw the generic Protestantism of the public schools as a blatant sectarianism itself, and thereby concluded that Catholic schools deserved public funding. Asking for support for eight run-down overcrowded Catholic schools, he claimed, "Roman Catholic parents face double taxation for the education of their children—one to the misinterpreted law of the land, and another to his conscience."[70]

The resulting firestorm of controversy over public funding of Catholic Schools eventually impacted the entire issue of funding for any form of religious education. Protestant leaders openly debated Hughes who held his ground repeatedly. In one speech, Hughes said, "We will not send our children where they will be trained up without religion, lose respect for their parents and the faith of their fathers, and come out turning up their noses at the name of Catholic. In a word, give us our just proportion of the common school fund!" Newspapers denounced "popery" and called upon politicians to deny Catholic school funding. In 1841, an editorial of the *New York Herald* stated, "Once we admit that the Catholics have a right to a portion of the school fund, every other sect will have the same right. We shall be convulsed with endless jarring and quarrels about the distribution of it, and little left for the public schools. The Catholics have a right to think and worship in their own way, but have no right to claim one cent of the public money to propagate their own faith."[71]

Ultimately the Public School Society offered to make changes to accommodate their Catholic families. They expunged numerous passages from textbooks deemed offensive. In 1842, New York's governor, William Seward, convinced the state legislature to bar funding to schools that practiced open sectarianism, and also legislate that Bible reading, without

---

69. Dierenfield, *Battle Over School Prayer,* 19–20.

70. Delfattore, *Fourth R,* 16–17; Hassard, *Life of John Hughes,* 231; Michaelsen, *Piety in the Public School,* 86–87.

71. Mondale and Patton, *School,* 36; Hamburger, *Separation of Church and State,* 221.

commentary, to not be a sectarian activity. By pushing for funding, Hughes effectively brought the larger issue of funding for all religious institutions to a head leading to greater secularization and uniting the Protestants firmly against future sectarian issues in public education.[72]

The Catholics also stirred controversy over the question of Bible reading. The accepted Catholic version, the Douay-Rheims Bible, an English translation of the Latin Vulgate from 1582, contained seventy-three books including such components as the Apocrypha. The Protestant King James Version of 1611 contained only sixty-six books and thereby rejected the extra books of the Douay translation. In addition, the version of the King James Bible still in use at that time contained a preface with particularly disturbing material. This introduction referred to the Pope as "that man of sinne," and blatantly denied the legitimacy of the Catholic Church by accusing it of hiding the truths of Scripture from the common man.[73] Obviously, the Bible reading in the new public schools promoted by Mann and others would create a problem for the Catholic immigrants that would sometimes turn confrontational.

In 1844, the city of Philadelphia experienced a riot over this issue. Francis Kendrick, an Irish born bishop, requested that anti-Catholic books be removed from the schools and that Catholic children be allowed to read from the Douay Bible or at least be excused from reading the King James Version. The local school board assured Catholic leaders that the students could be excused, but charges still persisted of abuse and humiliation being heaped upon immigrant children. Eventually, the Philadelphia School Board agreed to let students read from any version of the Bible as long as it had no printed commentary. This would exclude the Douay Bible. This very minor concession upset several Protestant groups including the American Protestant Association, a nativist organization convinced of a plot by the Catholics to take over the nation. Rallies resulted in the city with many of them turning violent. Full scale riots erupted in Irish neighborhoods. In the wake of this incident, eighteen people died, and fifty homes, a Catholic church, and a convent got torched. Ultimately, the rioting subsided with the arrival of the state militia and the decision of Catholic leaders in the city to start their own parochial system.[74]

Despite all of the incidents concerning Catholics and public education in places like New York or Philadelphia, the famous "Cincinnati Bible War" of 1869 stands as the most significant. This very heterogeneous Ohio

---

72. Delfattore, *Fourth R*, 28–29; Michaelsen, *Piety in the Public School*, 88.

73. Delfattore, *Fourth R*, 21; Dierenfield, *Battle Over School Prayer*, 17–18.

74 Feldberg, *Philadelphia Riots*; Delfattore, *Fourth R*, 41–43.

city became the scene of a Protestant / Catholic controversy that best illustrates the struggles over religion in education in the nineteenth century. Reflecting the changing face of America, this city possessed a variety of ethnic groups and religious beliefs that included conservative and liberal Protestants, Roman Catholics, Jews, and free thinkers. The school board of the city reflected this diversity and in the summer of 1869, they decided to try to bring all of the public and parochial schools together under their control for the purpose of establishing a unified school system acceptable to all. Opposition immediately arose from both Catholic and non-Catholic sources. A local nativist newspaper declared the existence of a "Jesuitical Scheme on Foot" to take over the schools. In addition, twenty-four German Catholic priests declared themselves "positively against all consolidation of our Catholic schools within the public schools." To solve this issue, one of the school board members, Samuel Miller, proposed that as a part of this consolidation, religious instruction and the reading of religious books such as the Bible should simply be prohibited in the public schools so as to allow children of all faiths to attend the schools and benefit from a common school fund. This proposal, though adopted, created a firestorm of protest from all quarters in the city. Protestant leaders screamed the loudest, proclaiming the Bible and the common Protestant religion to be irreplaceable pillars of American ideals. Ultimately, this proposal to have a non-religious school consolidation faced a court challenge. While lower courts overturned the Miller proposals, eventually this matter found its way in 1873 to the Ohio State Supreme Court. The court ruled that the Constitution of the state did "not enjoin or require religious instruction, or the reading of religious books in the public schools." Further, it went on to say that the courts had no real authority to interfere with the actions of local school boards in terms of the type of instruction to be given. Hence, the court upheld the decision of the school board.[75]

Even though the courts upheld the actions of the Cincinnati school board, Catholic leaders began to support separate parochial schools in the years after the controversy. Newspapers reported that the morals of the youth in the city did not seem affected whether or not the Bible reading occurred at school. Bible reading simply ceased in the Cincinnati public schools, while religious instruction continued as an integral part of the city's parochial schools.[76] The Cincinnati Bible War differed from previous incidents in that it foretold the direction of public education in the nation. Although the

75. Michaelsen, "Common School, Common Religion?," 201–17.

76. Michaelsen, "Common School, Common Religion?," 211–12; McGreevy, *Catholicism and American Freedom*, 116–17.

public schools in America would still retain their Protestant flavor well into the twentieth century, Cincinnati offered a picture of a movement toward religious neutrality and secularization in public education as the elusiveness of "non-sectarian" religious instruction became more evident over time.[77] Moving away from religious instruction simply reflected the evolution of common schools seeking to educate a citizenry of growing diversity.

Whether it be in New York, Philadelphia, or Cincinnati, the presence of more and more Catholics in the United States posed the most noticeable threat to the Protestant control of the public school system. Issues over public funding or the reading of the King James Bible necessarily wed nineteenth-century Protestants to public education as a critical institution for the perpetuation of their beliefs which they saw as intrinsically linked to the foundation of the nation. The conflicts mentioned above clearly illustrate the animosity of Protestants toward Catholics and the depth of their commitment to having Bible reading and religious instruction as a part of America's educational system. Decades later, Christian school pioneers would continue this battle against Catholic power while simultaneously building their own school system.

Beyond the struggles with Catholicism, Protestant control of education also faced attacks from new philosophies that ultimately infiltrated the public schools in varying degrees. John Dewey's progressive education provides the best example in that it challenged the traditional religious foundation of early American schools and greatly diminished Protestant influence. Dewey emerged in the late nineteenth century as the most dominant educational philosopher of his day. Born in rural Vermont in 1859, he studied at Johns Hopkins University under the teaching of George S. Morris and G. Stanley Hall, one of the founders of child and adolescent psychology. Their new ideas about the education of children, coupled with the Darwinian insistence on observation and scientific inquiry, influenced Dewey as he took up the cause of public education.[78]

Dewey took up educational reform at a time of great change in public education. He and others argued that educational functions traditionally carried on by family, neighborhood or shop were now failing due to the ravages of industrialism and the influx of vast numbers of immigrants. In their view, schools had to take on wider responsibility. Leading the Progressive movement's push for educational reform, Dewey published two significant books, *The School and Society* (1898) and *Democracy and*

---

77. Michaelsen, "Common School, Common Religion?," 201.

78. Anthony and Benson, *Exploring the History*, 330; Rury, *Education and Social Change*, 146–47.

Education (1916). Responding to the educational concerns of the day, he proposed that the classroom needed to provide not just basic academic skills, but discipline, character building, vocational awareness, and social development.[79] Dewey stated, "We must make each of our schools to be an embryonic community, active with types of occupations that reflect the life of the larger society, and permeated throughout with the spirit of art, history and science. When the school introduces and trains each child of society into membership within such a little community, saturating him with the spirit of service, and providing him with the instruments of effective self direction, we shall have the deepest and best guarantee of a larger society which is worthy, lovely and harmonious."[80]

This passage reflects Dewey's idea of what later became known as progressive education. A microcosm of the larger society could be found in his "embryonic community" with the educator being cast in the role of a social reformer. Dewey also sharply criticized "old school" teaching methods and strictly uniform curriculum.[81] He described it this way, "The educational center of gravity had too long been in the teacher, the textbook, anywhere and everywhere you please except in the immediate instincts of the child himself. The essence of new education was to shift this center of gravity back to the child."[82] Several key ideas permeated his theories about education, but at the heart of it all, he stressed child-centered education, focusing on their intrinsic motivations with emphasis on hands on activities, varied experiences, and social interaction.[83] For centuries education had been subject centered with the teacher serving as the authority and driving force in the classroom. Dewey encouraged just the opposite. A child's natural impulses toward conversation, inquiry, construction, and expression should now become the focus of the classroom as what he referred to as the "uninvested capital" of the educational process.[84] Dewey believed education to be a process of interaction between the child and the curriculum and between the school and society. Although criticized frequently, he was not a radical. He did not advocate doing away with traditional academic subjects and let the children follow their every whim. Instead, he felt that school lessons should be taught differently, utilizing a larger world of experiences

79. Cremin, *American Education*, 117.

80. Dewey, *School and Society*, 43–44.

81. Cremin, *American Education*, 118.

82. Dewey, *School and Society*, 51.

83. Reed and Prevost, *History of Christian Education*, 312.

84. Cremin, *American Education*, 118–19.

beyond just the teacher to impart the critical material about mathematics, history, biology and other fields.[85]

In his later work, *Democracy and Education* (1916), Dewey further commented on the role of education in a democratic society. Responding to the rapid changes facing American society, he argued that the school would be essential to imparting the tenets of a democratic life that would be threatened by widening social divisions. He believed that democracy prevailed when more and more points of view fed into the common beliefs of the people producing freer interaction and mutual understanding. A democratic society should be "intentionally progressive" meaning that it must be committed to change. Historian Lawrence Cremin states, "What more suitable theory for a society in flux, a society of immigrant groups engaged in a dramatic reshuffling of customs and allegiances, a society whose intellectuals sense a loss of community and a driving force to rebuild it? Democracy becomes a quest for the 'more perfect union,' a kind of continuing process of e pluribus unum." Placing the need for change at the heart of American democracy, Dewey obviously felt that this placed a compelling demand upon the educational system. Schools had to be restructured to develop citizens who could appreciate and adapt to rapid change of ideas and beliefs.[86]

Hence, according to Dewey, children will prosper in an educational system that allows for more ideas and experiences. The goal of education was not only to make students citizens or workers, fathers or mothers, but rather to make them human beings who will live life to the fullest by continuously adding to the meaning of their experiences. Teaching a broader range of subjects would better equip children for a more complicated world. Experiences that would enhance social interaction would eventually develop a more positive culture. Going further, Dewey wanted schools to inculcate habits that would enable individuals to control their surroundings rather than merely to adapt to them. Ultimately, John Dewey felt that you must transform school education in order to transform society.[87]

In terms of the role of religion in education, Dewey found it difficult to accept any particular orthodox faith because of their inherent limitations. He felt that if education supported the idea of a free, open-ended society, then it could not at the same time be hemmed in by a closed system of thought that one would find in religion, so the practice of Bible reading in the classroom would be contrary to his philosophy.[88] To put it another way,

85. Rury, *Education and Social Change*, 147.

86. Cremin, *American Education*, 121–22.

87. Cremin, *American Education*, 122–26.

88. Wilhoit, *Christian Education*, 89.

"It becomes the unique purpose of education, therefore, to keep all avenues to truth open, free, and accessible, as well as to point up the irreconcilable conflict between democracy and all forms of absolutism."[89] He therefore had little patience with the efforts of organized religion to influence the public school. In a 1908 article, Dewey warned that any attempt to teach religion in the common school constituted a clear violation of the true purpose of education because it would divert the school from the truly "religious" task of humanizing and communalizing Americans.[90]

Hence, for Dewey, religion was a "common faith" based upon consensus derived from experiences and a variety of points of view contrary to the notion that morals could be inculcated by direct authoritarian instruction. Progressive schools would actually perform "an infinitely religious work" in bringing together children of different nationalities, traditions, and creeds and "assimilating them together upon the basis of what is common and good." Dewey's words aimed to promote a spirit of unity, but to later critics they seem to promote a spirit of collectivism. However, it should be remembered that Dewey responded to the issues of his day, a time not far removed from the divisions of the Civil War, when thousands of immigrants poured into the country, when Jim Crow had become a reality, and when Jews and Irish faced numerous economic and social obstacles.[91]

The ideas of Dewey emerged as a major antagonist for conservative Christians in the twentieth century. Suggestions that truth was relative, and best determined by community consensus, would obviously create great problems for orthodox believers in the ensuing decades. Dewey's pedagogy would also find opposition in that he challenged the authority of the teacher and marginalized the role of religion. Making education child-centered based upon experiential learning rather than God-centered based upon the absolutes of the Bible would provide additional points of contention. No wonder that when the Christian school movement began to materialize in the decades of the 1920s through the 1940s, John Dewey would be a frequent target. Writing in 1947, an evangelical pastor would proclaim, "This so-called 'progressive education' with its emphasis on pupil-centered classes, basically rejects the thesis that past generations have anything to teach the individual. Instead, he is to learn from himself as the teacher is incidental in the classroom. Discipline is not to be tolerated as it will thwart the spirit of the child. We have with us a generation of young people who

---

89. Burns and Brauner, *Philosophy of Education*, 318.

90. Michaelsen, "Common School, Common Religion?," 146.

91. Michaelsen, "Common School, Common Religion?," 143.

have been taught not to obey, to feel that they know what is best for themselves, to follow their whims and do as they please."[92]

Another occurrence outside of the world of American Protestantism that would ultimately add to the debate over religion in schools would be the establishment of compulsory school attendance laws. In the years after the Civil War, with the pressures of immigration, urbanization and an industrialized economy, state governments became more active in legislative and regulatory efforts to assist children. More states began passing compulsory attendance laws with the result being a significant reordering of the relationship between the family and the state. While the state recognized the right of parents to educate their children, the state also asserted its authority by making sure all children attended school.[93]

For private schools, this legislation held great significance. Although most states recognized private schools as fulfilling compulsory attendance statutes, these laws became the legislative justification and legal mechanism through which the state could intervene and regulate the activities of a private school. Compulsory attendance regulations now made private religious schools instruments of state policy and thereby subject to supervision. A few examples from the final quarter of the nineteenth century illustrate the potential problems. In 1874, the California compulsory education statute contained a provision making enrollment in a private school a criminal offense unless the local board of education approved of a child attending such a school. Laws in Wisconsin and Illinois passed in 1889 required that certain subjects be taught in English. Germans in these states who had children attending Catholic or Lutheran schools viewed these laws as being clearly aimed at their private sectarian educational systems. At the close of the century, laws in Ohio and Rhode Island denied private schools a tax exempt status.[94]

The issue of compulsory attendance for private schools would eventually be resolved in the 1920s with the *Pierce v. Society of Sisters* case to be discussed later. However, the issue of state control would remain a point of contention. While the public schools in the nineteenth century remained distinctly Protestant and had the full support of the vast majority of American Christians, the issue of state regulation would emerge in the twentieth century as a great concern for conservative evangelical parents who desired to educate their children in their own way.

92. Edman, "New Lamps for Old," 4.

93. Randall, "Religious Schools," 90.

94. McLaughlin, *History of State Legislation*; Krausharr, *American Non-Public Schools*, 68; Randall, "Religious Schools," 90–91.

With challenges produced by immigration, Catholicism, and the educational philosophy of John Dewey, the practice of Bible reading in the schools began to decline in the second half of the nineteenth century, despite the fact that public education still enjoyed widespread support of all American Protestants. One of the earliest reports on this practice from the schools in Allegheny County, New York stated that of 105 schools surveyed, only twenty-seven opened their day with Bible reading. In 1846, the Reverend Charles Hodge, the moderator of the General Assembly of the Presbyterian Church, issued a report lamenting that "the common school system is rapidly assuming not a mere negative, but a positively anti-Christian character." The Massachusetts Board of Education in 1856, representing the state with probably more per capita Bible reading in schools than all of the others, reported moral training "as being looked upon as a purely incidental part of education, and is either neglected or treated in a desultory manner." John Eaton, the United States commissioner of education, wrote in 1880 that in the majority of the statewide reports the systematic instruction in moral teachings appeared extremely vague.[95]

Clear regional patterns of Bible reading emerged by the mid 1800s with the practice being most prevalent in the northeastern U.S. and least common in the South, Midwest and West. The South reported increases over the next fifty years, but no Southern state actually required it. The West practiced very limited Bible reading. In 1896, Nevada's state superintendent reported that not one school in the state had Bible reading or religious instruction. In the states of California, Wyoming, Colorado, and Oregon approximately one fourth of the schools on the average reported any kind of religious instruction and in Washington and Idaho, the law declared Bible reading illegal. An 1895 report of the United States commissioner of education best summarized the state of Bible reading and religious instruction in public schools. Noting that Bible reading in school districts across the country followed a wide variety of practices, the report concluded, "There is no considerable area where its use can be said to be uniform."[96] Mann's commitment to non-sectarian Bible reading began to gradually disappear by the end of the century as these schools adapted to the growing pluralism of the nation.

However, in terms of providing a universal education for all citizens, the sheer growth of public schools by the end of the nineteenth century certainly reflected Mann's vision. In 1870, expenditures for public schools stood at $69 million. By 1890, this number had risen to $147 million. In

95. Moore, "Bible Reading," 1581.
96. Moore, "Bible Reading," 1585–86.

terms of enrollment, the same decades saw 7.6 million students increase to 12.7 million. The United States had the distinction of providing more schooling to children than any other nation on earth. Historian Diane Ravitch concludes, "In 1900, the public school was one of the most treasured public institutions in the United States. Americans celebrated their tax-supported free schools as a quintessential symbol of the nation's democratic promise that all girls and boys could improve themselves and rise in the world in accordance with their talents and effort."[97] With this growth, public education in America had expanded to meet the needs of a changing nation. Although the Protestant Christian influence seemed to be slowly waning, most Protestants still possessed great loyalty to the public schools. The common school had succeeded in becoming a form of civil religion that combined the powerful emotions of patriotism with deep religious convictions. Failure to support this institution would still be viewed by most all American Christians in 1900 as a sign of disloyalty.[98] William Hutchison sums up the accomplishments of nineteenth-century Protestants this way, "A funny thing happened on the way to the twentieth century: the Americans, who were noted for overthrowing religious establishments, and were delighted with themselves for having done so, developed a very effective religious establishment of their own."[99]

However, by 1920, conservative Christian educators such as Mark Fakkema and Dr. Frank Gaebelein had begun to question this "quintessential" institution and as a result started to establish their own private Christian schools. For these leaders, the public schools had gradually drifted toward becoming secular and therefore unacceptable to their children. In their opinion, the educational system in early America had been thoroughly Christian, but over the course of the nineteenth century, the nation's schools had been undermined by Catholicism and new secular philosophies.[100] This virtually unnoticed minority of conservative Protestants saw the goal of a Christian America as now being actually threatened by the public school system. Believing that the nation had been founded on Christian principles, Fakkema called for the "re-establishment" of Christian schools.[101]

Even though the vast majority of American Protestants still strongly supported public education, when Fakkema, Gaebelein, and other early Christian school leaders emerged in the 1920s, they would look back at

---

97. Mondale and Patton, *School*, 58, 64.

98. Dierenfield, *Battle Over School Prayer*, 22–23.

99. Hutchison, "Diversity and the Pluralist Ideal," 59.

100. Fakkema, "Without the Christian Religion," 14–15.

101. Fakkema, "Without the Christian Religion," 1.

the previous century and a half with great concern. By the 1940s, as the movement reached nationwide status, these early Christian school leaders produced their own simplistic interpretation of the history of American education that disregarded the complex issues facing the new country. In their minds, a Christian nation, protecting freedom of religion and respecting biblical morality as the foundation of society had existed in colonial America. However, negative changes began to slowly occur. These individuals would praise the strong religious nature of the colonial schools with their extensive use of the Bible, but would be critical of Enlightenment ideas promoted non-sectarian beliefs in the schools and relegated Bible training to the churches.

In addition, they would have agreed with many of Mann's contemporary critics who saw his insistence upon Bible reading without commentary as a watered down form of Christianity. By the mid-twentieth century Christian school educators Kenneth Gangel and Warren Benson would see Mann's effort to keep Christian values in public education as a poor compromise that ultimately hurt the overall cause of Christian education. They state, "This system of compromises with respect to the religious issue, of which Mann was the principle advocate, set in motion a process that resulted in the legal secularization of most modern public education."[102] These conservative Christians were also greatly alarmed at the rising power of the Catholic Church in America and would have stood by the public schools in their refusals to fund parochial schools. However, the compromises made in places like Cincinnati, Ohio in the 1870s resulting in the complete elimination of Bible reading and religious instruction would only provide further proof of the gradual slide toward secularization.

The new public schools of the nineteenth century would have also caused alarm among the Christian school leaders over the issue of control. Mann's commitment to state supervision of schools that shifted responsibility away from the church and the home would eventually become a major issue. This system, supported by taxes and mandatory attendance laws, would, in the opinion of conservative Christian educator Rousas Rushdoony, "be bound to veer toward secularism and statism." Writing in the mid-twentieth century, Rushdoony would go on to say, "It follows that wherever government gets into the education business—whether local or national levels—its influence will tend to secularize the schools."[103]

Certainly, the new philosophies that emerged during the nineteenth century would likewise cause consternation among conservative Christian

102. Gangel and Benson, *Christian Education*, 274.
103. Rushdoony, *Intellectual Schizophrenia*, xix.

educators in the twentieth century. John Dewey would become vilified by the Christian school movement for decades in a variety of ways. While Christian educators appreciated Dewey's commitment to more modern teaching techniques, they would at the same time sharply criticize him for his belief in the relativity of truth. Perhaps most frightening to them was Dewey's commitment to changing society in ways that were seen by these conservatives as a direct affront to their faith and their view of the foundations of America. When Dewey died in 1952, Mark Fakkema said, "We appreciate Dewey's calling attention to a stilted, stifling educational practice, but we must condemn his God-denying, Christ-dishonoring educational philosophy."[104]

With the dawn of a new century, most Protestants in the United States would have still seen the public schools as a critical component in the fight for a Christian America. Despite the diminishing practice of Bible reading in many areas, the steadfast stand of public schools against Catholicism kept most Protestants firmly bound to this institution. However, by 1920 a minority of very conservative Christians became disillusioned about American public education. Because of their perception that Mann's common schools had started a gradual movement toward secularization, this minority of Christian leaders saw their goal of a "good society" being threatened. Whereas nineteenth-century Protestants looked to the future and hoped for the perfecting of a Christian America, by the early twentieth century this more conservative minority saw how far America had strayed from its Christian roots and pleaded for a return to the glorious Godly nation of the founding fathers, which, in reality was more of an illusion than reliable history.

But these conservative Christians would not despair. The solution to reclaiming a Christian America against this unwanted secularization could still be found in education. However, the challenge of educating children in a separate system would be daunting due to cost and long standing Protestant loyalty to public schools. Yet, despite this adversity, private Christian day schools would be founded in the early twentieth century laying a foundation for the later Christian school movement led by individuals such as Dr. Frank Gaebelein and Mark Fakkema. In the end, these educators would find themselves in surprising agreement with American Protestantism's nemesis, the Catholic Bishop of New York John Hughes, when he said, "We will not send our children where they will be trained up without religion, lose respect for their parents and the faith of their fathers."[105]

104. Fakkema, "John Dewey is Dead," 1.
105. Dierenfield, *Battle Over School Prayer*, 20–21.

Chapter 3

The Erosion of a Christian America

In the early twentieth century, America's educational system, like the rest of society, felt the influence of industrialization, immigration, urbanization, and growing cultural pluralism. A host of social problems emerged from these changes such as crowded cities, inadequate city services, poverty, and a population adapting from rural to urban living. Schools changed and responded to these issues. As Joel Spring summarizes, "The school was considered a logical institution to prevent these problems by providing social services, teaching new behaviors, and creating a community center." Schools expanded their services to include nurses, showers, cafeterias, and playgrounds. The changes in society made the school more than a center of instruction by turning it into a major social agency.[1]

A conflict also arose in the nation's very identity, between those who saw America as urban, cosmopolitan, heterogeneous, and progressive, and others who thought of their nation as homogeneous, rural, fundamentalist, and traditional.[2] With this conflict arose a fear that the new immigrants were destroying traditional America's values by bringing to its shores more radical economic, political, and spiritual ideas. To quote Spring again, "As the social center of the new urban America, the school became a bastion of Anglo-Americanism and anti-radicalism."[3] Hence, the schools became social agencies negotiating rapid change while simultaneously striving to uphold and rescue some of the traditional culture's core beliefs. Feeling this tension, many public school leaders felt it vital to develop in schools an artificial sense of community in which children could have traditional values

1. Spring, *American School*, 213–14.
2. Church and Sedlak, *Education in the United States*, 352.
3. Spring, *American School*, 214.

reinforced, while also encountering the social learning and group activities that were central to new ideas about progressive education.[4]

John Dewey's progressive pedagogy, outlined in the previously mentioned *The School and Society* (1898) and *Democracy and Education* (1916), sought to help children adjust to a new and rapidly changing world by addressing the concerns of many leaders of public education.[5] Dewey explained the new social functions of the school to educators who gathered at the 1902 meeting of the National Education Association. "Education must provide a means for bringing people and their ideas and their beliefs together," he argued, "in such ways as will lessen friction and instability, and introduce deeper sympathy and wider understanding." Modern schools, which Dewey characterized as "social centers," could pose as clearinghouses of ideas that would help the new urban industrial workers interpret the meaning of their place in the modern world. In addition, the school as a social center would continue to provide an Americanizing element for the sake of developing a unified American set of beliefs.[6]

As America's public schools passed through the first three decades of the new century, Dewey's progressive education gained ground. "Progressive education" has been described as simply the educational phase of American Progressivism writ large which made it an outgrowth of the overall humanitarian effort to deal with the perplexing new urban-industrial civilization developing in the late nineteenth century.[7] It became a multi-faceted effort to improve the lives of all children. Progressive education meant several things that included broadening the role of the schools to include concern about health, vocation, and family life. It also meant applying pedagogical principles in the classroom derived from new scientific research in psychology and the social sciences. In addition, progressive education implied a tailoring of instruction to different classes and ethnicities of children under the school's charge.[8]

The 1919 report from the Progressive Education Association entitled *The Cardinal Principles of Secondary Education* led to the implementation of significant changes in many public schools emphasizing experiential learning and an overall commitment to train children to be effective functioning adults in modern America. Teaching methods became more child

---

4. Cremin, *American Education*, 232–33; Church and Sedlak, *Education in the United States*, 391.

5. Church and Sedlak, *Education in the United States*, 392.

6. Spring, *American School*, 214.

7. Cremin, *American Education*, viii.

8. Cremin, *American Education*, viii–ix.

centered, flexible, hands on, and democratic moving decidedly away from the more rigid, subject-centered approach. The overall purpose of schooling shifted away from the mere acquisition of knowledge to a goal of "effective living" which meant providing more than just the standard subjects but also non-academic studies in family living, vocational training, and social issues. High school enrollments increased due to the broader range of courses and training available that appealed to more than just the minority going on to college.[9]

However, the changes associated with progressive education did not always go smoothly nor produce the desired results. Proposed curriculum changes created controversy in many schools. A sampling of school districts in the late 1920s noted a pronounced shift in the stated goals of some schools, from concern about intellectual development and mastery of subject matter to concern for social and emotional development and the adoption of "functional" objectives in areas such as vocation, health, and family life. According to Diane Ravitch, "Generally revised curriculum was not an effort to balance the intellectual, social and emotional needs, but a conscious attempt to denigrate the traditional notion of 'Knowledge for its own sake' as useless and possibly worthless."[10] As professional educators pushed progressive ideas, they often faced resistance from parents and teachers concerned about a shift in academics away from college preparation as well as the enlarged role of the school in family life. As the decade progressed, more complaints emerged, such as the comments of Professor Robert Hutchins of the University of Chicago, who wrote about poor discipline in progressive schools, poor mastery of the fundamentals, and the abandonment of Western culture for practical studies. In addition, laymen and parents felt the disdain of professional educators, and resented their attempts to constantly use children as guinea pigs in the latest pedagogical theories and fads. Perhaps most of all, many conservative educators and parents expressed concern over the neglect of standards of absolute truth coupled with emphasis placed on experience-based learning. More extreme measures also caused controversy and generated negative publicity. When one school attempted to abolish report cards and institute automatic promotion, parents complained loudly. A school district in Granite, Utah received much criticism because progressive officials felt a responsibility to have an "enlarged social role" by inquiring into the homes of their students and asking about their activities after school and in the summer.[11]

9. Ravitch, *Troubled Crusade*, 44–51; Cremin, *American Education*, 251–55.
10. Ravitch, *Troubled Crusade*, 55.
11. Patterson, "Curriculum Improvement," 48.

Overall, the progressive education that surfaced in the 1920s in public education brought much needed reform but also much controversy which retarded its accomplishments. The best summary of this struggle comes again from Diane Ravitch, "The positive contributions of progressive education were often at war with, and sometimes even submerged by, their own implicit distortions: the extremes of permissiveness in the child centered movement, the hostility toward books and subject matter that grew out of the emphasis on 'doing,' the excessive vocationalism that emerged from social utility, and the notion that the school was uniquely qualified to meet all needs without establishing priorities among them."[12] Some historians have argued that progressive education never possessed a clear definition beyond just an emphasis on experimentation. Consequently, this led to a wide variety of interpretations which in turn caused much controversy and criticism from conservative teachers, parents, and business leaders.[13] Even John Dewey criticized the movement in 1938. He rebuked educational zealots who seemed intent on ridding schools of any organized subject matter and disregarding any input of adults in the life of a child as if it were an invasion of freedom. He warned, "It is not too much to say that an educational philosophy which professes to be based on the idea of freedom may become as dogmatic as ever was the traditional education which is reacted against."[14]

Beyond the controversies associated with progressive education, the efforts to use public schools as vehicles for Americanization and the complementary issue of the role of religion in education also added to the turmoil in the educational world of the 1920s. Going back as far as Horace Mann, public school leaders had felt pressure to instill in children, native and immigrant, the virtues that many considered essential to both the American Republic and Protestant Christianity. By the 1920s, the concern over immigrants, and the push to use the schools as an agent of Americanization, reached a crisis point in a court case involving a public school law in Oregon.

In the fall of 1922, the voters of the state of Oregon passed a referendum on a bill designed to make public school attendance compulsory for all children between the ages of eight and sixteen. The Ku Klux Klan had gained a political foothold in the state and succeeded in convincing the voters that only public schools properly inculcated the important American values to

12. Ravitch, *Troubled Crusade*, 51.

13. Cremin, *American Education*, 252; Pulliam and Patten, *History of Education in America*, 222.

14. Dewey, *Experience and Education*, 21–30.

their children.[15] Over the next three years, many church leaders spoke out harshly against this law since the most immediate impact of this legislation would be to close down all private and parochial schools in the state. Catholic leaders raised the issue of religious freedom and defended the value of their own form of education which promoted the beliefs of their church. Before the law was even passed, a Catholic newspaper in Oregon stated, "those who imagine that they are attempting to enforce conformity as a purely educational issue apart from religion should realize that the real issue at stake here is religion and the animus behind the measure is directed especially at one religion."[16] The Oregon School law, driven by conservatives concerned about Americanization, not only highlighted compulsory attendance laws, also brought to light the issue of religion in education.

Not surprisingly, the constitutionality of this law was challenged and in 1925 it was argued before the Supreme Court under the name of *Pierce v. Society of Sisters*. On June 1, the Supreme Court ruled unanimously in favor of the Society of Sisters. Upholding the opinion of the lower federal court, the high court ruled the Oregon compulsory school law unconstitutional. Justice James Clark McReynolds expressed the view of the court that the state's parochial schools "are engaged in a kind of undertaking not inherently harmful, but long regarded as useful and meritorious. Certainly there is nothing in the present records to indicate that they failed to discharge their obligations to patrons, students, or the state."[17] The ruling did not directly mention religion in education. However, *Pierce v. Society of Sisters* did raise the issue of the teaching of religion in public schools while also strengthening the position of private schools in American society. Obviously, this case would later be foundational to the Protestant Christian school movement.

While private schools came out of the *Pierce* case validated, its significance can be found in what it represented about the tension that existed between religion and education in the 1920s. Continuing to struggle to provide an education to an increasingly pluralistic society, advocates of the Oregon school law hoped to keep a homogeneous form of white Protestant values intact in public education and leave no room for the Catholics. The failure of their attempt exposed the growing religious diversity of the nation, ultimately leading to more controversy about religion in public schools. This renewed debate would again raise the question about the feasibility of religious teaching in the schools, a question unresolved since the Cincinnati "Bible War" of 1869. In addition, Dewey's progressive education, which

15. Holsinger, "Oregon School Controversy," 329.

16. "Real Issue," 4.

17. "Pierce Case," 1.

raised doubt about the role of religion in public schools, only added to the debate and the gradual march toward secularization.

However, while controversy certainly existed in the 1920s over the place of religion in American schools, public school educators did strive to keep religious instruction in their institutions. Educational journals and minutes of professional educator conferences from the decade show many concerns about Christian principles disappearing from the classroom. In 1916, *School and Society* published a report from the annual convention of the Religious Education Association of America. According to the editors of the journal, this organization of leading Protestant churches reported on an emerging awakening of the American people toward the need for religious education. This organization specifically called for religious training during the week, curriculum materials approved by school and church officials, and professional standards for teachers of such classes. The report ended by exhorting churches and parents to seize the great opportunity that existed to enhance the religious life of children.[18]

In 1918, the issue arose again in an edition of *School and Society*. Drawing on patriotic themes in the midst of the world war, the author called for a reconsideration of democratic education that included an emphasis on character development. By using literature and Christian hymns teachers could effectively communicate moral truths while also stirring a love for God and country. "If we emphasize character and morality," the author concluded, "Thus shall we make the pattern laid up in heaven incarnate on earth. Thus shall we build the city of God."[19]

At the 1922 meeting of the National Education Association, a report presented from a committee on the teaching of democracy had a notably religious tone. The committee described its work as "epoch making" and discussed a movement underway to strengthen Protestant church education through renewed cooperation with public schools. This could be accomplished by establishing week-day church schools which would meet for two or three hours twice a week, using a trained teaching force and a "scientifically organized" course of study. The students would leave their public school campus for such instruction, but would receive academic credit for these religion courses. At the same time, the committee asked church leaders, who would teach these classes, to link their religion courses to democratic principles and also lessen the sectarian elements of the instruction. In sum, this NEA committee advocated weekday church

18. "Religious Instruction and Public Education," 540.
19. Boodin, "Education for Democracy," 724–31.

schools, claiming that they would benefit the nation by bringing religious instruction back into the public schools.[20]

In October 1923, *The Educational Review* reported on an example of a weekday religious school in New York City. Certain schools dismissed children one hour early once a week for religious training at the request of two Catholic archbishops. Protests from the board of education resulted on the grounds that the plan violated the separation of church and state and this arrangement was only short lived. However, the article did note that efforts to have off campus religious instruction at the university level appeared to be successful in nine states. Despite the mixed success of weekday religious instruction, the journal made a strong appeal for continued attempts to bring religious training into public schools. Charles Eliot, the former President of Harvard University, bolstered this argument by proclaiming, "The failure of our public schools to turn out good citizens and voters is conspicuous. We shall have to look it squarely in the face. First teach children their duty to parents, brothers, and sisters. Children in the public schools are getting none of it at the moment. Many are getting nothing of it at home. Teach the meaning of loving their neighbors. Beyond that is the motive of putting into children's hearts the love of God."[21]

Eventually, legal challenges to the idea of "weekday religious schools" or what later became known as "released-time religious instruction," arose in the 1920s and would continue into the 1950s. In 1926, a case involving such programs reached the Supreme Court of the state of New York. In the city of Mount Vernon, a suit alleged that the weekday religious schools curtailed the amount of instructional time for the public schools and thereby indirectly allowed for religion to be taught during school hours. The court agreed with the suit seeing the program as a violation of the separation of church and state.[22] Later, the editors of *The School Review* pointed out that this case indicated a growing problem facing many school systems desiring to teach religion. School leaders all across the nation found it difficult to refuse the many requests of citizens to have their children pulled out of school for religious training. As a result, these weekday schools became very diverse and often sectarian, making it "quite impossible to devise any general system of religious education and that supervision of the methods and the quality of such training as is given is hopeless."[23]

20. Yocum, "Report of the Committee," 505–10.

21. "Religious Instruction in Public Schools," 170–72.

22. "Religious Instruction in Co-operation," 170–74.

23. "Religious Instruction in Co-operation," 172.

Despite these valiant efforts, secularism in the public schools seemed to be inevitable. F. Ernest Johnson, Executive Secretary of the Federal Council of Churches, when asked about the decline of religion in schools, stated, "It is a mutual badge of ineptitude that Protestants, Catholics, and Jews should have found no way to combat the common foe, antisocial secularism, except to remove from our most influential institutions for character building the resources of spiritual living that we hold in common."[24] The loss of religious studies in public schools concerned Christians all across the theological spectrum.

In sum, public education in the 1920s became embroiled in controversy associated with the rapid changes in American society. The rural, homogeneous America rooted in traditional conservative Protestantism clashed with the modern, progressive, urban America characterized by religious pluralism. Public educators, feeling the pressure of traditional high expectations from their constituents, struggled with the complexities of diversity. Progressive education reflected a response to this challenge by promoting innovative pedagogical strategies focused on the needs of the child with a goal of preparing them for a constantly changing society. However, conservative educators opposed the apparent lack of emphasis on traditional studies as well as progressive theories about how children learn. Public schools strained to continue their task of Americanizing immigrants resulting in a failed attempt to force compulsory attendance in the *Pierce v. Society of Sisters* case. Inadvertently, they forced the courts to uphold the validity of private education, which would only add to the growing pluralism. Finally, public education dealt with diversity in the issue of religion in their schools. Attempting to provide religiously based character education for a student body that reflected more and more religious pluralism resulted in controversial released-time programs that faced challenges from those who felt that the practice violated the principle of separation of church and state. The question of religious diversity necessarily drove the schools to eliminate specific teaching of religion. Public educators in the first two decades of the twentieth century, seeking to address social issues of the day and meet the needs of an increasingly complex populace, faced great resistance. Continuing to evolve into a "common school," they received much criticism from those uncomfortable with their changes and the changes in society in general. Among their many critics would be a tiny contingent of conservative Christians led by Mark Fakkema and Frank Gaebelein.

Protestant Christianity, so long the dominant religious force in America and so long associated with public education, simultaneously faced its own

24. Marty, *Noise of the Conflict,* 381.

unique set of challenges in the twenties. The attempts in the nineteenth century to create a Christian America through revivalism on the frontier and the presence of biblical teaching in the schools seemed to be initially effective in maintaining a strong Protestant value system in the new nation. However, between the end of the Civil War and the end of the 1920s, the power of the American Protestant church faced a heavy assault from forces both within the Protestant faith and from the external American culture. According to historian Robert Handy, this period ultimately led to what he refers to as a "second disestablishment" of American Christianity that left Protestants weakened, their goal of creating a Christian America fading rapidly.[25] The result of this trend would ultimately lead to serious division within the church and more significantly, a loss of cultural prestige and power.

But, as the twentieth century began, many in the Protestant faith still held to the goal of realizing a Christian America, sure that the United States was a Protestant nation, God was Protestant, and Americans were God's chosen people.[26] In the 1873 meeting of the Evangelical Alliance, an early attempt to unite the growing number on Protestant sects, a delegate expressed optimism about the nation's future despite the growing presence of unbelief, Darwinism, and liberal theology. In the 1892 Supreme Court decision of *Church of the Holy Trinity v. United States,* the court made this comment in its majority opinion, "our civilization and institutions are emphatically Christian. This is a religious people. This is historically true. From the discovery of the continent to the present hour, there is a single voice making this affirmation . . . we find everywhere a clear recognition of the same truth. . . . These, and many other matters which might be noticed, add a volume of unofficial declarations to the mass of organic utterances that this is a Christian nation."[27] Evangelicals assumed their continued dominance.

However, this confidence, based on decades of previous success, overlooked the vast changes occurring in American society. In the thirty years following the Civil War, uncomfortable realities in the form of industrialization, immigration, urbanization and an ongoing scientific revolution posed serious challenges to their optimism, long nurtured in the predominantly rural atmosphere of the early nineteenth century. As a result, serious divisions and tensions arose.[28] In 1800, there were approximately three dozen major denominations in the nation; by 1900, this number had risen to

25. Handy, *Christian America*, 184.
26. Tyack and Hansot, *Managers of Virtue*, 19; Randall, "Religious Schools," 67.
27. Anthony and Benson, *Exploring the History*, 288.
28. Handy, *Christian America*, 65.

more than two hundred.[29] The Civil War had caused serious rifts in many denominations as both north and south each saw their respective causes as a part of God's plan for a Christian America. In addition, perceived heretical movements such as Deists, Owenites, Unitarians and spiritualists grew and new indigenous sects such as the Mormons, Seventh Day-Adventists, and Christian Scientists surfaced by the end of the century.[30]

The rise of liberal theology and Darwinism also increased the divisions within the Protestant faith. According to Handy, "The intellectual revolutions of the nineteenth century influenced the thinking of increasing numbers of Protestant clergy and laity. Traditional views of biblical authority, chronology, and interpretation were upset for many as the theory of evolution was popularized and as the techniques of historical criticism were applied to the sacred documents." To a growing group of modernist liberal theologians, the Bible no longer seemed inerrant and immutable. In regard to Darwinism, liberal theologians attempted to marry the theory of evolution to Christian belief. For example, Henry Ward Beecher, a well-known Brooklyn pastor, preached in 1886 that "the great truth" of Darwinism would bring aid to the already established truths in scripture as set forth by Jesus Christ.[31]

George Coe, a professor at Union Theological Seminary and a leading Protestant liberal, promoted a new type of religious education within the church that embraced modern thought. Coe supported teaching a reconciliation between Darwinism and Christianity and as well as acceptance of the educational theories of John Dewey. Coe's 1917 book, *A Social Theory of Religious Education*, criticized the revivalist approach to Christian education that stressed salvation and emotionalism in favor of a faith committed to the reconstruction of the culture through social welfare, social justice, and internationalism. By the late 1920s, Coe had written *What is Christian Education?*, which embraced a Deweyian approach to education within the church that emphasized the creative discovery of students' spiritual experiences while eschewing the traditional approach based solely upon the transmission of religious truths.[32] An academic revolution had changed the cultural balance of power in America. The modern research universities then emerging in the early twentieth century replaced the theistic foundations of earlier academic life with naturalistic presuppositions. Educators

---

29. Wuthnow, *Restructuring of American Religion*, 20.

30. Randall, "Religious Schools," 67; Hutchison, *Religious Pluralism in America*, 140–41; Mosley, *Cultural History of Religion*, 84.

31. Handy, *Christian America*, 72–73; Marty, *Noise of the Conflict*, 219.

32. Elias, *History of Christian Education*, 167–69.

and scientists, armed with these ideas, gained influence as authorities. To the more conservative Christian community, liberal ministers worsened the situation by readily attaching themselves to these educational and scientific elites and joining in the attacks on the Bible's divine inspiration by proposing evolutionary models of moral progress in its place.[33]

Conservatives had reason to be worried. In the three decades from 1890 to 1920, liberalism emerged as the most dynamic force in white Protestantism. Liberal theology managed to become dominant in one-third of the nation's congregations, seminaries, and Protestant publications. For example, a liberal Christian newspaper, *The Outlook,* listed a readership of fifteen thousand in 1870. By 1900, circulation stood at one hundred thousand, the largest readership of any religious newspaper in the nation. In addition, liberals had also come to control a substantial number of foreign mission boards.[34]

Beyond the internal schisms, there existed the on-going concern about the expanding Roman Catholic Church, which threatened the long held Protestant hegemony and dominance in the United States. Catholic challenges to Protestant control of public schools in places like New York and Cincinnati and their continued efforts to establish their own separate schools in many places served to make traditional Christian leaders suspicious of the challenge Catholicism posed to their dream of a Christian America. In 1885, Josiah Strong published the widely read *Our Country: Its Possible Future and Its Present Crisis* in which he outlined the "seven perils" facing the nation. In order, he placed them this way: immigration, Romanism, Mormonism, intemperance, socialism, wealth, and the city. Strong viciously attacked these perils, calling them direct threats to the future of America. Referring to Catholic immigrants, many of whom he characterized as criminals, illiterates, drunkards, and member of the pauper classes, Strong stated, "during the last few years, we have suffered a peaceful invasion by an army, more than twice as vast as the estimated number of Goths and Vandals that swept over Southern Europe and overwhelmed Rome." By 1906, numbers backed up this claim that the country faced a "peaceful invasion," as 40 percent of American church members now belonged to the Roman Catholic faith.[35]

Therefore, by the early 1920s, many forces within education and within the church itself posed serious challenges to traditional Protestant

33. Carpenter, *Revive Us Again,* 36; Marty, *Noise of the Conflict,* 187.

34. Hutchison, *Religious Pluralism in America,* 141.

35. Randall, "Religious Schools," 67; Hutchison, *Religious Pluralism in America,* 139.

power. An article by Philip Hammond summarized the changes in this era, "Just as early nineteenth-century Protestants woke up to the inevitability of a voluntary church, so early twentieth-century Protestants woke up to the inevitability of pluralism, the authority of science, and to the realities of an urbanized, capitalistic society."[36] Ever since the 1880s Protestants had witnessed the absorption of Biblical criticism, evolutionary thought and modern secular philosophy into mainline liberal denominations.[37] With conventional Protestant power structures under attack by the second decade of the twentieth century, the dream of a Christian America appeared to be dying. It would take an aggressive force of conservative believers to revive their vision.

36. Hammond, "Protestant Twentieth Century," 281–94.
37. Marty, *Noise of the Conflict,* 211.

Chapter 4

The "Devoted Few"

I n 1921, the newly formed Stony Brook School for boys in New York chose twenty-two year old Frank E. Gaebelein as its first headmaster. Over time, the school emerged as one of the first notable Christian schools in America and Gaebelein, in turn, became known as one of the movement's philosophical leaders. Though not initially as visible as Mark Fakkema, he nonetheless spoke ardently of the need for Christian schools in the United States. Many years later, in his definitive 1951 book, *Christian Education in a Democracy,* he made clear his view that the nation was imperiled, the vision of a Christian America lost. He lamented the fact that, "the Bible, the greatest moral and spiritual source book in the world, has no place on the required reading list of our American youth."[1] Painting a gloomy picture of America, he went on to say, "Whether we like it or not, we are now in a dark wood. Our generation has lost the direct way."[2] Despite his negative views, Gaebelein continued to believe that the Stony Brook School of the 1920s, like many others in the early twentieth century, held the key to restoring America to greatness. He summed up the introduction to his book in this way, "This, then, is a manifesto, not a mere dispassionate survey. On controversial questions, it takes sides. Like all Christian witness, it seeks a verdict. Its sponsors are quite aware that its appeal is not a majority one. But we have faith in the power of dedicated minority. We know that Christian history abounds with examples of the decisive influence of **the devoted few**: an Athanasius contra mundum, a Luther at Worms, a Carey attempting and accomplishing great things for God, a Niemoeller defying a Hitler—these are only some of a noble army. Men and women, administrators and teach-

1. Gaebelein, *Christian Education in a Democracy,* 5.
2. Gaebelein, *Christian Education in a Democracy,* 9.

ers, schools and colleges willing to go all the way in Christian education may not be numerous; but under God their influence may yet tip the balances in favor of the spiritual revitalization needed to bring America victoriously through the ordeal of this age."[3]

Dr. Frank Gaebelein, along with Mark Fakkema, first appeared in the 1920s as part of this "devoted few" who established the prototypes of a Christian school and an eventual national movement. Gaebelein's Stony Brook School (1922) and Fakkema's Dutch Reformed National Union of Christian Schools (1920), both set standards for the Christian schools that would bloom in the 1940s. These prototypes did not occur in a vacuum; rather they emerged during the tumultuous early decades of the twentieth century felt in both in education and Christianity that sparked some conservative Christians to break with the majority of their fellow Protestants, who still kept their faith in the nation's public schools.

This revolt started with an aggressive force of conservative Christians known as fundamentalists in the 1920s. With deep roots in the evangelical and revivalist traditions, the fundamentalists have been defined as "militantly anti-modernist Protestant evangelicals." Beyond their close ties to nineteenth-century revivalism, this group sought in the twentieth century to oppose both liberal theology and the cultural changes that modern theology endorsed. Consequently, a nationwide patchwork coalition bloomed consisting of groups such as traditional Baptists, Reformed Calvinists, and other conservative Christian sects.[4] This group shared common goals but lacked genuine homogeneity. Theological differences existed, but in an overall sense, they could be seen as conservative orthodox Christians committed to the infallibility of scripture, a firm stand against modern liberal theology, and a commitment to dispensationalism which focused on the prophecy of the end times and the return of Christ.[5]

From World War I to the mid-twenties, fundamentalism became more militant, more galvanized, and more popular. Fundamentalists, like the rest of the nation, found themselves immersed in the patriotism of the Great War and the pervasive anti-German attitudes. Liberal theologians faced assaults because of their links to the German philosophy of biblical criticism. Modern theology and science, now linked to German culture, provided common enemies for conservative Christians to attack in their efforts to protect the nation. Fundamentalists moved this debate beyond theology to a moral issue over which the future of civilization precariously hung. In 1918,

3. Gaebelein, *Christian Education in a Democracy*, 19.

4. Marsden, *Fundamentalism and American Culture*, 4.

5. Sandeen, *Origins of Fundamentalism*, 4–5.

Pastor Howard Kellogg gave an address at the Bible Institute of Los Angeles and proclaimed, "Let the German culture now be identified with Evolution, and the truth begins to be told as a monster plotting world domination, the wreck of civilization, and the destruction of Christianity itself." Marsden stated, "Evolution now became a symbol. Without the new cultural dimension it is unlikely that the debate over Darwinism could have been revived in the spectacular way it was or that fundamentalism itself could have gained widespread support. Americans had just fought a war that could be justified only as a war between civilization and barbarism."[6]

Several notable traits eventually surfaced in this reactionary group of Christians. For example, fundamentalism exhibited a strikingly paradoxical tendency to identify sometimes with the "establishment" and sometimes with the "outsiders." The movement emerged from the revivalism in the nineteenth century and yet in the twentieth century circumstances forced this group to take on the role of a beleaguered minority with strong sectarian or separatist tendencies.[7] These outsider tendencies came from the intellectual insecurity that fundamentalists felt in light of their loss of prestige in many American universities and seminaries. However, at the same time, they enjoyed widespread support in the nation for most of the decade. R. Laurence Moore explains, "If fundamentalists suffered from hurt feelings in twentieth-century America, they have also had available to them a large cushion of public support on which to rest their bruised egos."[8] Despite the apparent victories of the liberals, fundamentalists used their status as outsiders to separate themselves from perceived heresies and distinguish themselves as the protectors of historic biblical truths. In turn, they embarked on an ambitious program of forming their own congregations, denominations, publishing houses, colleges, Bible institutes and eventually elementary and secondary schools.[9]

Another significant characteristic of fundamentalists during this time would be their commitment to premillennialism, an eschatology based upon certain books of prophecy in the Bible. Studying such books as Daniel and Ezekiel, coupled with statements of Jesus about the end times, fundamentalists believed that a hidden plan for the end of the ages could be discovered. Premillennialists pointed to significant events such as the restoration of the Jews to Palestine, the emergence of a new powerful empire in Rome led by Benito Mussolini, the emerging Communist Soviet Union

6. Marsden, *Fundamentalism and American Culture*, 148.

7. Marsden, *Fundamentalism and American Culture*, 6–7.

8. Moore, "Bible Reading and Nonsectarian Schooling," 165.

9. Balmer, "Age of Militancy," 349.

and devastating wars as fulfilling prophecy. They believed that out of this chaos a new leader would arise promising peace and security to the world. Ultimately, this individual would be revealed as the prophesied antichrist, but not before all of the nations had submitted to his authority. However, just before this occurred, premillennialists believed that all of the faithful Christians would be "raptured" to heaven to be with Christ. Afterward, the world would endure seven more years of tribulation and at the end, Jesus and his saints would return for a thousand year reign of peace and prosperity.[10] This set of beliefs made fundamentalists watchful of world events that appeared to point to the end times while also making them suspicious of governmental authority.

Premillennialism, originating with British evangelist John Nelson Darby in the 1870s, stood in contrast to postmillennialism, the dominant eschatological belief of the nineteenth century. Postmillennialism offered a more optimistic mood, believing that the thousand year reign of Christ would come soon for the faithful. It led followers of Christ into action based on a hope in the imminent return of Christ that could be ushered in by the benevolent work of the faithful. Premillennialism was more pessimistic about the future believing that tribulation and totalitarian rule by the antichrist was coming. However, this served to motivate twentieth-century Christians into action to make a stand for righteousness in a dying world. They felt a need to bring Christianity into the culture so as to save as many as possible in the last days.[11] Hence, they had no hesitation speaking out about the evils they perceived at home and abroad. If Armageddon was approaching, they wanted America to be on the right side of history. Premillennialism would become a major tenet of fundamentalism and would remain an influential component of their attitudes toward politics, the economy, and education up until the present time.

Fundamentalism also never neglected its close ties to America's earlier evangelical heritage. Older revivalism and pietism sat at the center of their beliefs and traditions resulting in constant efforts to return to the notion of "the Bible alone." Reformed church leaders often made references to the colonial Puritans and their desire to build a "Christian civilization."[12]

Closely tied to this, fundamentalists felt a strong "trusteeship" of American culture. Historian Joel Carpenter says it best, "The mythic chords of 'Christian America' have played loudly in their memories and their periodic

---

10. Sutton, "Was FDR the Antichrist?," 1056–57; Boyer, *When Time Shall Be No More*, 2.

11. Collins, *Evangelical Moment*, 35.

12. Marsden, *Fundamentalism and American Culture*, 7.

public crusades have displayed their determination to regain their lost cultural power and influence. Even when fundamentalists have expressed their alienation toward American cultural trends and advocated separation from worldly involvement, their words have been more of wounded lovers than true outsiders. They have seen themselves as the faithful remnant, the true American patriots."[13] They explained that their uncompromising attitude developed only because of the enormous challenges to their traditional faith that a successful liberal movement had presented. With a belief that they are right and others are simply wrong, fundamentalists comfortably divided the world into good and evil, right and wrong, ally and enemy, American and foreigner, Christian and anti-Christian. They idealized a golden age of their nation's past and fought hard to restore an earlier version of America.[14]

Fundamentalists were primarily white, middle class. Great attention was paid to the messages they received from preachers, radio, and magazines. Contrary to what many believed, they thrived in predominantly northern and western urban areas, such as New York, Boston, Philadelphia, Chicago, Detroit, Minneapolis, Los Angeles and Seattle. According to Matthew Avery Sutton, the reason for this demographic had to do with the fact that these areas were places where the differences between the fundamentalists and the broader culture were most pronounced. Hence, they distinguished themselves and became more attractive. Fundamentalism did eventually grow in the rural South, but this took longer because conservative Christianity already fit quite comfortably within existing churches.[15]

Fighting to restore their vision of a Christian America, fundamentalists in the 1920s provided impetus to the first Christian elementary and secondary schools. Dewey's controversial progressive education, debates over the role of religion in public schools, the growing power of the Catholic Church, divisions within the Protestant faith, and the overall concern about the loss of power within the traditional American Protestant Church all provided an ideal setting to stir a sense of urgency among some fundamentalists for Christian education. Corresponding with the rise of fundamentalism, Christian schools appeared in this decade as a response to a changing culture marked by rising secularism. The desire of a "devoted few" surfaced with the intent to bring America back to its perceived spiritual heritage.

The roots of a national Christian school organization first appeared decades earlier in the Dutch Reformed schools of the American Midwest.

13. Carpenter, *Revive Us Again*, 6.

14. Hughes, *Christian America and the Kingdom*, 137–38; Hutchison, *Religious Pluralism in America*, 148.

15. Sutton, "Was FDR the Antichrist?," 1055.

As previously noted, the mid 1800s witnessed the establishment of many church based sectarian educational institutions, most notably Roman Catholic schools. Calvinist Dutch immigrants came to America as early as 1847, settling in western Michigan. One of their leaders, Albertus Van Raalte, immediately began promoting the idea of Dutch Reformed Christian schools and as a result, the first parochial Reformed Christian School opened in 1857.[16]

These initial Dutch parochial schools emerged from the Reformed Church, which claimed the need for children to learn foundational truths of their faith. In an 1870 ecclesiastical conference of this church, one official passed a resolution stating, "The elementary school is the nursery of the church." Although great fervor seemed to accompany the establishment of these schools, they possessed inferior instruction, poorly prepared teachers, and inadequate equipment.[17] Hence interest in the schools waned as evidenced by the fact that by 1875 only four of these schools existed in Michigan. Reasons for this stagnation include a loss of conviction about Christian education from the Dutch settlers more concerned with surviving in the wilderness, and the fact that the schools only used the Dutch language.[18]

A Calvinist revival in the Netherlands in the 1880s spread to America and brought new life to the struggling parochial schools. Led by the minister Abraham Kuyper, the new movement stressed that the Reformation ideals of the sovereignty of God should inspire Christians to express their beliefs through, among other things, the creation of distinctly Christian institutions of learning. Going further, the revivalists asserted that the primary responsibility of the education for a child's education belonged to parents, not the state or even the church.

These schools enjoyed the support of some new Dutch immigrants of the 1880s and 1890s who came with professional credentials as educators, including the Reverend Klaas Kuiper, in 1891.[19] Kuiper brought new life to the Dutch Reformed schools by suggesting a new organizational structure. Under his leadership, several schools in western Michigan adopted a resolution in 1892 stating that schools could be better maintained through parental associations rather than a parochial arrangement through the church. Each associational leadership structure varied, but most would be led by a school board. With this resolution, the first such group, known as the Society for Christian Instruction on Reformed Basis, emerged to

16. Simpson, "Development of the National Organization," 75.

17. Vander Ark, 22 Landmark Years, 15.

18. Simpson, "Development of the National Organization," 76.

19. Vander Ark, 22 Landmark Years, 15.

support twelve existing Michigan schools.[20] The establishment of a parent governance model reflected their firm conviction about parental responsibility as noted in certain scripture passages (e.g., Deut 6:4–9). While the role of the church might be diminished with this model, the commitment to Christian standards remained firm. This idea also held great appeal to conservative Christians who desired more control over the education of their children. More debate over this issue would occur later, but the establishment of these parent societies laid a significant foundation block for the future. Today, a large majority of Christian schools still operate in this manner, satisfying the desires of tuition paying parents to have direct influence in the school attended by their children.

In 1894, the Society held its second meeting to discuss a variety of concerns, including the need for trained Christian Reformed teachers and the desire for Reformed based textbooks. However, the central area of debate focused on the reasons for the lack of parental interest in these Christian schools. Three answers to this concern emerged which led to important changes and noticeable growth. First, these schools taught exclusively in the Dutch language. Second, local Reformed ministers did not support the movement. And third, continued unease existed among some parents in regard to the new parent associations that took over the leadership of these schools from the traditional role of the church.[21]

Addressing these concerns took time, but gradually these small Dutch schools universally transformed into English speaking Reformed Christian Schools led by parent associations. From there, the associations banded together to form Christian School alliances. Four such groups eventually materialized—the Michigan, Chicago, Western, and Eastern Alliances. The largest, the Michigan Alliance, began to write a course of study for their schools. They also established an annual teachers institute in 1914 and the Michigan Principals Club in 1916.[22] With the rise of these alliances, some local pastors took more interest in the movement. The Reverend Jan Van Lonkhuyzen, pastor of the First Christian Reformed Church of Chicago, threw his support toward the schools by writing several enthusiastic endorsements of the Chicago Alliance as the editor of a Dutch weekly paper *Onze Toekomst*. The Chicago Alliance, led by Mark Fakkema, the principal of the Chicago Christian High School, quickly advanced as a leading

20. Kuiper, "From the First Union," 16.

21. Simpson, "Development of the National Organization," 80.

22. Simpson, "Development of the National Organization," 80–82.

organization serving as a driving force in the birth of the National Union of Christian Schools in 1920.[23]

Mark Fakkema, whose influence can hardly be overstated, arose from humble beginnings to become one of the founding fathers of the entire Christian school movement. Born in 1890 and reared on a farm in Oak Harbor, Washington, Fakkema attended school through the third grade until his father asked him to quit and help more around the farm. The youngster pleaded for further education and eventually made a deal with his father by agreeing to work on the farm on sunny days, while being allowed to attend school on rainy ones. Slow progress resulted, but young Fakkema graduated from the eighth grade at the age of eighteen in 1908. Following his love for the classroom, he then went to Seattle to earn a teaching certificate and returned a year later to teach at his old school. Because of his strong Calvinist upbringing, Fakkema desired to become a minister and this led him to enroll in Calvin College in Grand Rapids, Michigan. He went on to earn a Master's degree from the University of Michigan and later pursued additional graduate studies from the University of Chicago.[24]

Throughout his life, Fakkema found himself constantly working in pioneering ventures. After his year of teaching in Washington, he assisted with the establishment of a Christian school in Holland, Michigan and worked as a teacher there for several years. While teaching in Holland he struggled to overcome a lifelong fear of public speaking, which he eventually did, giving a massive number of speeches over the next few decades. In 1918, a Christian high school association organized for the purpose of launching a new Christian high school in Chicago. Fakkema accepted the position of principal that same year despite the fact that the school had only nine students enrolled. After asking one of the few automobile owners in Chicago to drive him around, Fakkema began a relentless recruiting campaign in the summer to bring in more students to the school. He visited scores of parents asking them to consider this new school for their children.[25] Strong marketing skills aided the young principal as he also created relationships with several Reformed Christian elementary schools in the Chicago area.

Serving as the principal of the Chicago Christian High School put Fakkema in a leadership role in the Chicago Alliance. Realizing great differences in the level of instruction among the various Christian schools, the Alliance appointed a committee consisting of Fakkema and fellow

23. Benson, "History of the National Association," 20.

24. Vander Ark, "Tribute to an NUCS Founder," 6.

25. Mark Fakkema interview in Benson, "History of the National Association," 76–78.

principals Andrew Blystra and Henry Kuiper to engage the problem of creating a unified course of study for all elementary and secondary students. The Alliance also set up other committees for such issues as textbooks and teacher training.[26]

Sitting around a kitchen stove on a cold, damp afternoon in 1919, Fakkema, Blystra, and Kuiper realized that the Reformed Christian schools faced a common set of problems. The Chicago Alliance, seeking to establish a unified course of study, mirrored similar efforts of other groups, most notably the Michigan and Western Alliances. In addition, the Michigan group had already started looking into sponsoring a normal school similar to the one at Calvin College. Taking all of this into consideration, the committee of Fakkema, Blystra, and Kuiper first conceived of the notion of starting a national Christian school association. They saw their concerns as not simply local, but rather much larger in scope. Hence, a national organization composed of all associations and alliances could more effectively cope with the problems of normal training, teacher needs, school board issues, Christian textbooks, and a publication for teachers and school board members.[27]

At the January 1920 meeting of the Chicago Christian School Alliance, Fakkema, Blystra, and Kuiper made a recommendation to start the process of forming a national league of Christian schools that would unite all of the various alliances. Through letter writing and a regular column by Fakkema in *Onze Toekomst*, an appeal went out in the spring of 1920 to seventy-three of the Reformed Christian school associations in the upper Midwest. As a result, thirty-seven associations sent representatives to a meeting in Chicago on September 1, 1920. Eight associations had already authorized their delegates to join this group. The eight charter members came from schools in Chicago, Indiana, Iowa, and Wisconsin. Meeting in the First Christian Reformed Church of Roseland in Chicago, various speakers, including Mark Fakkema, spoke on the need for Christian schools in the current American society. In addition, delegates elected a board that reflected equal membership of all the member associations. Also, participants adopted an official name, The National Union of Christian Schools (NUCS).[28]

The Constitution and by-laws, penned at this occasion, defined the mission of this new organization. Article three read "The purpose of the Union is to further the interests of Christian education which our schools have in common." The by-laws included additional commitments to Christian Normal training, publishing professional journals, raising overall

---

26. Kuiper, "National Union of Christian Schools," 2–3.

27. Kuiper, "National Union of Christian Schools," 3.

28. Kuiper, "National Union of Christian Schools," 4.

educational standards, improving teacher compensation, assisting one another and supervision of the individual schools.[29] The meeting ended with the members of the union giving the board the responsibility of taking on some immediate challenges.

The most urgent matter confronting the board of the fledgling NUCS revolved around financing this new venture. A treasurer's report from 1921 revealed a balance of funds at $19.72 with outstanding bills of over $200. NUCS board member James DeBoer suggested that an appeal be made to all Christian Reformed churches for support. Churches responded generously enough to carry the organization through its first few years.[30]

Expanding membership in the NUCS also needed attention in those first years. Board chairman A. J. Visser and Mark Fakkema volunteered to meet with the boards of local Christian school associations to promote joining the union. Recruiting the associations to unite with a national organization proved a challenge as most of these groups operated in isolation with complete autonomy.[31] Gradually progress did materialize and by 1922, membership increased from eight to thirty-seven associations. By 1924, the number of associations rose to fifty-one.[32] Mark Fakkema compiled the first set of statistics for the NUCS in 1922. He reported that at that time, the NUCS consisted of seventy-three individual schools, 341 teachers, and a total student enrollment of 10,401.[33]

Despite these encouraging numbers, many major issues still confronted the NUCS beginning with the issue of control and oversight. The Dutch Reformed Christian schools traditionally exercised a great deal of individual autonomy. Even with the formation of Alliances, the schools retained a local flavor and solved problems within their own associations. With the formation of the NUCS, the question naturally arose in those early years about how this organization should function. One group felt that the Union should focus on its goals listed in the Constitution and by-laws which mentioned teacher training, textbooks, the economic status of teachers, and the publication of professional journals. Natural unity would be achieved by addressing these more global issues and leaving the schools to run their own affairs. However, the Constitution and by-laws also listed "supervision of the individual schools" as a goal. Hence, this led some within the movement to press for a centralized authority under

29. Kuiper, "National Union Begins to Function," 16.

30. Kuiper, "National Union of Christian Schools," 4.

31. Kuiper, "National Union of Christian Schools," 5.

32. Benson, "History of the National Association," 22–23.

33. Fakkema, *Survey of the Free Christian Schools.*

a superintendent which could meld the schools into a unified system.[34] Others favored a more decentralized system that allowed for a national organization but leaving much autonomy in the hands of individual parent associations and their respective schools. This struggle eventually settled in 1926 with the appointment of Mark Fakkema to be the General Secretary, a post he would hold for the next twenty-one years. In an attempt to bring unity and respect the individuality of each school, Fakkema and the board followed the tradition of the Dutch Reformed schools and organized the NUCS as a decentralized, confederation of schools.

This conflict mirrored the establishment of parent associations several years earlier. Klaas Kuiper promoted parent associations to run the schools, instead of relying upon direct church supervision. The chief reason for this commitment to the independence of the schools came from the tradition of decentralized authority in Protestant churches, especially among Reformed congregations. In addition, this foundational characteristic of all Christian schools speaks to one of the driving forces of the movement, the issue of control. As will be outlined later, one of the major impulses behind the rise of Christian schools came from the desire of parents to possess more control over their families and their child's education in the midst of rapidly changing world that seemed to be moving headlong toward a secular society. Reclaiming power within communities, conservative Christians felt better equipped to battle the forces of secularism and eventually bring revival back to America as well as restore the prominence of Anglo-Protestantism through a "bottom up" approach.

Beyond this struggle, other issues faced the NUCS in the 1920s. The early NUCS commitment to providing teacher training attracted many schools to join, and hence became another key matter to address. The Union board heard frequently from their member schools about the need for the establishment of a Christian normal college. However, few realized what it would take in terms of finances and personnel to pull off such a venture especially when the young NUCS could barely meet expenses. Cognizant of this reality, the NUCS board opted to select an alternative provision of the Constitution that mentioned, "the NUCS shall give strong moral support to existing institutions which give reasonable guarantees of furnishing our schools with thoroughly equipped teachers." Over time, some of the schools, such as the Chicago Christian High School, created their own normal training courses and received NUCS approval.[35]

---

34. Kuiper, "National Union of Christian Schools," 5.
35. Kuiper, "National Union of Christian Schools," 6.

The publishing of Christian textbooks also garnered attention from the NUCS in its early years. As previously mentioned, both the Michigan Alliance and the Chicago Christian High School published a course of study outlining the specifics of what children in Christian schools should study. The Western Alliance submitted a supplementary reader, *Sketches from Church History*, written by B.J. Bennink to the Union in 1926. This book contained stories about some of the great leaders in church history with emphasis upon the Reformation. The Union also published a systematic study of the Bible in five volumes produced by Fakkema and Andrew Blystra. In 1928, the NUCS employed Dr. Garrett Heyns and Mr. Garritt Roelof to write *A Christian Interpretation of American History*. Gradually more and more books of this type emerged although the Union did not have a universal set of texts and did not require the schools to adopt any of these materials.[36]

A final issue that the NUCS sought to address in its first decade centered on teacher compensation. Staying with its now established role of non-intervention, the Union board realized that individual schools held the chief responsibility for teacher salaries. However, the board did immediately explore setting up some type of pension fund for the teachers in their schools. A report on the subject of a teacher retirement fund first surfaced in the 1922 NUCS annual meeting drawing only mild interest. The board later submitted a plan for consideration in the 1928 meeting and again negative sentiment prevailed among most of the member schools primarily due to cost. However, this issue did revive some twenty years later in the midst of better economic times.[37]

Enrollment of students in the National Union rose steadily throughout the 1920s. By 1925, enrollment increased to 13,243 students and by 1929 it peaked at 14,002. The NUCS struggled through internal dissension while simultaneously seeking to address issues of teacher training, textbooks, and teacher compensation.[38]

Not surprisingly, the Great Depression of the 1930s posed a great challenge to the NUCS. Between the years 1930–1938, the NUCS monthly bulletin, *Christian School and Home,* published no less than eighty-five articles concerning finances in their schools. A central theme focused upon sacrifice for the cause of Christian education and the need for Christian parents to place God's priorities ahead of the luxuries in life. Some school leaders went so far as to say that if parents took their children out of the Christian school it reflected a denial of the faith. NUCS leaders also urged

36. Kuiper, "National Union of Christian Schools," 7.

37. Kuiper, "National Union of Christian Schools," 8.

38. Fakkema, "Christian School Statistics," 42.

schools to seek alternative sources of revenue and cut expenses to keep the doors of their schools open.[39]

Mark Fakkema exhorted the schools to do all they could to keep students and keep solvent. He tirelessly promoted the need for the schools stating in one article, "It is a serious thing to close a Christian school. It deprives Covenant children of spiritual food. The school was opened as a result of prayer; let it not be closed without it being a result of prayer."[40] Fakkema set an example by refusing during these years to accept any salary from the Union. He contacted numerous schools and urged them to notify him if they faced possible closure as he wanted to find some additional financial support.[41]

The enrollment of children in NUCS schools did decline during the 1930s, although not in significant numbers. The peak enrollment of 14,002 students in 1929 dropped only to 13,710 in 1931. 1933 brought the lowest numbers of the decade with an estimated student enrollment at 13,000. From there slight increases came in succeeding years with a total enrollment of 13,930 students listed in 1940. While little new growth occurred, the NUCS could at least claim to have survived the Great Depression.[42]

As World War II approached, the National Union of Christian Schools could look back upon almost of twenty years of growth and struggle. This small contingent of Dutch Reformed Christian schools managed to establish a national organization and survive terrible economic times. Their leader, Mark Fakkema, emerged from the obscurity of a small Christian school to become a visible propagandist for this movement and his presence would only increase in the years ahead.

The NUCS accomplished much that influenced the future of the Christian school movement in America. Their organizational structure became the model for future national associations. The Union's commitment to teacher training, Christian textbooks, and communication through monthly magazines all established precedents for later Christian school groups. Most importantly, the NUCS set in motion several key philosophical ideas which affected future Christian schools. Reflecting the rise of religious fundamentalism, this association demanded a strict adherence to conservative Christianity in the schools with the teaching of the Bible being non-negotiable. Scripture memorization and required courses in Bible would be found in all NUCS schools. Departing from a parochial model,

39. Benson, "History of the National Association," 25–26.
40. Fakkema, "Closing of Schools," 9.
41. Benson, "History of the National Association," 26.
42. Fakkema, "Christian School Statistics," 9.

the NUCS also encouraged parent associations. Empowering parents in the education of their children no doubt led to the steady growth in enrollment throughout the first decade of NUCS existence. The issue over the supervision of the schools finally settled, making the national organization decentralized and more focused on providing services rather than being an authoritative supervisory presence.

At the same time, the National Union faced a notable limitation. A strict denominational commitment to Reformed theology gave the NUCS a sectarian appearance that would limit its appeal to the broader world of evangelical Christian parents. The establishment of alliances in the early years allowed for more Reformed congregations to set up Christian schools, but this still constrained the overall movement. While being called the "national" union, in reality, the NUCS only covered states in the upper Midwest such as Illinois, Michigan, Iowa, and Indiana during its first two decades, places where Reformed Presbyterian churches dominated. Over the next twenty years, as fundamentalism evolved into evangelicalism, a form of the faith which de-emphasized denominational and doctrinal differences among conservative Christians, the NUCS would encounter parent groups beyond the upper Midwest sharing their desire for Christian education, but not willing to adhere to the Union's strict Calvinist doctrine.

Along with the birth of the NUCS, another significant event in the Christian school movement occurred simultaneously in the early 1900s when a handful of pastors from the New York City area began contemplating a new Christian venture. *The New York Times* announced in July 1907 the establishment of the Stony Brook Assembly in the small village of Stony Brook, New York situated on Long Island Sound. Dr. John F. Carson, pastor of the Central Presbyterian Church of Brooklyn, founded the assembly. This picturesque beachfront area would be ideal for summer camps and Bible conferences to address relevant topics of the day and respond to the serious challenges of modern liberal theology. Other pastors, primarily Presbyterian, eventually joined with Carson to form a corporation known as the Stony Brook Assembly. They targeted the summer of 1909 for their first Bible conference. The founders created a statement of faith that would identify their beliefs and set a standard for all conferences. They devised a broad and orthodox doctrinal statement free from denominationalism or sectarian labels. Reformed Calvinist theology, seen in the NUCS, did not appear in their statement of faith. In addition, this document distinguished this assembly from liberal theology by emphasizing the authority, inspiration, and integrity of the Bible as well as proclaiming the deity of Jesus Christ.[43]

43. Lockerbie, *Way They Should Go*, 22–25.

Stony Brook reflected the new fundamentalist commitment to developing their own Christian institutions.

Over the years, the Stony Brook Conferences grew in number and prestige. In 1912, *The Brooklyn Daily Eagle* devoted an entire page of an issue to news of the conferences as well as abstracts of the various speakers. Carson invited many of his Presbyterian pastor friends to speak at the summer conferences as well as other renowned pastors and Bible teachers. Carson sought out highly educated speakers from European seminaries as well as ones from Yale and Princeton. By World War I, the conferences grew to the point that several thousand attended evening meetings open to the public. Over the course of a given summer, hundreds stayed in neighboring cottages or newly constructed summer hotels.[44]

In the summer of 1918, Carson shared a broader vision for Stony Brook with his associates. Seeing the camp idle for many months of the year, Carson introduced the idea of a Christian based, secondary college preparatory school. He delayed sharing this dream for many years, feeling that the assembly needed to gain stability and a constituency of faithful supporters. The war also suspended Carson's aspiration for some time. In addition, the Stony Brook leaders all believed they needed a strong leader to start such a school and in 1918, they knew of no one holding the qualifications they sought.[45]

Pastor Arno Gaebelein frequently spoke at Stony Brook. Already well known as a fundamentalist preacher in the New York East Conference of the German Methodist Church, he published a magazine, *Our Hope*, which focused much of its attention on his premillennialist views of Biblical prophecy. Gaebelein traveled the country speaking at evangelistic conferences and also teaching about eschatology. He became well known at the Stony Brook conferences as a featured speaker at the Assembly's annual Prophetic Conference. In 1899, Arno and his wife Emma, had a son, Frank, who developed a strong Christian faith, in addition to an appreciation for academics and the fine arts. A talented writer with great intellect, Frank began writing articles for *Our Hope* at the age of 15.[46]

In the fall of 1916, Frank Gaebelein began classes at the Bronx campus of New York University. He majored in English, joined a fraternity, and ran track. Having learned to play the piano as a child, he also pursued studies in classical piano and often performed at school functions. In 1918, he had brief stint in the army in the midst of the Great War. Returning to school

44. Lockerbie, *Way They Should Go*, 27.

45. Lockerbie, *Way They Should Go*, 27.

46. Rausch, *Arno Gaebelein*, 95, 193–96.

soon afterward, Gaebelein eventually focused his energy on writing, giving up the chance to join a musical conservatory. In 1920, Gaebelein, a newly elected member of Phi Beta Kappa, became a candidate for a Rhodes Scholarship and subsequently found his way to Harvard to study English and comparative literature.[47]

In the spring of 1921, Ford Ottman, one of the Assembly's trustees, suggested to John Carson that they interview Arno's son Frank for the position of headmaster of the still visionary Christian school at Stony Brook. Meeting with Ottman and Carson at a downtown New York restaurant, the young Harvard graduate student nervously answered several questions from the two men about how he would start a Christian preparatory school, how he would obtain a quality faculty, and about the kind of curriculum needed in such an institution. Gaebelein later recalled his feelings of inadequacy, "I was wholly without experience of the kind being required of me. And I had never attended this kind of school." Gaebelein returned to Harvard with mixed feelings as he already had an offer to teach at a college and had never really considered being involved in secondary education, much less being the headmaster of such a place. However, Ottman and Carson felt differently, seeing in young Gaebelein a man of a strong Christian background and impeccable academic credentials making him ideal for the position. In the summer of 1921, Gaebelein accepted the offer of the Stony Brook Assembly with an annual salary of $2400.[48]

By September of 1921, Frank Gaebelein commenced his duties as the principal of the Stony Brook School for boys. However, at this time the school possessed no students, no faculty, no classrooms or books. Gaebelein and the board of trustees committed to prayer the goal of opening the doors in the fall of 1922. Gaebelein set up an office in the Presbyterian Building on Fifth Avenue in New York and began the task of making Carson's dream a reality.[49]

For Gaebelein, the development of the school's philosophy and curriculum ranked first among his priorities for Stony Brook. In one of his first brochures, the phrase "Character before Career" appeared and subsequently remained the school's motto over the decades. This initial publication went on to say, "The aim of the school is to provide, in a Christian atmosphere and through Christian teachers, a sound education with a spiritual content, an education that has regard for the souls of our youth as well as for their bodies and minds. To this end, the study of the English

47. Lockerbie, *Way They Should Go*, 29–31.
48. Lockerbie, *Way They Should Go*, 31–32.
49. Lockerbie, *Way They Should Go*, 32.

Bible and the fundamentals of Christianity will have a place of first importance in the curriculum."[50]

Gaebelein desired for the school to place the Bible squarely at the center of the curriculum while at the same time refusing to diminish the intellectual standards and the overall pursuit of academic excellence. He recognized that having Bible study in his school did not make it unique or even unusual. Public schools, universities, and many denominational Christian schools had long offered courses in religion and the Bible. Stony Brook proposed a philosophy that made it stand out and become a prototype for the future. The school would not just simply include the Bible in its curriculum, but rather the curriculum would take its shape around the central belief in the Scriptures as the absolute truth of God and central to all learning. Gaebelein also made it clear that the Bible must not be merely tangential to the rest of the courses, but must be worked into each of course of study. While separate courses in Bible would be taught at the school, the teachers would avoid the promotion of any doctrines that seemed "sectarian," in contrast to the approach adopted by both NUCS and Catholic schools.[51] Gaebelein stated, "The central aim of this school is to correlate Christian principles, the great and eternal verities, with education of a type high enough to merit intimacy with such exalted ideals."[52] His intense commitment to integration of the Bible in every subject even caused him once to propose that the Bible department of Stony Brook be eliminated so as to increase the integration of the Bible into other subjects. Math, physical education, and even the fine arts felt the push for integration of scriptural principles. For example, rather than just simply teach math, students at Stony Brook would be instilled with the idea that math was created by God and reflected His perfect, orderly nature. To Gaebelein, no disconnect existed between God's truths and every aspect of education and life.[53]

The first catalog of Stony Brook announced how the school intended to create and maintain its Christian quality and as such, the faculty had to be completely committed to the Christian faith and to its exemplification in their lives. Gaebelein stated in the catalog, "No man will be employed whose religion is a mere profession. No matter his antecedents, he will not have a place on the faculty unless his Christianity is vital, unless he burns with the desire to lead others to the faith that creates true character. For upon the teacher rests the problem of making Christianity real to the boy."

---

50. Lockerbie, *Way They Should Go*, 32.

51. Lockerbie, *Way They Should Go*, 33–35.

52. Gaebelein, "Christian, the Arts, and Truth," 32.

53. Lockerbie, *Way They Should Go*, 81.

Over the next few months Gaebelein hired a variety of men and women with credentials hailing from Columbia University to the University of Bern in Switzerland to the National Conservatory of music in Helsinki. With the later hire of a registered nurse and a secretary, the total number of employees came to nine.[54]

The teacher stood at the heart of Gaebelein's educational philosophy. He stressed again and again that "Christian education must be rooted in the idea that the foundation of all knowledge is the divine revelation of Jesus Christ which can be properly interpreted only by those who have been regenerated by the Spirit of God." Beyond the ability to integrate scriptural principles into a particular discipline, the teacher should embody a personal Christian faith and model the integration of faith and life each day for the students. Many years later, Gaebelein summed it up this way, "The fact is inescapable; the worldview of the teacher, in so far as he is effective, gradually conditions the worldview of the pupil. No man teaches out of a philosophical vacuum. In one way or another, every teacher expresses the convictions he lives by, whether they be spiritually positive or negative. This is why the school or college that would develop a Christ-centered and Biblically grounded program must fly from its masthead this standard, 'No Christian education without Christian teachers,' and must never, under any condition, pull its colors down."[55] Whereas Dewey saw the teacher as more of a facilitator guiding students toward the development of their own philosophy, Gaebelein put the teacher in the role of being the source of truth in academics and lifestyle.

With a faculty of committed believers in place, the task began of recruiting students for the fall 1922 semester. It proved a difficult challenge. In a later interview, Gaebelein confessed that in the summer of 1922, they had virtually no enrollment. The young headmaster relentlessly made personal calls to the homes of families that had made inquiries. A few unexpected enrollments occurred such as Tom and Marius Brohard from El Paso, Texas. On September 13, 1922, the first day of school at Stony Brook registered a total of twenty-seven students. A student body quite diverse in age, ability, and background inhabited the campus of this infant school. Their ages ranged from eight to nineteen. They came from eight states stretching from New York to Texas and two were from China. The group contained excellent scholars as well as boys who experienced severe academic difficulty in their previous schools.[56]

54. Lockerbie, *Way They Should Go*, 38.

55. Lockerbie, *Way They Should Go*, 55.

56. Lockerbie, *Way They Should Go*, 41.

At the inaugural ceremonies, Gaebelein made a speech reflecting his commitment to the uniqueness of Stony Brook. Focusing on the main priority he stated, "Education without character is a dangerous thing. For character, not intellectual agility is the source of right living. But character itself has a source. It springs not from moral maxims, rules of conduct, proverbs, or thou-shalt-nots. Its derivation is higher. It grows out of religious experience-the effective religious experience that is the result of the gospel of our Lord and Saviour Jesus Christ." The main speaker of the day was Francis L. Patton, former president of Princeton University. In his remarks this distinguished educator created an expression, "the Fourth R," referring to religion taking a place alongside reading, 'riting and 'rithmetic. This phrase would also become synonymous with the school. As Stony Brook's first year got underway, Gaebelein faced the enormous task of making this experiment work and fulfilling all of the pledges made in conversations, writings and public addresses. The responsibility rested solely in his hands, a task he would bear for the next forty-one years.[57]

School facilities immediately posed challenges. Hopkins Hall, a dormitory used for the summer conferences, served as the housing for the entire school operation since it was the only building on the grounds equipped with heat. Within a short time, eleven additional boys enrolled bringing the number of students to thirty-eight. Some commuted from the city, but most lived in the dormitory. The faculty and their families resided there as well. It proved to be quite cramped but the operation ran smoothly. At the end of the first year, Gaebelein reported to the trustees, "There has been no friction among the teachers—or the wives of the teachers." However, tight quarters did cause problems. A student found it impossible to perform laboratory experiments because no room existed. Gaebelein later remarked that he shuddered when he thought back about how they solved the problem. "The only place available for the chemical experiments was in the basement— right next to the boiler room!"[58]

Activities beyond the classroom emerged as another issue. Despite small numbers, a football team competed in the very first year, beginning a long tradition of athletics at the school. A literary society published a journal the first year named *The Adventurer*. In addition, the small campus saw the formation of a chess club, a radio club and an instrumental ensemble in which Gaebelein often joined with his piano expertise.[59]

---

57. Lockerbie, *Way They Should Go*, 39–41.

58. Lockerbie, *Way They Should Go*, 41–42.

59. Lockerbie, *Way They Should Go*, 42.

Gaebelein himself proved a role model for all of his students in that he possessed all of the qualities of a Christian "Renaissance man." While respected all over the campus as a scholar who went on to write scores of books, he also performed frequently as a concert pianist. Being a former college track athlete, Gaebelein could be seen constantly competing with the boys around campus in such tasks as punting a football or hitting a baseball. Students also realized he possessed a vibrant sense of humor by telling a good joke or by reading aloud from a popular comic author of the day. In addition, Gaebelein would act out scenes from Shakespeare's *Twelfth Night* based upon his own high school experience.[60] In 1980, he reflected upon his wide of interests by remarking, "Intellectually, I should describe myself as a Christian humanist. I am, of course, using the term in its classical renaissance sense, rather than in its contemporary usage, as 'secular humanism' for example. I am a generalist, not a specialist, and my interests are not restricted to just one discipline."[61] Gaebelein's wide range of interests showed at Stony Brook as the curriculum did not just focus on the sole study of the Bible, but rather embraced all disciplines, interpreting them from a biblical perspective.

Stony Brook weathered its first year of existence, holding true to its principles of Christian character and strong academics. With just a handful of students, the school could not afford to lose any of them and yet, in the first year, Gaebelein did expel one of the young men. This particular student used profane language and in the opinion of the faculty had a detrimental influence on the rest of the school. On the positive side, Stony Brook graduated its first student at the end of this inaugural year. Gilbert P. Inglis received his diploma in the spring of 1923 and then went on to give the school a notable commendation by being admitted to Princeton. In addition, the Regents of the University of the State of New York gave their support to Stony Brook by approving its academic program after only one year. Gaebelein reflected an optimistic spirit when he reported to the board on October 18, 1922, "It is the unanimous opinion of the faculty that the great principle upon which the school has been founded has already been proved true."[62]

As the 1920s progressed, Stony Brook experienced much growth and change. By 1927, the school had a student body of approximately one hundred boys. The school now offered all twelve grades, divided into elementary and secondary divisions. The curriculum in the secondary level

60. Lockerbie, *Way They Should Go*, 50–51.

61. Hull, "Frank Gaebelein," 15.

62. Lockerbie, *Way They Should Go*, 42–43.

offered courses in Bible, English, Latin, French and New Testament Greek. In addition, the course of study included ancient, modern, and American history, biology, chemistry, algebra, geometry, and business principles. The campus saw several new buildings rise and attractive landscaping installed. In 1928, the Stony Brook scholarship fund, totaling $14,000, assisted twenty boys of lower income to attend.[63]

In 1929, the education editor of *The Christian Science Monitor* visited the Stony Brook campus and reported back many positive findings. Commenting on growth, the article stated that the school now had 133 students, eleven faculty members, and ten buildings on the campus. The editor went on to praise the school's academic standing, reminding readers about its recognition from the University of the State of New York, and that 90 percent of Stony Brook graduates attended institutions of higher education. Summing it up, the correspondent said, "A visitor (to the school) observes that although religion is the fourth R at Stony Brook, and Bible study is a major subject, the boys are as fun-loving and active as normal schoolboys are everywhere. The development of the spiritual side is as natural as breathing and is accepted as a part of true education." Dr. Mather Abbott, headmaster of another private school in New Jersey, commented, "There is not another school like it in the country. It takes courage to put spiritual things first nowadays."[64]

Not surprisingly, Stony Brook faced grave challenges during the Great Depression of the 1930s. Gaebelein asked the faculty to accept a graduated reduction in salary. Not everyone agreed since the school maintained its policy of giving scholarship aid despite the financial pinch. At the same time, the school hired its first financial officer, Gilbert Moore, who quickly discovered accounts in disarray and a $20,000 deficit. Moore tightened accounting procedures and cut expenses to reduce the shortfall. Issues also arose over property boundaries as a dispute surfaced with neighbors who claimed the school practiced football on their land. Several months of new surveys revealed great inaccuracies in the original Stony Brook land plots. Eventually, the school purchased the tracts in question.[65]

As the thirties progressed and the Depression worsened, Stony Brook struggled but also held fast to its principles. Enrollment dropped to below a hundred students. Reductions in salaries totaled almost $35,000 from 1932 to 1939. However, the scholarship fund that had topped at $14,000 annually in 1929 only dropped to $13,000 for most of the decade. Gaebelein kept

63. Lockerbie, *Way They Should Go*, 73–74.

64. Delfattore, "Fourth R," 9.

65. Lockerbie, *Way They Should Go*, 75–76.

insisting on high standards of character for the students and proved this by not allowing five full paying students to return for another year because he felt their "influence had been detrimental." Academics remained strong as the school received a charter in 1930 from *The Cum Laude Society*, an honors society akin to Phi Beta Kappa. Only sixty schools in the nation belonged to this organization at this time. In 1931, Princeton recognized the Bible courses at Stony Brook by having its admissions committee fully accept this course for college credit. In 1932, the Association of Colleges and Secondary Schools included Stony Brook when it published its first listing of accredited schools. Gaebelein would reflect later upon the Great Depression years by saying, "During those years the promises of God in the Scriptures, especially the promises of His faithfulness, became especially precious to me." Despite the financial crisis, which proved fatal to many private schools of this era, Stony Brook survived.[66]

Stony Brook School, a tiny, struggling educational enterprise of the 1920s and 30s, set a standard that would eventually expand the movement to much larger dimensions than Mark Fakkema's National Union of Christian Schools. Notably, Stony Brook sharpened the principles of Christian education, setting it apart from Dewey's popular progressive ideas. To illustrate, many years later Gaebelein commented on a speech given by Ohio State professor, Dr. Howard Bode, a Dewey disciple and leading educator of his day. Professor Bode asserted that morality could only be derived from naturalistic forces and that the public schools had an obligation to be "made an agency for the propagation of secularistic and anti-religious philosophy." Bode went on to say that religion had to be removed from education because of its authoritarian nature, which he deemed as undemocratic. Gaebelein responded by saying that on the contrary, Christian schools actually better represented democracy in that they respected the most cherished liberty of freedom of worship. Outlining his philosophy of Christian education, Gaebelein concluded his criticism of Dr. Bode by saying, "Every Christian parent recognizes that his children belong first of all to God, who entrusts them to the home to be brought up for Him. It is a basic right of free Americans to educate their children in accord with their own religious convictions. This means for Christian parents the right to provide schooling in harmony with the Word of God. And in the gap today there stands the independent school as the means whereby parents who dissent from the prevailing naturalistic philosophy of public education may provide their children parallel opportunities under Christian direction."[67]

66. Lockerbie, *Way They Should Go*, 79–82.
67. Gaebelein, "Christian Education," 8.

Gaebelein's insistence upon "Character before Career" also established a standard for the development of morality based upon biblical truth beyond any academic or vocational goals. Gaebelein himself embodied this concept in that he did not possess the expected professional credentials of the day for being an educator, much less the head of a school. However, Gaebelein felt he owned spiritual qualities needed to lead young boys. He believed his school represented a return to the first tradition of American education character-ized by training young men in Christian principles for Christian service. The teaching of religious and moral principles ranked highest in his priorities, followed by a commitment to gentlemanly conduct and the development of intellectual ability. Many years later Gaebelein's daughter Gretchen noted that her father consistently taught his students that in considering any course of action in life, the first question should never be, "How will it enhance my career?," but rather, "Is it the right thing to do?"[68]

Perhaps most importantly, Stony Brook broadened the appeal of Chris-tian schools to the larger Christian community. Whereas the schools of the NUCS represented a narrow theological persuasion which framed them as sectarian, Gaebelein's school appealed to a wider Christian constituency. Departing from fundamentalist tendencies toward separatism and distrust of educational standards of the day, Stony Brook embraced academic ex-cellence and a well-rounded curriculum which included activities beyond the classroom. As already noted, the school achieved accreditation and recognition from secular educational institutions.[69] While teaching specific Christian values remained Stony Brook's clear distinction from public edu-cation, Gaebelein's devotion to strong academics, fine arts, and sports also revealed his commitment to a proper balance between religious, scholastic, and recreational matters.

Even though he considered himself a fundamentalist, Gaebelein sometimes differed from this group in his views on biblical truth. He felt that discerning God's truth required openness to new light, fresh transla-tions, and the latest in biblical research. Although unyielding in his affir-mation of the authority of Scripture and the basics of salvation, he willingly re-examined the hard questions of the faith. His daughter quoted him once as saying, "Sometimes evangelicals tend to be afraid of newly discerned truth. If so, they may have been equating some cherished doctrinal for-mulation or historical position with final truth. So when some hitherto unrecognized truth, some breakthrough into wider knowledge faces them, it may seem a threat and they may react in fear and anger." In developing

68. Hull, "Frank Gaebelein," 16.
69. Hull, "Frank Gaebelein," 17.

integrity in his students, Gaebelein challenged the boys to remember that a person of integrity can be well meaning but come off as legalistic if he does not understand that maintaining integrity includes a constant and sometimes difficult effort to discern truth.[70]

This more moderate approach also invited criticism from fundamentalists who perceived liberal trends in the school. When the 1925 Scopes trial branded any discussion of evolution as a cardinal sin, Gaebelein did not interrogate his science teachers or make an issue of Darwinism on the Stony Brook campus. When asked about his apparent passivity toward the hot button issue of the day he simply stated, "I let my Christian teachers teach. I trusted them as teachers just as I trusted them in other capacities. We didn't ignore evolution as a hypothesis in the history of ideas; we just didn't allow it as dogma." Later, in the 1930s when the Presbyterian denomination faced division over theology, Gaebelein welcomed both Dr. J. Ross Stevenson, president of Princeton Theological Seminary and Dr. J. Gresham Machen of the more conservative Westminster Theological Seminary to the Stony Brook campus.[71]

Perceived liberalism also surfaced in terms of expectations of student conduct. Gaebelein did insist upon strict rules as a basis of integrity, but at the same time applied reason to his rules for the boys. He avoided authoritarianism by working to explain to his boys the reasons for these rules. Examples included a ban on smoking not because of its sinfulness, but rather because of the risks of fire hazard and suspected health issues. Likewise, card playing was not treated as evil in itself, but rather the school administration gave strict admonishments to avoid gambling with card games. Of course, drinking had no place in such a school, but Gaebelein's sermons against drink stressed the notion of personal character against mindless conformity rather than condemning drink as a sin. With permission the boys attended movies and the school also encouraged students to visit New York performances of the theater, ballet and opera. Gaebelein disagreed with the school trustees over social dancing. The board took a strong stand against this activity, while Gaebelein simply felt that far greater pitfalls in life existed. He questioned why young people could find so little to converse about at a party and hence depended upon dancing as a substitute.[72]

Stony Brook's uniqueness lay in its ability to clearly oppose the emerging progressive philosophy of public education while at the same time moving beyond its fundamentalist roots to establish a more broad-based Christian

---

70. Hull, "Frank Gaebelein," 17.

71. Lockerbie, *Way They Should Go*, 101.

72. Lockerbie, *Way They Should Go*, 102.

school that would become a prototype for the decades ahead. Gaebelein opposed those who felt that Christian schools should be a haven for young people to hide from the world. Some outsiders mistakenly regarded the school as a glorified Sunday school from which emerged angelic adolescents stamped out to be missionaries or preachers. Gaebelein recoiled at this image seeing it as totally contrary to a true Christian education. Embracing the idea of a liberal education, he stated, "The essence of a sound liberal education is its power to unshackle the mind from the ignorance that binds it. A Christian liberal education frees the mind from all that is untrue, including some of the legalistic taboos adopted by some Christians. Our primary function is to educate children of superior ability and character. After all, our chief aim is training for Christian leadership. A school can't achieve that aim by hedging its students against the realities of life beyond the campus."[73]

Gaebelein's Stony Brook School for boys emerged as a glimpse of the future of Christian schooling. Qualities such as a strict adherence to scripture, a commitment to biblical integration, teachers who lead in the truth, a priority of academic excellence, a well-rounded curriculum, and an emphasis on Christian leadership eventually became the model for numerous Christian schools over the course of twentieth century. Stony Brook's move toward mainstream education that did not compromise on God's truth provided a more effective tool that would enlarge the movement for the future.

Both Stony Brook and the National Union of Christian Schools arose from the changes of the new century in educational philosophy and Protestant Christianity. Challenges from Roman Catholicism, liberal theology, progressive education, and an urban industrialized society caused these schools to seek a return to upholding the Bible as the basis of all truth and educating children in the ways of their ancestors. These schools also mirrored the rise of fundamentalism. Reformed theology dominated the National Union, but both institutions held fast to conservative biblical standards. By starting their own schools, both the NUCS and Stony Brook stood as challenges to public education which would have been seen by many as anti-American and yet clearly in line with the militant anti-modernist tendencies of fundamentalism. The NUCS also reflected the "outsider" tendencies of fundamentalism, while Stony Brook reflected the "establishment" side of fundamentalism. The unique characteristics of both entities combined later to form the basis of a larger and more sophisticated Christian educational community.

The Christian school movement began to take shape in the 1920s, though this trend remained imperceptible in contemporary, mainstream

73. Lockerbie, *Way They Should Go*, 102–3.

American education. In 1931, the United States enrolled a total of 29,061,000 in public and private schools.[74] In the prior year, statistics revealed that a total of 254,068 students attended private religious schools and of that number, roughly 200,000 of these children attended Roman Catholic schools. At the same time, the NUCS reported an enrollment of only 14,000 students. Hence, the Christian school movement comprised less than half of 1 percent of all schoolchildren. By 1940, 28,043,000 children attended America's public and private schools, with total enrollment in private religious schools rising to 361,000. The NUCS enrollment still hovered at pre-Depression levels of 14,000 students.[75] The 1930s made the Christian school faction seem even smaller when compared to the overall educational landscape of the nation.

Despite these numbers, leaders of the Christian school movement faced the 1940s with optimism. The National Union of Christian Schools had been established and survived despite internal bickering and crushing economic times. A structure for a national Christian school organization now existed along with precedents for parent control and local autonomy. Likewise, the Stony Brook School survived its infancy and similar financial pressures. A broader program had been developed at this little school on Long Island Sound encompassing a well-rounded education possessing a distinct biblical philosophy. Breaking from the strict theology of the NUCS, Stony Brook also encouraged its graduates to interact with the outside world while not straying from its commitment to "Character before Career."

Though virtually unnoticed by most Americans, both the National Union and the Stony Brook School laid the groundwork for a future Christian school movement. In a period of change and division within the educational world and the Christian church, Mark Fakkema and Dr. Frank Gaebelein stepped forward as a part of the "devoted few" to establish an educational alternative. As a result, they not only started schools, but also planted the seeds of a movement which would expand beyond their lifetimes and go a long way toward assisting conservative evangelicals in their quest to restore a "Christian America."

74. Carter, *Historical Statistics*, 400.

75. US Department of the Interior, *Biennial Survey of Education*, 786.

Chapter 5

"Moving Forward as a Mighty Army"

On April 7, 1942 in a crowded St. Louis hotel ballroom, the Boston pastor, Dr. J. Elwin Wright, stood before 149 conservative Christian ministers, seminary professors, and missionaries to make an earnest plea. As the opening speaker of this unique get together, he stated, "It is becoming apparent that we have arrived at a time when there is at least an earnest longing for better understanding, closer fellowship, and the development of a new and more effective grand strategy in the task of the Church of Jesus Christ. Concerted action, and that without delay, is imperative if the tide of secularism is not to engulf it. It does make a difference whether we move forward as a mighty army or merely by squads and platoons."[1] Wright believed that, after years of struggle and division, a united force of committed evangelicals was the only solution for the perilous times facing the nation.

Wright's call for a "mighty army" came in response to an October 1941 letter inviting hundreds of Christian leaders to attend the first convention of what would become known as "The National Association of Evangelicals." The visionaries behind this unprecedented meeting expressed a desire to bring unity to the various conservative evangelical churches, schools, missionary organizations, radio ministries, and publishers.[2] For conservative Christian leaders, this new nationwide group served as a crucial building block in their movement to restore a Christian America and would ultimately provide a vehicle for Christian education to broaden its scope and become partners in this vision.

Dr. Wright initiated the idea of trying to unify the conservative churches in the wake of the defeats and divisions that came out of the 1920s.

---

1. Wright, "Historical Statement," 3–13.
2. Wright, "Historical Statement," 3–13.

In 1929, Wright organized the New England Fellowship (NEF), an association of many churches in the region willing to unite across denominational lines for the sake of strengthening traditional Christianity, and to challenge the new liberal trends. In the early organizational meetings, Wright and several other pastors determined that some twenty denominations never affiliated with the liberal-leaning Federal Council of Churches (FCC). They also estimated that roughly twenty million believers who stayed in the FCC churches remained committed to conservative Christian truths despite the liberal shift of their denominations. In addition, hundreds of congregations simply withdrew from their denominations and became independent due to their association with the Federal Council of Churches.[3] Wright traveled extensively in the late 1930s and early 1940s and found pastors and leaders of missionary organizations all over the nation concerned about the decline of long established Christian values and consequently, he found a common desire for some kind of national organization to restore and strengthen these conservative believers. In 1939, 1940, and 1941, church leaders from fifteen denominations attended Pastors Conferences of the New England Fellowship, and drafted resolutions calling for some kind of national organization of evangelicals. As a result, the NEF board sent Wright on a tour of thirty-one states to discuss concerns and to gauge interest in such an association. In this same year, Reverend Ralph T. Davis, director of the Africa Inland Mission, wrote to many pastors and mission boards to discover the extent of their interest in attempting greater cohesion among evangelicals, especially those in the mission field. A temporary committee consisting of Dr. Wright as chairman and Davis as Secretary set up a Brooklyn office in 1941 which became the site of a series of meetings. In the meantime, Dr. Wright continued to travel the South and Midwest.[4]

Ministers from all over the nation responded to the invitation to this inaugural meeting of the NAE. David Otis Fuller of Wealthy Street Baptist Temple of Grand Rapids, Michigan wrote to the temporary committee and promised to attend even though he expressed disappointment that the preliminary information he had received about this new organization did not seem to indicate that it would take a clear stand against the liberal FCC. However, he promised to come "with no axe to grind and no divisive spirit" and stated in his correspondence that he would come to the meeting praying the evangelicals of America would unite for the sake of common "mighty principles" and forget personalities, minor doctrinal

3. Taylor, "NAE Celebrates 30 Years," 8–9.

4. Wright, "Historical Statement," 4–5.

differences, and petty jealousies in order to take a stand against the apostasy and sin of modernism.[5]

Out of these concerted efforts came the first annual meeting of the National Association of Evangelicals in St. Louis on April 7, 1942. One hundred forty-nine delegates from twenty-two states attended, representing several denominations ranging from Presbyterian to Assemblies of God. They came from cities such as New York and Chicago, but also from places like Mount Pleasant, Texas and Salina, Kansas. The majority of those present consisted of pastors, but others at the conference came from Christian colleges, seminaries, missionary boards, magazines, and para-church organizations such as the Cleveland Christian Business Men's Committee.[6]

Appropriately, the first address of the convention came from Dr. Wright, the first to call for the formation of a "mighty army" of evangelicals. To build this force, Wright admonished the delegates about the need to drop denominational differences and cling to the basic historic truths of the Bible. He described it this way, "We are here met in conference, not to discuss a union of denominations, but to explore the possibilities of resolving misunderstandings, to find common ground upon which we may stand in our fight against evil forces, to provide protective measures against the dictatorship of either government or ecclesiastical combinations in restraint of religious liberty, and to seek ways and means of carrying on for Christ unitedly and aggressively, but with freedom of action within our respective organizations." Wright outlined a basic statement of faith that stressed fundamental biblical truths and retained a firm commitment to the infallibility and inspiration of Scripture while remaining broad enough to appeal to all conservative evangelicals. He ended his rousing speech proclaiming, "I believe that God is in our midst and that the prayer of Jesus will yet be fulfilled, 'That they all may be one.'"[7]

Over the next few days, other evangelical leaders addressed the convention, but none more passionately than Dr. Harold J. Ockenga, pastor of Park Street Church in Boston. In his opening day keynote speech, "The Unvoiced Multitudes," Ockenga exhorted his brethren about the desperate need for a renewal of unified evangelical Christianity in the midst of turbulent times. Describing himself as a "lone wolf," he exclaimed, "I see ominous clouds of battle which spell annihilation unless we are willing to run in a pack." He lamented the state of the church in this way, "Evangelical Christianity has suffered nothing but a series of defeats for decades. The programs of few

5. Fuller, "Letter to the Temporary Committee."

6. National Association of Evangelicals, "Roster of Delegates," 92–100.

7. Wright, "Historical Statement," 3–16.

major denominations today are controlled by evangelicals." Keenly aware of world events, Ockenga compared the state of traditional Christianity to the world war now raging. He saw evangelical Christianity as being attacked in a manner similar to the small nations defeated by the Nazis and the Japanese. He criticized the passive, defensive nature of these weak countries. According to Ockenga, the same thing had happened in the church as step by step, liberal Christians discredited traditional beliefs and their leaders. Liberals had organized under the Federal Council of Churches in 1905 and as a result gained significant power. Gradually, the conservative Christians lost their long held positions of leadership due to their own lack of unity and an unwillingness to confront erroneous teachings. Ockenga summed up his point by pleading for unity and a call for aggressive action by stating, "Let us learn from the Soviets and the Nazis. If the children of this world are wiser than the children of light, then it is time to open their eyes and learn how to carry on God's work. This is the time, the day for the offensive. Personally I am just as tired of defensive tactics in ecclesiastical matters as Americans are tired of defensive tactics on the part of the democracies of the United Nations. In fact, our defensive tactics threaten to be fatal to us as they have been disastrous to nearly a score of nations of the world. One by one we shall be overwhelmed. Do not be so foolish as to think that though your own personal work is thriving at the present time you will escape."[8] While the nation united against the forces of Hitler, Ockenga used the war as a metaphor calling for the faithful to adopt the aggressive tactics of the Nazis and Soviets against the forces of liberalism.

Ockenga outlined three distinct threats to Protestant Christianity that had to be directly confronted by this new organization. First, he pointed to the rise of Roman Catholicism by claiming that his hometown of Boston, once a stronghold of Protestantism, now saw 80 percent of its citizens practicing the faith of Rome. He also cited nationwide numbers that showed an increase in Catholics from twenty million to thirty-five million in the previous decade. Second, Ockenga decried liberalism as being just as much a menace as the Catholic Church. He noted again how liberals, united under the Federal Council of Churches, gained control of many metropolitan church councils and other prominent denominational positions. The FCC had also recently signed exclusive agreements with two national radio networks and hence posed serious challenges by threatening to silence the conservative voice of Christianity on the nation's airways. Third, Ockenga cited secularism as an additional threat to traditional Christian beliefs. He described the rise of drunkenness, immorality, corruption and "utter

8. Ockenga, "Unvoiced Multitudes," 19–26.

atheism" as a wave that had swept America since the Great War. He blamed the rise of secularism and a passive Christian church for the rise of Hitler in Germany. In his most impassioned plea, Ockenga stated, "Unless we have a true revival of evangelical Christianity, able to change the character of men and build up a new moral fibre, we believe Christianity, capitalism, and democracy, likewise, to be imperiled." With this sense of urgency, Ockenga joined with Wright in calling for the creation of an official organization of evangelical Christians to combat liberalism and restore America to its true Protestant roots. He concluded this portion of his keynote address saying, "The crisis is greater than any of us realize. Now, if ever, we need some organ to speak for the evangelical interests, to represent men who, like myself, are 'lone wolves' in the church." Just as Wright called for a mighty army, Ockenga called for the lone wolves to run in a pack and move forward to bring a revival to the nation.[9]

The words of Wright and Ockenga did not go unheeded; the 1942 St. Louis convention led to the official birth of the National Association of Evangelicals and the group did not adjourn until they established an organizational plan. These leaders put together a constitution and doctrinal framework that would be subsequently refined and adopted at the next convention. The tentative constitution made clear the voluntary nature of the organization and a commitment to function democratically and not infringe upon the operation of each individual ministry represented. The doctrinal statement, though conservative, avoided denominational distinctions so that each delegate could subscribe to its tenets without any mental reservation. In addition, the delegates passed several resolutions and set priorities for the focus of this new organization. These seven priorities consisted of evangelism, government relations, national and local use of radio, public relations, preservation of the separation of church and state, Christian education, and the guarantee of freedom for home and foreign missionary endeavor. They elected Ockenga to be the first president and chose Wright to be executive secretary. Upon the conclusion of this first NAE convention, the leadership called for seven additional regional meetings across the nation over the next year in preparation for the next annual conference to be held in Chicago on May 3, 1943.[10]

The establishment of the NAE represented the culmination of several forces and events in American Protestant Christianity in the first few decades of the twentieth century. As noted in chapter three, liberal theology, the rise of science, and the growing pluralism of the nation brought

9. Ockenga, "Unvoiced Multitudes," 26–31.

10. Paine, "Report of the Policy Committee," 101–15.

about by industrialization and immigration served to weaken traditional Protestant hegemony by the early 1900s. As a result, fundamentalist Christianity, a militant coalition of conservative believers arose in the 1920s bent on restoring more traditional biblical beliefs, such as the inerrancy of the scriptures, to America. This group took on characteristics of a beleaguered minority, while still maintaining a strong sense of "trusteeship" of American culture, committed as they were to bringing the nation back to its historic Christian heritage.[11]

According to Robert Garson, these fundamentalists of twenty years later possessed an overarching concern about the transformations in society that shifted power from local communities to a larger secular culture. Changing social and sexual habits and new modes of knowledge and education became widely disseminated through new media in the form of radio and movies. Fundamentalists believed that a diverse but powerful group of cultural elites not bound by historic tradition or popular consent had managed to take over the role long held by Protestant churches of influencing and shaping the mores of society. Hence, an important characteristic of conservative Christians in the years prior to World War II centered on their desire for a closer vigilance over the political, social and educational standards in their communities. In an earlier age, tradition-bound communities found it easy to immunize themselves from cultural and political change, but this seemed to be fading quickly in a more diverse, liberal, and progressive America of the 1920 and 30s.[12]

As a result, there emerged increasing emphasis of conservative Christians on the family and the church during this same era. Realizing they lacked control in a public world that seemed to be careening out of their control, watching as many public institutions became more secularized, fundamentalists sought out more control in the private world of their own homes, schools, and churches.[13] By focusing on their families and communities, fundamentalists hoped to get more control of their world and eventually bring about a spiritual revival that would expand into the wider culture resulting in a "bottom up" restoration of their Christian heritage.

Joel Carpenter points out that during the 1930s, conservative Christians did not disappear but rather temporarily retreated, reorganized, refocused, and established their own subculture that would later serve as a launching pad to reassert themselves back into American culture. He notes how conservative Christians did indeed reflect separatist tendencies during

11. Marsden, *Fundamentalism and American Culture*, 4, 6–7.

12. Garson, "Political Fundamentalism," 130–32.

13. Watt, "Private Hopes," 165–66.

the 30s and 40s, but this tendency had a definite purpose, "In retreat from public embarrassment, fundamentalists cultivated distinctive religious communities, or 'shelter belts' as one person called them, to provide some respite from the gales of modern secularity and a home base from which to launch evangelistic campaigns."[14] In seeking to gain control of their world and ultimately renew their prominence, fundamentalists cultivated a network throughout the nation consisting of magazines, radio programs and Bible conferences. In addition, they also established and strengthened Christian liberal arts colleges such as Wheaton College in Illinois, Bob Jones College in Tennessee, and Gordon College in Massachusetts. A survey of seventy Christian colleges from 1929 to 1940 revealed that enrollment doubled during this time.[15]

As previously noted, premillennialism also exerted great influence over fundamentalism in the 1930s and 40s. With a strong commitment to biblical prophecy, fundamentalists saw the rise of European dictators, a collapsed economy, the expansion of governmental power under the New Deal, and even FDR's longevity in office as ominous signs pointing to a one world government and the rise of the antichrist. This led them to become more active in the culture with a conservative, antiliberal political philosophy. Hence, the formation of an activist group of evangelicals that came to be known as the NAE, culminated years of organizing a network of conservative Christians intent on reclaiming America for Christ.[16]

In addition, historian Patrick Allitt notes that after this temporary retreat and emerging subculture, the fundamentalist movement by 1940 morphed into a broader "evangelical Christianity." Although these "evangelicals" remained staunch in their commitment to the infallibility of scripture and their opposition to Roman Catholicism, Allitt sees this development as a departure from the negative connotations of the fundamentalists. He put it this way, "In 1942, two evangelical ministers, J. Elwin Wright and Harold J. Ockenga, trying to create a more upbeat and harmonious image for their brand of Protestantism, founded the National Association of Evangelicals. It was a pointedly nondenominational organization, drawing members from many different churches and trying to restore the old revival tradition, emphasizing Jesus' love and personal salvation, while avoiding harsh polemics and doctrinal hair splitting. It also aimed to modernize the image of evangelicalism."[17] By 1940, the combination of fundamentalist

14. Carpenter, *Revive Us Again*, 3.

15. Carpenter, "Fundamentalist Institutions," 62–75.

16. Sutton, "Was FDR the Antichrist?," 1069–70.

17. Allitt, *Religion in America*, 13–15.

concerns over a loss of prestige, their commitment to restoring America to its so-called Christian heritage, their desire to wrest control of their world from liberal and secular society, premillennialist theology, and their consolidation of a conservative subculture all merged leading to the rise of the National Association of Evangelicals.

From the beginning, the National Association of Evangelicals had a direct impact upon education and Christian schools. As stated before, the delegates of the first NAE convention listed Christian education as an area of critical concern. Ockenga made a reference to education in his "The Unvoiced Multitudes" address when he lamented "materialistic education is the great poison which is spoiling the testimony and message of the majority of our young preachers today."[18] The policy committee at the St. Louis convention stated, "We believe that true education and all true culture must of necessity be in harmony with the Gospel of Christ, who is Himself the truth." They recommended that an Educational Committee be formed to encourage Christian colleges and schools to affiliate with their new organization. In the final session of the first convention education again surfaced as an important issue and with it another call for unity, "Education must not continue to be used as an agency for the destruction of the faith and morals of the young people of our land. Ten million or more evangelicals will constitute a sufficiently powerful minority to win the respect and attention of educational authorities when they act together through such a central agency as this Association."[19] Evangelical activism, ignited by the NAE, would lead to educational activism that would partner with Christian educators such as Mark Fakkema and Frank Gaebelein.

Evangelical pastors and educators provide ample evidence of their distress about godlessness in public education as criticism arose from many Christian leaders of the time. Dr. Harold Ockenga, the Boston pastor chosen as the first president of the NAE, preached a series of messages in 1939 which he titled "Emergency Sermons for the Nation." In the third of this series, Ockenga provided a lengthy discourse on what he perceived to be danger signals of the greatest contemporary threats to America. His list included Japanese Imperialism, the "Red Monster" of the Soviet Union, Nazi Germany, rising crime in American cities, indecent publications, divorce, and the false philosophy of the nation's schools. He lamented the rejection of Christian doctrine in the public schools that had been replaced by a progressive, evolutionary, naturalistic, and materialistic philosophy which reduced man to a mere beast rather than a creation in God's image. Ockenga

---

18. Ockenga, "Unvoiced Multitudes," 28.

19. National Association of Evangelicals, "What Next?," 129.

concluded, "As a result, expression rather than restraint is advocated. The entire progressive education program is based upon the expression of the desires and instincts of children. It ridicules the idea that man's tendencies are evil and need to be curbed." Ockenga concluded his sermon this way, "The coming generation is rapidly developing into a lawless, self-willed race and its posterity will undoubtedly witness an increase of insanity deformity, moral weakness, and vacillation of character. We have taught men that there is no God and they are living on that theory."[20]

Numerous conservative Christian publications in the 1940s also spoke loudly about the problems of public education. Three times over the decade the evangelical publication *Moody Monthly* featured stories by M.H. Duncan, a thirty-year veteran of Texas public schools. Duncan frequently called for a return to absolute standards in education but stopped short of actually promoting Christian schools. In 1941 he wrote, "When modern education refused to make the Bible the basis of its program and thus gave no place to the Christ of the Book, it was doomed to failure."[21] Duncan also connected the lack of moral standards to immigration by saying, "One great source of trouble in America today is that men and women with other moral conceptions have come to us so fast that we have not been able to assimilate them. As long as we had a common measure of morals and stood as a unit in our acceptance of the Bible as a supernatural book, a standard of morals given us from another world, we could absorb all who came to us and mold them into our way of thinking. But when we ceased to accept the Bible as a supernatural book, we lost our ability to assimilate, and today a foreigner who comes among us is a potential source of danger."[22] Duncan's final article appeared in 1947, again bemoaning a lack of spirituality in the public schools and warnings about the nation's doom if a Christian revival failed to take place in the educational system.[23]

Between the years 1941 and 1952, *The Sunday School Times* published fourteen articles on public school education while also advocating Christian day schools. Examples include Dr. Robert L. Cooke's article, "What is Wrong with American Education?" from June 1941. Dr. Cooke, a Wheaton College professor, directly challenged Dewey's progressive education ideas. He claimed that today's youth had found neither happiness nor success in the mere self-expression of progressive education and as a result they had become "confused morally, ethically, and religiously and they desperately

20. Ockenga, "America Pay Attention or Beware!," 48–55.

21. Duncan, "American Education Needs a Standard," 569–70, 587.

22. Duncan, "Bible in Life and Education," 425, 438–39.

23. Duncan, "Something is Missing," 673–74.

need something to believe in and hold to." He attacked Dewey from many angles, but centered most of his attention on religion. Cooke frequently challenged the father of progressive education in such areas as his call for a "common faith" based upon a devotion to intelligence. He also pointed out Dewey's rejection of original sin and his claim about the divisive nature of Christianity that supposedly stood in opposition to the inclusiveness of the democratic ideal. Cooke stated the main goal of Dewey's philosophy this way, "a fundamental feature of the Progressive educational doctrine is that it condemns on the ground of opposition to all indoctrination, all effort of the school toward inculcating in the youth those moral values traditionally considered fundamental." Dr. Cooke ended his article with a plea to return to the basics of the Christian faith. "Does the modern educator indeed turn to science and human philosophy for enlightenment?," he asked. "Let him rather look for his guidance to the Author of all knowledge and the Searcher of all hearts, to Him who "made the world and all things therein."[24] Over the ensuing decade, various writers for *The Sunday School Times* produced more articles with titles such as "Clouds on the Educational Horizon," "The Increased Need for Christian Education," "Undermined Foundations," "Public Education, a Propaganda for Atheism?," and "Saving Children Through the Christian Day School."

Beyond the issues raised by a few pastors in St. Louis, American education faced widespread criticism throughout the 1930s and 40s. During the Depression and on into the Cold War years, public education and its progressive programs faced internal schisms and also drew attacks from conservative politicians and business leaders. Progressive educators such as George Counts, a Dewey disciple, teacher union organizer, and Columbia professor of education, who authored numerous books advocating the Soviet educational system, drew much fire from traditional school leaders. His speech "Dare Progressive Education Be Progressive?," delivered at the 1932 Progressive Education Association convention, caused great concern because it outlined a more radical Marxist agenda for progressive education and called upon teachers to drop fears of conservative imposition and indoctrination of tradition.[25] Speaking during some of the worst days of the Depression, Counts believed that Dewey's idea of schools being a transforming agent meant that teachers should identify prevailing social ills and then use the schools to correct them. Counts felt that teachers should embrace a new socialistic economic system and instill these values directly into the

24. Cooke, "What is Wrong?," 459–61.

25. Counts, "Dare the School," 257–58; Cremin, *Transformation of the School,* 259–64.

students in order to bring about needed social change. However, another faction of educators, who also saw themselves as progressives, did not necessarily agree with Counts. More conservative educators still felt the task of social reform belonged to others and that as progressive educators their responsibility remained giving the child the noetic and social skills necessary to function as an intelligent and socially effective adult. From there, as a fully equipped progressive minded citizen, the students could then identify for themselves the best way to bring about change and continue the evolution of a democratic society. Divisions in the progressive ranks existed by the 1930s and they would not be settled for many years. However, the most vocal faction, led by Counts, created a negative image about public education during this era by appearing to favor Marxist ideals.[26]

Not surprisingly, some newly organized teacher unions also faced charges of favoring communism. In 1940, the New York State Legislature organized a committee to investigate communism in the schools, especially in New York City. The Rapp-Coudert Committee attacked teacher unions and schools for allegedly hiring communist sympathizers. Foreshadowing McCarthyism, this committee eventually managed to have several teachers removed and effectively damaged the power of the unions.[27]

There also existed a "conservative vigilantism" toward public schools in the 1930s by individuals who sought to exploit American fears of communism. A former army officer General Amos Fries became notable for his relentless attacks on the Washington DC public schools. Circumventing the local school board, he convinced a number of conservative Congressmen to pass a law in 1935 that forbade "teaching or advocating" Communism in the schools. Fries also succeeded in banning textbooks written by progressive historian Carl Becker whom Fries labeled as a "well known communist writer." Fries proved to be very effective in promoting his central tenet, "Communists and progressives were of one mind in subverting the schools."[28]

Additional clashes arose between professional educators and community business leaders over spending for education during the Depression and the war. While local school boards wanted to cut expenses, professional educators wanted to maintain their programs. At the same time, some leading educators felt that the economic pressures of the Depression and World War II years should force the schools to make to take a more active role in

26. Bowers, *Progressive Educator*, 4–7.

27. Hartman, *Education and the Cold War*, 40–41.

28. Hartman, *Education and the Cold War*, 48–49.

re-shaping society leading to further concerns among conservatives about radicals taking over the schools.[29]

More anxiety came from the formation of the Life Adjustment movement, a progressive education trend that began in the 1920s and culminated in the early 1940s that shifted priorities away from traditional studies and more toward the teaching of practical everyday life skills, based on a belief that education should meet the needs of the majority of average students who would not be attending college. Foreign languages, the classics, advanced sciences, and mathematics became obvious casualties.[30] Despite good intentions of progressives, Life Adjustment came under fire from conservatives who demanded a return to a traditional curriculum. Cold War fears about falling behind the Russians only added to the worries that progressive schools were failing to provide American children with a strong education.[31]

According to historian Andrew Hartman, public education in the U.S. during the 1940s and 50s underwent what he characterized as "the great condemnation." Widespread feeling that the schools were woefully out of step with the needs of the nation led to "undifferentiated fury" toward progressive education. Pressure coming from the Cold War only intensified the "shouting match" over education. John Dewey's ideas of a flexible, child-centered education did not fit in a nation now engaged in a global struggle against communism. Desiring a unified nation against the Soviet threat, conservative educators and politicians roundly criticized what they perceived as Dewey's epistemological relativism which could lead to confusion and push the masses toward communism. But, Hartman also states that the Cold War only fanned the flames of the educational crisis. Issues with teacher shortages, racial integration, the later "Baby Boom," and rapidly changing demographics after the war all created an atmosphere of tension and uncertainty in the bulwark of American democracy, the public school.[32]

However, the Supreme Court case *McCollum v. Board of Education of Champaign County* stands as arguably the single most important event in this decade that led conservative Christians to sharpen and amplify their condemnation of public education. As discussed in chapter three, public schools across the nation, in an attempt to accommodate expanding religious diversity, began a practice in the 1920s of released-time programs that allowed students during the school day to attend classes in their particular faith taught by outside teachers approved by local religious councils. Despite the fact that

29. Spring, *American School*, 338.
30. Ravitch, *Troubled Crusade*, 65–70.
31. Church and Sedlak, *Education in the United States*, 401.
32. Hartman, *Education and the Cold War*, 2–3.

the program proved difficult to manage, it nevertheless grew to the height of its popularity by the mid-1940s, enrolling approximately 2 million students or roughly 10 percent of the entire student population in some 2,200 communities in forty-six states. Ten of these states allowed the released-time classes to be held on the public school campuses.[33]

In one of these ten states, Illinois, the practice of released-time programs came under fire in 1945 in the city of Champaign by the mother of fifth grader Terry McCollum. Terry's mother, Vashti, resented the treatment her son received by teachers and classmates because of his refusal to attend such classes. Ultimately, this situation developed into a case before the United States Supreme court which challenged the constitutionality of released-time programs for religious instruction in public schools.

The McCollum case garnered close attention from the Christian community and Christian school leaders. *United Evangelical Action,* the official publication of the NAE, kept a watch on the developments of the case. A 1945 article by Ray Cartlidge, a Presbyterian minister from Champaign, considered the case in his hometown as promoting irreligion, and overturning the democratic process. He feared that if the school lost the case, it would be a "precedent–setting victory for the anti-religion forces—a blow from which we will not recover for years." He went on to explain how this action went against the wishes of the community, "Here we have the spectacle of one parent opposing the desire of the parents of 754 children to have religious training in our schools. Did the framers of our Constitution mean that a minority of one should stand in the way of a majority of 754?"[34]

The McCollum's endured three years of public abuse before being vindicated in the 1948 decision of *McCollum v. Board of Education of Champaign County.* In a vote of eight to one, the court ruled in favor of the McCollums stating that released-time programs violated the establishment clause of the First Amendment. Religious instruction on public school property violated the concept of separation of church and state.[35]

Predictably, outrage erupted from all corners of the evangelical Christian world and with it came increased calls for establishing Christian day schools. *United Evangelical Action* responded immediately in a May 1948 news brief by proclaiming, "However contrary the Court's decision may be at some particulars it has made clear the fact that evangelicals can no longer look to the public schools for the type of education that will make Christian citizens. The decision is therefore a challenge to all Christian Americans to

33. Dierenfield, *Battle Over School Prayer*, 52.

34. Cartlidge, "Battle of Champaign," 3–4.

35. Dierenfield, *Battle Over School Prayer*, 54.

build Christian day schools and guarantee the perpetuation of those principles which have made America great in the past and without which she is doomed to destruction."[36]

Mark Fakkema's comments in regard to the *McCollum* case reflect indignation but also his talents as a propagandist for the Christian school cause. Fakkema had never supported released-time programs in the first place. In a 1942 radio interview he stated, "Regarding such supplements as vacation Bible schools and week-day religious education, I merely wish to say that such measures—good as they are in themselves—cannot change the character of secular instruction."[37] However, his disdain for released-time programs did not stop him from using the *McCollum* case to ramp up his message about Christian schools. In a scathing newsletter, Fakkema blasted the court decision and used the opportunity to paint a very black and white scenario for Christian parents and their children. He saw the choice as clear, "Religiously interpreted, this court decision warns us: If we want our children to be religious, we must not send them to the public school. Stated positively, it implies: If we want our children to be Christians, we must send them to a Christian school. Morally interpreted, this decision suggests to the thoughtful: If we would train our children in moral virtues, we must not send them to the public school—instead we must send them to a private school whose moral instruction is based upon the Christian religion."[38] Writing many years later about the *McCollum* case, Fakkema continued to use it as a marketing tool by directly correlating the case to enrollment statistics. He claimed that prior to the case the percentage of children attending private schools stood at approximately 10 percent. In the ensuing years it increased to 15 percent.[39]

Another event which further condemned the public schools in the eyes of some evangelical Christians came from the publication of *General Education in a Free Society*. Produced in 1945, it reflected three years of work by a committee of Harvard professors who studied the present state of education in America for all grades. This report called for a fresh examination of general education for all citizens, not just a privileged few as had been the case in the previous century. In the nineteenth century, the students who attended high school almost all attended college and consequently engaged in a rigorous curriculum designed to prepare them exclusively for the university. However, the report noted that in the twentieth century, three fourths

36. "Christian Education Report," 21.
37. Fakkema et al., *Round Table Discussion*, 13.
38. Fakkema, "Educational Significance," 1.
39. Fakkema, *Result of a High Court Decision*, 2.

of high school students now went directly into the work force. Hence, much of the report focused on changing curriculum of secondary schools so as to more effectively prepare the larger general public, those not going on to college, to be productive citizens.[40]

Educational issues aside, the report's comments about religion in education quickly caught the attention of Christian leaders. In discussing the nation's colleges, the report stated, "Sectarians, particularly Roman Catholic, have of course their solution, which was generally shared by American colleges until less than a century ago: namely, the conviction that Christianity gives meaning and ultimate unity to all parts of the curriculum, indeed to the whole life of the college. Yet this solution is out of the question in public supported colleges and is practically, if not legally, impossible in most others. But whatever one's views, religion is not now for most colleges a practicable source of intellectual unity." The report also showed strong support for the progressive ideas of Dewey and noted his commitment to the premise that the "full truth is not known and that we must be forever led by facts to revise our approximations of it." In the report's recommendations for a new curriculum for high schools, religion appeared noticeably absent.[41]

The Harvard Report received notable attention at the fourth annual convention of the National Association of Evangelicals, held at Minneapolis in April 1946. Responding specifically to *General Education in a Free Society*, the Commission on Christian Educational Institutions called for the formulation of a clear Christian philosophy of education for all students. In addition, the Commission proclaimed the need for an educational system from kindergarten to university focused upon the Christian philosophy of life supported by a Bible-based curriculum.[42]

The editor of *United Evangelical Action*, Dr. Carl F. H. Henry, commented on the Harvard report in 1947. While commending parts of the report, Henry honed in on the phrase about religion not being a source of intellectual unity among colleges and its implication that religion had no place of significance in modern education.[43] At a 1947 meeting of business leaders and professional men at the Montrose School of Essex Fells, New Jersey, Dr. Clarence Roddy of Eastern Baptist Theological Seminary, expressed similar concerns. Proclaiming that "there is something radically wrong with the public school of America today," he also pointed out that the Harvard report implied that religion had been abolished from public education. Specifically,

40. Harvard Committee, *General Education*, v–x, 6–9.
41. Harvard Committee, *General Education*, 39, 47, 103–76.
42. Paine, "Report of the Commission," 4.
43. Henry, "Harvard Report," 15.

Dr. Roddy lamented the fact that colleges and universities no longer recognized the value of Christian truth and hence American education had lost its way since breaking traditional ties with the church.[44]

Therefore, it is evident that one of the major reasons for the growth of Christian schools in the 1940s came from widespread criticism in the evangelical community toward public education. The most common charge leveled toward public schools centered on the decline of teaching religion and the subsequent neglect of the spiritual life of the student. To many conservative Christians all of this came from the systematic rejection of the Bible in the nation's classrooms over many years. John Dewey and his theories of progressive education that rejected traditional religious beliefs also served as an easy target of this criticism. The *McCollum v. Board of Education* case and the publication of *General Education in a Free Society* intensified the attacks and emboldened Christian school advocates. The loudest and most audacious statements came from individuals such as Mark Fakkema, but the entire evangelical Christian community also expressed concerns about the "godless" public schools.

However, a closer look at the public schools and the issue of religion throughout the 1940s portrays a different picture. Whereas individuals like Ockenga, Fakkema, or Gaebelein painted the world of public education as totally divorced from God, evidence indicates that the public schools continued to struggle with the question of religion in the classroom throughout the 1930s and 40s and well after the *McCollum* decision. Seeking to accommodate a variety of faiths, actions of the public schools in this decade reveal the charges of "godlessness" to be exaggerated. Recent studies on the Cold War have also made the point that despite constitutional limitations, the federal government actually supported the teaching of Christian values in public education due to a belief that religion served as an important tool for combating communism. Jonathan Herzog found that during the late forties a whole new relationship developed between government and public schools that went against the gradual secularization of the previous century.[45]

As already noted, public schools continued to employ released-time programs for religious instruction well into the 1940s with numbers reaching their peak just prior to the *McCollum* case. Reports from the National Education Association indicate that from 1938 to 1948 the number of children participating in release programs increased 323 percent.[46]

---

44. "Increased Need for Christian Education," 402.

45. Herzog, *Spiritual-Industrial Complex*, 136–39.

46. National Education Association, *Research Bulletin*, 27.

Clearly, religious release time multiplied during this period despite the charges of rampant atheism.

In the years just after the *McCollum* decision, minutes of the proceedings of the annual conventions of the National Education Association provide even more clarity from public school leaders about religion in their schools. At the 1948 convention in a report named, "The Role of the Public Schools in the Development of Moral and Spiritual Values," NEA secretary Willard Givens stated, "In our opinion, this decision of the Supreme Court in no way voids the responsibility of the public schools to inculcate those moral and ethical principles which are the essence of the good life. One of the important objectives of public education has been, and always will be, to inspire in youth a deep appreciation for the basic spiritual and religious values which give meaning to existence, provide the foundations of good character, and are guides to a high order of human conduct." The report went on to devote several paragraphs explaining the great worth of teaching moral and spiritual values to students, which encourage admirable character traits. This same report also noted that American democracy possessed roots in Christian belief and hence the perpetuation of its democracy depended on a continued commitment to teaching spiritual values. NEA leaders made their most definitive statement by repeatedly claiming that the court ruling did not banish the teaching of moral and spiritual values, but rather banned sectarianism.[47]

The NEA concluded its 1948 report with several recommendations. First, it suggested a Commission be established to foster and promote the development of moral and spiritual values in the public schools by issuing publications and materials on this matter. Second, the report expressed a desire for the Commission to influence teacher-training programs across the nation to recognize the obligation they have to adequately prepare teachers in this area. Third, they asked this new Commission to investigate ways to use mass media as a tool of inculcating moral and spiritual values. Finally, the NEA leadership made a mass appeal to all public school educators to reaffirm their faith in, and support of, a strong program of teaching values and unite together behind this important cause.[48]

In 1950, the NEA made more reports on the issue of teaching moral and spiritual values. Much discussion focused on the importance of instilling individual responsibility for each child as well as responsibility for their peers. The Commission also responded directly to the criticism coming from such groups as the NAE and the Catholic church by saying, "We do wish to

47. Garrison, "Role of the Public Schools," 169–71.
48. Garrison, "Role of the Public Schools," 172.

answer the criticism of some people that schools are Godless, perhaps immoral in their influence, we do advise them that moral, spiritual values are being stressed, are understood and are definitely a part of the responsibility of the public school system. We do also recognize that the home and the various agencies within the community also have their responsibilities, we will try to do our share with all of these other institutions."[49]

In 1952, the NEA again addressed the issue of teaching moral and spiritual values and on this occasion produced conclusive opinions while also responding sharply to its critics. Dr. Henry Hill, chair of the NEA policies commission, described the recently published NEA document, *Moral and Spiritual Values* by saying, "The public school can teach objectively about religion without advocating or teaching any religious creed. To omit from the classroom all references to religion and the institutions of religion is to neglect an important part of American life. Knowledge about religion is essential for a full understanding of our culture, literature, art, history, and current affairs."[50]

Dr. Hill went on to directly address those who charged that the public schools were godless. He made several points which received thunderous applause, such as, "There is now in some quarters a demand that the public schools teach religion. Whose religion? What creed or ritual? However much we may like the plan of teaching that religion common to all recognized religions in the United States, the religious leaders have not produced such a text. Nor are they likely to do so." Hill also referred to his many years of being a public school superintendent and the numerous teachers he had hired and made this insightful comment, "Without a single exception, every teacher I hired was a member of a recognized church—Protestant, Catholic, or Jewish. If we may identify church membership with goodness—and surely most of the good people are in the churches; if we may identify membership in any or synagogue with godliness as contrasted with godlessness, then how and at what moment do good and perhaps godly teachers become godless as they step from the churches and homes to their posts of duty in the public schools? Are all places of assembly or work—the stores, factories, courts, farms, trains, and market places—to be regarded as godless because in them man does not thru ritual or formal act worship God or study or recite the dogmas of his church?" Hill concluded by clarifying the charge that secular necessarily means godless with this statement, "The word secular is sometimes substituted for godless. There is being read into this word, which has been used to designate civil as separated from religious affairs, the pejorative

49. Selke, "Education for Moral and Spiritual Values," 172–73.
50. Hill, "Report," 141–44.

idea that secular is evil. What else can schools open to all American children be except nondenominational? They must remain secular unless we change those underlying concepts and practices which have to date made and kept America relatively free from the religious quarrels, wars, and intolerances which drove many of our forefathers, fettered by oppressors, to escape to America. Are we willing as members of church groups to insist that the homes and churches handle matters of religious beliefs and that the public schools deal with common and moral spiritual values?"[51]

Professional journals of public school educators from this same decade also illustrate a spirited dialogue on religion in schools. One such publication, *The Nation's Schools,* published numerous issues about the role of religion in public education displaying a wide range of opinions on the topic. One such piece, "Teaching Religion in Public School is Playing With Fire," argued that religious instruction violated the establishment clause and hence could have grave consequences for personal liberties.[52] A year later, in another editorial, a professor from the University of Michigan wrote, "These teachings of the Nazarene need to be inculcated in the home, the church, the schools in private and public life not merely as desirable truths but rather as the absolute essentials for the survival of our race and as a matter of the truest self-interest of every individual."[53] Many articles reminded educators of the fact that public schools had always sought to teach character and morals. One commentary attacked evangelical Christians directly by saying, "Apparently, the churches want an evangelical Christian nurture introduced into education. They want the child taught to depend on supernatural forces, such as grace and the sacraments, as a means of achieving upright character. Yet, such Christian nurture leads straight to the door of controversial sectarian issues."[54]

Despite the loud and frequent claims of the NAE and numerous Christian leaders about godlessness in public education in the 1940s, clear evidence to the contrary exists. Public school leaders consistently claimed a long commitment to teaching moral and spiritual values while at the same time emphasizing a strong commitment to non-sectarianism in the tradition of Horace Mann. The mere presence of released-time programs illustrates the fact that public schools recognized the value of church instruction while trying to respect religious pluralism. For public school educators, The *McCollum* case did not negate the teaching of values but

51 Hill, "Report," 141–44.

52. Sisson, "Teaching Religion," 43–44.

53. Waterman, "Without Religion Education is Incomplete," 53–54.

54. Brubaker, "Why Force Religious Education?," 23–24.

instead kept the separation of church and state intact. The decade of the 1940s again demonstrated the century long struggle of trying to provide a common education to America's school children in the midst of ever expanding social and religious pluralism. To call the schools "godless" during this decade grossly oversimplifies the era, reflecting a previous mentioned characteristic of fundamentalists—that being their ability to frame everything in basic terms of good and evil.[55]

But for Christian school pioneers of the 1940s, public school claims of teaching moral and spiritual values rang hollow. They could not see how this could be accomplished apart from the specific teachings of the Bible, which they believed to be the only source of truth and morality. Dr. Robert McQuilkin, the president of Columbia Bible College, responded to the 1948 report of the National Education Association regarding the McCollum case in this way, "So the public schools are to inculcate moral and ethical principles which are the essence of a good life. Where are we to find these? Do they come from God? Are they in the Bible? Are they separate from religion? All educators agree that character and good citizenship are the chief ends of education. Will it be character without Christ? Shall we rule out God and the Bible? What are the educational leaders of America putting in its place? The answer is plain. They are putting secularism in its place. They are putting atheism in its place."[56] Hence, after years of seeing their power wane in American education, Christian school leaders would accept no compromise and continued their relentless assault on public schools for the purpose of promoting their own school system.

A few years after the McCollum case, a similar situation also reached the Supreme Court. The city of New York had a released-time program in place that allowed some three thousand Catholics, Protestants, and Jews to receive religious instruction. However, the New York program differed from that of Champaign County, Illinois in that the students attended classes away from their campuses and the public schools incurred no expense. A court challenge ensued and in 1952, the Supreme Court ruled in the case of Zorach v. Clauson by a vote of six to three that the New York program did not violate the Constitution because the religious instruction did not take place on public facilities and no public monies were utilized. Justice William Douglas claimed that the proper function of government toward religion should be one of cooperation, not neutrality. Douglas had no problem with the New York released-time program seeing it as akin to the schools allowing students

55. Hughes, Christian America and the Kingdom, 137–38.
56. McQuilkin, "How Can We Have Moral Education?," 497–99.

to miss classes to observe religious holidays.[57] The point seemed to be clear; the government respected religion and had no intention of forcing a "godless" education upon America's children. Interestingly, the *Zorach* decision produced no comment from the NAE leadership.

The debate about the role of religion in public education in the 1940s only served to stir the anxiety of conservative Christians and increase discussion about the establishment of separate Christian schools. The second annual NAE convention met in May, 1943 in Chicago and education remained a central topic of discussion. The NAE leadership specifically criticized education as having been infiltrated by modernism and liberal ideology that excluded God. Dr. J. Elwin Wright commented in his opening keynote address, "When we contemplate the fact that our institutions of higher education are, in so many instances, in the grip of infidel leadership we must realize that a well-integrated program in the field of education is one of the great necessities of our times. We must be delivered from the domination of organized modernism which has its tentacles in every phase of educational work if we hope for a revived and spiritually healthful church."[58] Dr. Harold Ockenga criticized educators and called upon the delegates to establish a distinct program of Christian education to redeem the nation. In his usual passionate style, Ockenga concluded his remarks this way, "It is to our everlasting disgrace that we have allowed this field to be almost wholly possessed by the proponents of modernistic conviction. The creative elements in religious education have been taken out of our hands. The result is that in many major universities the Christian faith is so transformed that we as evangelicals cannot recognize that it is Christian at all. We must take note of the thousands of youth who get their education in such an atmosphere. There is not much sense in our allowing modernistic education to depose our evangelical heritage."[59]

The NAE exhibited a strong conviction about education based on Christian values, but initially most of the emphasis centered upon colleges, seminaries, and churches. The comments of Wright and Ockenga clearly articulated evangelical concerns about liberalism and secular trends apparent in education, but specifically their comments pointed to their concerns about colleges. Most of the work of the Educational Committee formed in 1942 delved into issues surrounding higher education and Sunday schools in local churches. However, in the 1943 report of the Educational Committee, a brief recommendation appeared at the end of the report which

57. Dierenfield, *Battle Over School Prayer*, 59–60.

58. Wright, "Report of the Promotional Director," 12.

59. Ockenga, "Christ for America," 12–13, 22.

began a relationship with the NAE and the fledgling Christian elementary and secondary schools. It stated, "We recommend that a sub-committee on Education, as far as possible, conduct research into elementary and secondary Christian education in its entire scope, the findings to be given wide publicity."[60] This proposal, although yielding little initial fruit, did acknowledge the presence of such Christian schools and placed them into the overall NAE debate about American education.

Over the next year, the NAE continued to express trepidations about public education and in some instances already suggested Christian schools as an alternative. After the request for a subcommittee on elementary and secondary Christian education at the 1943 Chicago convention, the topic surfaced frequently. In the official NAE publication, *United Evangelical Action*, several articles during the 1940s addressed concerns over the state of education in America and often called for the support of Christian schools. Pastor William Haverhouse in his 1943 UEA article "A Plea for a God Centered Education" stated, "The lack of a concerted effort to establish Christian schools would prove that evangelicals were 'flabby' and unwilling to exercise sacrifice or discipline for such a valid cause."[61] Dr. Ockenga wrote an article in 1943 that called upon the nation's evangelicals to plan a program of Christian schools and Christian education that would provide leadership for generations to come.[62] In the October 1945 edition of UEA, Mark Fakkema wrote the lead article, "Shall the Church Build its Own Schools?" In this piece, Fakkema argued for a return to education based on religion as envisioned by the founders of America. He quoted such historical examples as the Northwest Ordinance of 1787 and then related how secularism had gradually destroyed America's Christian heritage in education and as a result the nation and its government faced peril. Hence, he pleaded, "Establish private Christian schools while this is still the privilege of our waning democratic form of government. We cannot rear a generation without God and expect it to submit to the rule of God. What we sow we may expect to reap. Sow in the hearts and minds of our youth a view of life that knows not God and we may expect to reap a harvest of godless men and women."[63]

However, it would be simultaneous events taking place some thirty miles west of Chicago, in the town of Wheaton that would eventually bring the Christian school movement and the NAE together. As the home of Wheaton College, this small town had stood as a bastion of conservative

60. National Association of Evangelicals, "Report of Committee," 35.
61. Haverhouse, "Plea for a God Centered Education," 4.
62. Ockenga, "Christ For America," 3–5.
63. Fakkema, "Shall the Church Build Its Own Schools?," 3, 4, 20.

fundamentalist Christianity since the mid nineteenth century. Organized in 1860, Wheaton College resisted the growing liberalism in the church guided by the leadership of its first president, Congregationalist educator Jonathan Blanchard. Blanchard believed America to be a Christian nation and even worked for a Christian amendment to the U.S. Constitution that would highlight religious values and promote temperance, honoring the Sabbath, and racial equality. Later, his son Charles Blanchard continued this conservative tradition for the college building close ties to the popular evangelical preacher D.L. Moody and actively portraying Wheaton as a light to the dark world of twentieth-century modernism.[64] By the 1930s and 40s, Wheaton College appeared to be a throwback to the earlier revivalist era, with a pervasively evangelical emphasis and atmosphere, an accent on Christian service, and a strong penchant for training young apologists to defend the faith. J. Oliver Buswell, president of Wheaton College from 1926 to 1940, prided himself on the school's academic standards and champion debate teams often referring to the school as "the Harvard of the Bible belt."[65]

In this overwhelmingly fundamentalist town with a strong academic tradition, it is not surprising that the idea of a Christian elementary school surfaced in the early 1940s. In the summer of 1941, Dr. Paul Culley, the Dean of Men and professor of anthropology at Wheaton, first shared the idea of a local Christian elementary school with some of his colleagues. Culley, and three other Wheaton professors notified local parents about a meeting to be held on September 12, 1941 to discuss the possibility of starting such a school. This group of parents and educators, from a variety of local churches, met in Blanchard Hall on the Wheaton campus. The professors invited none other than Mark Fakkema of the National Union of Christian Schools to come and explain all of the issues involved in starting a Christian school. In this meeting Fakkema's enthusiasm and his statement, "we are in urgent need of distinctively Christian instruction in the plastic young lives of early school age" struck a chord with these individuals, who agreed with this pressing concern. Three months later on December 9, 1941, Fakkema again met with the group and following his lead, fourteen individuals established a parent association known as the Wheaton Society for Christian Instruction.[66]

Over the next few months, the Society publicized the opening of the school and recruited students. Fakkema continued to advise the parents and assisted in hiring the first teacher. On September 8, 1942, the Wheaton

64. Marsden, *Fundamentalism and American Culture*, 29–32.

65. Carpenter, *Revive Us Again*, 21–22.

66. Knowles, "Wheaton Christian Grammar School," 6–8; "Suburb to Hail $80,000 School," 6.

Christian Grammar School (WCGS) opened at Wheaton Bible church serving grades 1–6 with a total of fifteen students.[67] However steady growth occurred throughout the decade with the WCGS enrollment rising to a total of 117 students by 1950.[68]

From the start, the school board of Wheaton Christian Grammar School showed a strong pledge to keep the school independent. They rejected any type of denominational affiliation feeling the school could better serve the entire community without being tied to any one particular church. Along with this, the board also committed to the notion of remaining independent as they did not want to be distracted by minor theological details. The Declaration of Faith of WCGS reflected a definite conservative flavor in such areas as belief in the Trinity, the virgin birth, the inspiration of scripture, and the atoning death of Christ, while at the same time showing no connection to denominational distinctions. The organization of the school under a parent association followed the pattern of many NUCS schools and no doubt reflected the influence of Mark Fakkema who consulted with school leaders from the beginning. However, WCGS differed from the strictly Reformed theology of most NUCS schools by admitting families from a variety of denominations including Reformed, independent Bible, Church of Christ, Brethren, Baptist, Evangelical Free, Methodist, Lutheran, and Episcopal churches.[69]

In terms of educational philosophy, WCGS reflected the same conservative yet non-denominational stance adopted at Gaebelein's Stony Brook School. A promotional booklet from the time stated that all the fundamental subjects of public school elementary education would be stressed along with classes in the Bible.[70] The curriculum did indeed carry out all of the basic subjects but also provided for a thorough integration of scriptural principles in every course. Instructors understood that they held the position of not only teaching curriculum but also serving as spiritual mentors to the children. In regard to textbooks, WCGS used both Christian-based publications as well as secular materials. None of the school's teachers or administrators felt that the use of secular textbooks would be harmful to the goals of the school, as long as they were integrated with biblical concepts.[71]

The founding of Wheaton Christian Grammar School in 1942 eventually came to serve two distinct purposes. First, it reflected the new evangelical

67. Knowles, "Wheaton Christian," 13–16.

68. Campbell, "Wheaton Christian," 2.

69. Knowles, "Wheaton Christian," 82, 121.

70. Wheaton Society, *Announcing*, 3.

71. Knowles, "Wheaton Christian," 81, 83, 88.

Christianity of this era. Like the National Association of Evangelicals, WCGS possessed a broad appeal to a variety of Protestant families from many different denominations, while at the same time maintaining its commitment to conservative biblical truths. Hence, it helped to define Christian education as a broader pan-evangelical movement, not the more limited denominational enterprise that characterized the NUCS schools. The school also served as a concrete response to the wide and growing evangelical concerns about education. In an early prayer letter to parents at WCGS, school leaders outlined the purpose of Christian education while also criticizing the purposes of progressive education, "Parents and teachers are to train up a child in the way he should go, not the way he would go, for the bias of inbred sin, strengthened by actual sin, tends to direct his actions in the downward way. Although some of us may be called eccentric—and we surely are out of center in the opinion of many educators—yet we are more interested than they in integrating the personality; but, whereas they put 'self' on the throne and magnify 'self,' we seek to build a life with Christ Jesus magnified and enthroned in the heart of each child."[72]

Second, Wheaton Christian Grammar School served as a catalyst in starting similar schools and a larger national movement. Due its broad statement of faith and more liberal admissions policy, WCGS fit the mold established by Stony Brook which stood apart from the NUCS for many years. But ultimately, the new Christian school at Wheaton had a greater impact. Heightened concerns of conservative Christians about public education, secularism, and the loss of influence and control in American society in the two decades after Stony Brook's founding in 1920 set the stage for WCGS to spark the growth of a larger, more visible and ultimately more influential Christian school movement.

In 1946, *United Evangelical Action* hosted its most extensive number of articles about Christian education to date. Over the course of the year, no less than five major stories appeared in this official NAE newsletter as well as countless small articles announcing the establishment of Christian schools all over the nation. With titles such as "Education Without Christ— Public Enemy Number One" and "Shall We Educate Teenagers Without Christ?"[73] NAE members made evident their feelings about the state of public education at this time. In one 1946 article, "Christian Schools For Such a Time as This," Mark Fakkema outlined three types of school systems in the nation: parochial, public, and parent—society. The parochial system

72. Wheaton Christian, "Prayer Letter."

73. Warren, "Education Without Christ," 3–8; Friend, "Shall We Educate Teenagers Without Christ?," 3–4.

of the Catholics, under the directives of the Vatican, had obvious problems for Protestant families. Public schools did have locally elected school boards, but Fakkema noted how they still fell under the supervision of the government with a state-prescribed curriculum based on "evolutionistic teaching" and a clear directive to keep religion out. Hence, Fakkema argued that Christian schools, under the supervision of parent societies consisting of parent boards and officers in the NUCS model, produced better scholarship, better moral training, and best reflected the democratic ideals of the nation. This commitment to democracy came from the fact that parents had the power to establish their own schools and determine the character of the instruction given. Most importantly, Fakkema argued, the parent society Christian school rendered a service that public schools could not, namely, the constitutionally guaranteed privilege of parents teaching their own religion to their offspring.[74]

With the establishment of the National Association of Evangelicals in 1942, conservative Protestants united behind their great concerns about the direction of American society, an agenda that included a call for major educational reform. The emotional debate over the *McCollum* case and the publication of *General Education in a Free Society* further eroded the trust between evangelicals and public education that had been waning for decades. At the same time, the founding of Wheaton Christian Grammar School represented an educational alternative that possessed the nondenominational tendencies of the NAE. With apprehensions about family, community, and a loss of influence in an increasingly secular and pluralistic society, conservative Christians had indeed regrouped in the 1930s and 40s with a goal of reclaiming their perceived heritage. As the 1940s unfolded, more events would push these evangelicals to further question the nation's public educational system. To these believers, public schools now threatened their dream for a Christian America and the time seemed ripe to move forward as a mighty army and establish a larger, more effective Christian school movement.

74. Fakkema, "Christian Schools," 3–5.

Chapter 6

"The Christian School is a Substitute for the Public School"

B y the late 1940s, public education felt the throes of conflict in trying to meet the changing needs of American society and the divisive discussion about the teaching of religion and moral values in the classroom. At the same time, a handful of conservative Christians saw the issue as very black and white in terms of religion in education. To individuals such as Mark Fakkema and Frank Gaebelein, the future seemed quite ominous, the need for Christian schools urgent. The newly formed National Association of Evangelicals was striving to unite conservative believers so that the nation could return to it's perceived Christian heritage. As the turmoil in public education raged and a handful of infant Christian schools, formed in the twenties and thirties, struggled to take their first baby steps, the NAE created a national assembly for conservative believers and provided a forum for the discussion about Christian education.

Consequently, on April 14, 1947, Mark Fakkema stood before the fifth annual convention of the National Association of Evangelicals in Omaha, Nebraska to make an earnest plea. After several months of preparation, he came to speak to fellow evangelicals about the need for a new national Christian school organization that could include Christian schools from a variety of denominations. Fakkema attacked public education but also challenged the Christian education children received in churches as simply inadequate. This "minor Christian educational influence," as he called it, could "never make right the major anti-Christian influence of the average public school of today." The only solution, he argued, was to create Christian day schools, not a supplement and correction to public schools, but a replacement for them.[1] He asked the NAE, with its emphasis on evangelical unity, to form and sponsor a nationwide association of these kinds of schools. After Fakkema spoke, the Committee on Christian Day Schools, a subcommittee of the Commission on Educational Institutions led by its new chairman, Frank Gaebelein, met to consider this request. The Committee recommended to the NAE board that a national Christian school organization be formed along the lines proposed by Fakkema. This organization would adhere to the NAE statement of faith and it would assist and oversee all Christian elementary and secondary schools desiring membership.[2]

Fakkema's speech to the NAE culminated several months of discussion and activity. The establishment of Wheaton Christian Grammar School in 1942 coincided with the founding of the NAE and both institutions revealed the changing nature of Protestant Christianity in America. After years of sectarian division, the NAE brought together the members of many Protestant denominations longing for a return to more conservative orthodox beliefs under the broad banner of "evangelical Christianity." Likewise, WCGS attracted students from a myriad of Protestant churches and thereby moved away from more traditional sectarian Christian schools. At that time, Fakkema served as the General Secretary of the National Union of Christian Schools, an organization of Christian schools committed to a strict Presbyterian Calvinistic theology. He decided that in order to grow, the Christian school movement needed a newer organization with a much wider attraction among Protestants.

The new school at Wheaton had indeed posed a problem for the NUCS concerning the issue of non-Reformed schools. Dr. John Van Bruggen, an NUCS leader, expressed alarm about this matter in *Christian Home and School Magazine*. "With the coming of Christian schools sponsored by groups other than those of the Reformed tradition, we are faced with a danger," he wrote. "We must encourage these fellow Christians and cooperate with them, but how far should we go? May we never cooperate with them to the extent of giving up the Calvinistic interpretation of life that our Christian school founders sought so vigorously to impart to their children."[3] Reformed theology, directly associated with the Presbyterian Church, contained several points that had long been a source of contention among Protestants. With such notions as predestined salvation, the total depravity of man, and eternal security, Christian schools under this set

---

1. Fakkema, "Christian Day School," 37.
2. Paine, "Report of the Commission," 7.
3. Bruggen, "At the Crossroads," 7.

of beliefs emphasized an exclusiveness that did not fit a school like WC-
GS.[4] In the early part of the decade, several non-Reformed schools sought
membership in the NUCS for the sake of its many resources; however, the
Union consistently refused them because of a fear of setting precedent and
the obvious theological differences.

In March 1945, the issue reached a climax when Wheaton Christian
Grammar School applied for membership in the NUCS. The statements of
faith of WCGS did not include Reformed theology and therefore NUCS
leaders simply could not agree to accept this school. Mark Fakkema had
a long and close relationship with WCGS and denying membership to
this school proved difficult for him. The rejection of WGCS's application
represented the dilemma of a growing number of non-Reformed schools
and hence, Fakkema addressed the issue with the NUCS board. He stated
his frustration with helping schools like WGCS get started and then being
compelled to push them away like orphans.[5] Over the next year and a half,
Fakkema frequently mentioned the idea of a broader organization to NUCS
board members. In a later report to the NAE, Fakkema described his feelings
this way, "Either the National Union must tell the 'outsiders' to erect their
own schools and eventually form their own unions or the National Union
in cooperation with the 'outsiders' must form an overall school organization
which would do for all evangelical schools what the National Association
of Evangelicals attempts to do for all evangelical churches."[6] Fakkema's relationship with WCGS clearly caused him to question the effectiveness of the
NUCS as a national organization.

Beyond the issue of Wheaton Christian Grammar School, Mark Fakkema had begun questioning his role as General Secretary of the NUCS, a
position he had held for almost a quarter of a century. In 1943, the NUCS
board began to address the issue of the implementation of their philosophy
into actual classroom teaching and found that while Fakkema possessed
great skills as a promoter, he lacked graduate training in education. More
and more schools sought textbooks and curriculum materials and Fakkema,
with his heavy travel schedule and his lack of educational training, could not
meet this need. According to an interview with Dr. Van Bruggen, by 1945,
Fakkema began to feel that his skills might be better utilized in pioneering a
larger, more inclusive national movement.[7]

4. Benson, "History of the National Association," 30–32.

5. Mark Fakkema interview in Simpson, "Development of the National Association," 131–32.

6. Fakkema, "For a Time Such as This," 2.

7. John Van Bruggen quoted in Benson, "History of the National Association," 34.

Mark Fakkema attended the annual NUCS business meeting held on August 22, 1946 in Pella, Iowa with concerns about the questions raised by Wheaton Christian Grammar School. He had already corresponded with several NUCS board members about the idea of creating a more broad-based Christian school organization and hence came prepared to take up this cause. In a lengthy address to the board, Fakkema stated, "Our contribution of a God-centered life for children applied to all spheres of activity is not something which is immaterial to the well-being of these other churches. It is basic to their as well as our future development." Making it clear to the convention that NUCS must make the most of the present opportunity, Fakkema went on to say, "We must have a new type of national organization-one that embraces all Christian schools that proceed from private initiative rather than from parish authorization. Membership in such an organization should not be on a doctrinal basis other than the doctrine that parents must train their own children in the light which God has given them to see the light."[8]

The NUCS leaders at the 1946 business meeting received Fakkema's comments favorably while still maintaining their approach to education based on Reformed theology. In a resolution, the leaders explained the historical reasons for their existence and made it clear that children from non-Reformed churches should not be admitted to their type of schools. However, they also endorsed the idea of a larger Christian school organization. In one particular resolution, the NUCS maintained its commitment to its own distinctive character while at the same time saying, "That this body supports the formation of an overall national organization, similar to the NAE to promote the cause of Christian education everywhere."[9]

Dr. Roger Voskuyl, the current acting President of Wheaton College and President of the Wheaton Society for Christian Instruction, attended the meeting at Pella, Iowa. He came for the expressed purpose of encouraging the establishment of a new organization. Fakkema later reported that Dr. Voskuyl appreciated the unified spirit of the board and the General Secretary toward this new idea and immediately withdrew the request of WCGS to join the Union. He returned to Wheaton to meet with his school leaders and discuss ideas toward the creation of a new nationwide association.[10]

The National Association of Evangelicals met for its fourth annual convention on April 24, 1946 in Minneapolis, Minnesota. For several days,

8. National Union of Christian Schools, "Proceedings of Annual Business Meeting," 9–10.

9. National Union of Christian Schools, "Proceedings of Annual Business Meeting," 34–35.

10. Fakkema, "Report to the Promotion Committee," 3.

various NAE commissions met and this included the Commission on Christian Educational Institutions. In their report to the entire convention, leaders of this Commission related that on April 27 they met with representatives of approximately fifty evangelical schools and discussed a wide range of topics concerning Christian education. The chief recommendation of the Commission expressed their concern over the neglect of Christian education at the elementary and secondary level and proposed that this topic be given serious consideration at the next year's convention. In addition, the Commission requested that several new members be added to the group. Among the thirteen names to be added to the NAE Commission on Christian Educational Institutions were Mark Fakkema, General Secretary of the National Union of Christian Schools, Frank Gaebelein, Headmaster of Stony Brook School, and Dr. Enock C. Dyrness, Vice President of Wheaton College.[11]

Hence, when Mark Fakkema made his request at the fifth annual NAE convention at Omaha, Nebraska, the establishment of a new national Christian school organization seemed almost a foregone conclusion. After the Committee on Christian Day Schools acted upon Fakkema's recommendation, more decisions followed. They voted to open an office and hire appropriate personnel, with expenses covered through contributions accrued through services rendered by this new organization. Noting with appreciation that the NUCS had endorsed this new endeavor, the Committee made a final recommendation that included approaching the NUCS and requesting that they loan the services of Mark Fakkema on a part-time basis to give assistance in setting up this new enterprise.[12]

A month later, the NAE board met to consider these requests. Dr. Dyrness of Wheaton College and a member of the Committee on Christian Day Schools gave a report. The board sought clarification about the theological stance of this new organization so as to distinguish it from the NUCS. Mark Fakkema, invited to attend by the board, addressed this issue again by stating that this new association would be based on the premise that education is the responsibility of the parents and would not fall under the auspices of a particular denomination or theology. Since the schools in this new organization would be established by a group of parents in each community from different churches, known as a parent society, each school could set standards while still adhering to the NAE statement of faith.

After this discussion, the body voted unanimously to found an affiliate organization of the NAE in the field of Christian day schools. With this NAE board decision, the National Association of Christian Schools

11. Paine, "Report of the Commission," 55–57.
12. Paine, "Report of the Commission," 7.

(NACS) officially became established.[13] In a later interview, Fakkema explained the importance of this meeting, "This was so important because it implied that home training was not enough, Sunday school training was not enough, released-time training was not enough and all the other agencies that we have that are for the betterment of youth were not enough, that we also need a Christian day school. They were virtually telling the folks back home, 'We need something else beside all these other agencies.' So that morally, they took a position in favor of the Christian day school."[14] At the end of this meeting, the NAE board asked Fakkema if he would consider serving on a temporary basis as the director of this new organization if the NUCS would agree. Fakkema responded affirmatively based upon working out details with the NUCS.

Over the next few weeks several other events occurred to set in motion the future of the National Association of Christian Schools. On June 10 the NAE authorized the selection of a board to oversee the NACS and this inaugural group included Dr. Frank Gaebelein. The other critical issue of the next few weeks surrounded the question of Mark Fakkema and his release from the NUCS. The NAE had originally asked for him to lead this new organization on a part-time basis. On June 24 and 25, the NUCS board met to consider a letter they received from Dr. Dyrness requesting Fakkema's services for the NACS. At the same time, the NUCS board and Fakkema discussed their recent decision to hire an educational secretary to oversee the creation of educational materials and curriculum. Apparently, this move caused tension between Fakkema and the NUCS board with Fakkema perceiving this hire as a demotion since it relieved him of some of his responsibilities. The board agreed to pay Fakkema's salary for the next year and allowed him to become the new General Secretary of the NACS beginning September 1, 1947.[15] While it may appear initially that Fakkema would be "loaned" to the National Association, events clearly point to the fact that Fakkema would not return to the NUCS. A month earlier at the August 1947 convention of the National Union, Fakkema submitted a letter of resignation and the NUCS board presented him with a watch and expressed gratitude for twenty-one years of service.[16]

With a new director, a new board, and under the auspices of the NAE, the National Association of Christian Schools embarked on its mission in

13. Benson, "History of the National Association," 45.

14. Fakkema in Simpson, "Development of the National Organization," 134.

15. National Union of Christian Schools, "Proceedings of the Board of Directors," 141–44.

16. Benson, "History of the National Association," 47–51.

the fall of 1947. Understandably, some issues needed attention in those early years. One of the first centered on the relationship of the NACS to the NAE. When Fakkema first accepted the role of General Secretary, he did so with a condition. He requested that this new organization be started as an affiliate member of the NAE, which meant that it would not be under the direct supervision of the NAE, but would instead have its own board. In addition, the NACS would not accept financial support from the NAE but would raise its own revenue. Hence, from the beginning, Fakkema wanted to make sure that the NACS actually had only a cursory relationship to the NAE. In a later interview, Fakkema explained that this was "because the board by and large of the National Association of Evangelicals knew nothing about the Christian day school. It was new to them, and they would not be able to give really good direction if they were ignorant of the movement or the organization. So I personally felt that it should be governed by those who are Christian school minded, and who know what the problems are." Mark Fakkema insisted upon autonomy from the start while at the same time wanting the publicity and connections that would come being associated with the NAE.[17] However, limitations did exist in this relationship. All NACS board members had to be approved by the NAE administrative board. The NACS also had to submit a report at the annual convention. Most importantly, the constitution and by-laws of an affiliate such as the NACS had to be approved by the NAE administrative board.[18]

Hence, another early task facing the new NACS focused on the creation of a constitution. Fakkema and his board set to work on this immediately and submitted a preliminary draft in 1949 that received final approval in 1950. The preamble stated, "Recognizing that each generation is responsible to God to transmit to its children a true and adequate knowledge of the Holy Scriptures and of God's general revelation in nature, we feel that it is our God-given duty to establish Christian schools. Knowing that such schools have many problems and needs which can best be met by concerted planning and action, we do herewith establish a national Christian school organization which shall be known as the National Association of Christian Schools." In terms of its purpose, the constitution said, "To give stimulation and advice in the establishment and operation of Christian schools; to devise ways and means of securing and placing Christian teachers; to cooperate with other agencies to provide the necessary Christian textbooks; to provide expert advice for cooperating school groups; to encourage high

17. Fakkema quoted in Simpson, "Development of the National Organization," 135–36.

18. Benson, "History of the National Association," 61.

scholastic standards; and perform such other functions as the Association may do more effectively than individual schools, denominational schools, or groups of schools can do separately." The constitution also called for individual and institutional memberships in the NACS distinguishing between educators and actual schools. The NACS constitution also contained a doctrinal statement similar to the NAE's reflecting broad evangelical principles, while avoiding denominational or theological differences.[19]

Perhaps the most distinctive and compelling statement in the NACS constitution appeared at the end in regard to individual schools affiliating with this new organization. It read, "By joining the National Association of Christian Schools local school organizations do not in any way compromise their distinctive doctrinal positions, neither do they assume responsibility for the doctrinal tenets held by other members of the Association. Individual schools or groups of schools retain all of their sovereign rights. It is not necessary, either, that they be members of the National Association of Evangelicals in order to have membership in the National Association of Christian Schools."[20] Thus, the NACS followed the NUCS organizational plan by granting a great deal of autonomy to member schools, but differed in its theological stance by its inclusiveness to all evangelical Christians. Fakkema arranged the NACS constitution based on his long experience with the NUCS while holding to the philosophy of its parent organization, the NAE.

By allowing each Christian school to retain a great deal of sovereignty, the NACS also reflected the long held NUCS standard that education was first and foremost a parental responsibility. As General Secretary of the National Union, Mark Fakkema had long promoted and supported the idea of Christian schools being controlled by parent associations. In the mid-1950s, Fakkema wrote an article for *United Evangelical Action* stating that nowhere in the Scriptures can it be found that the education of children primarily belonged to the church or the state. Rather, in passages found in Deuteronomy, the Psalms, Proverbs, and Ephesians a clear mandate existed for parents to educate their children.[21] Since parents could not assume complete responsibility for the instruction of their children, they could meet this obligation by forming "parent societies" that ran Christian schools through the supervision of a school board run by parents. This board would enforce policy and hire all personnel.[22] Hence, to evangelical Christians, a locally controlled Christian school, led by the parents, fit this God mandated role perfectly.

19. National Association of Christian Schools, *Constitution*, 1.

20. National Association of Christian Schools, *Constitution*, 2.

21. Fakkema, "Case for the Christian Day School," 8.

22. Postma, "School Board," 7.

Another early issue of the NACS involved finances. Striving to be an independent affiliate and thereby trying to accept limited funding from the NAE posed challenges from the start. The offer of the NUCS to pay Fakkema's salary for a year helped tremendously. Fakkema then sought out businessmen he knew from around the country and asked for donations for the administration of the National Association. He eventually secured annual donations of $100 from approximately one hundred men for the first few years. Later, proceeds from the sale of literature, curriculum and membership fees all contributed to the NACS budget.[23] A report submitted by Fakkema to the NAE in September 1948 reported the largest source of income to be from "Founders" with the greatest expense being salaries and office rental and utilities. The NACS reported a bank balance of just over $4,000 on September 30, 1948.[24]

Judging by Mark Fakkema's commitment of time, the highest priority of the early years of the NACS focused on the promotion of Christian schools and this new organization. Just as he had done with the NUCS, Fakkema immediately began to produce publicity materials. For twenty years prior, he had written numerous articles and editorials for the National Union's *Christian Home and School* magazine. The NUCS later reprinted some of these articles in the form of brochures. When he left the NUCS, Fakkema asked if he could keep these materials and use them for the NACS and the Union agreed. So for many years, some of the promotional materials used by the NACS came from the NUCS.[25] At the 1948 NAE convention, Fakkema reported that six pamphlets had been produced with titles such as "Christian Schools and How to Organize Them," "How to Teach Children Morally," and "How to Teach Obedience."[26] Over the next two years, scores of articles and pamphlets appeared addressing a variety of topics all related to selling the notion of Christian education to the evangelical community. Titles include "Christian Education Against Modern Paganism," "Christian Schools or a Pagan Nation—What Shall it Be?," and "Christian Day Schools—Why?" The NACS first anniversary pamphlet, "For Such a Time as This" mentioned that the association printed 80,000 pieces of promotional literature in its first year.[27] Using strong rhetoric, these writings stirred Christian parents to seriously consider the need for a Christian school in their respective communities.

23. Simpson, "Development of the National Organization," 179–80.
24. Fakkema, "Statement of Income and Expense," 6.
25. Benson, "History of the National Association," 66–67.
26. Fakkema, "National Association of Christian Schools," 23.
27. Fakkema, *First NACS Anniversary*, 1.

One of the most widely read pamphlets produced by the NACS at this time was "Popular Objections to the Christian School." Responding to six common questions parents would receive by taking the bold step of removing their children from the public schools, this short work received widespread distribution. Examples included the question, "By replacing public schools with Christian schools are we not breaking down an American institution?" Fakkema answered that these schools did not break down an American institution, but rather restored an American institution. This pamphlet went on to remind readers that all schools in early America had a religious orientation and that the move toward secular education only appeared in the nineteenth century. Moreover, since America possessed religious freedom, parents had the liberty to establish schools based upon their beliefs and if they neglected this responsibility, they ran the risk of being overwhelmed by secularism and ultimately losing that freedom. Another question raised in this pamphlet centered upon the issue of sending Christian children to be missionaries in the secular public school rather than sheltering them in a private school. The response maintained that unfortunately, the influence would most likely work in the opposite direction with Christian students becoming more worldly in a public school rather than vice-versa. Putting children in a Christian school would be more prudent because, "Before a soldier goes to the front he must pass through a period of strenuous military training in the homeland. To send a Christian child to a worldly school is to rush a volunteer of the army of the Lord to the scene of battle un-tutored and untrained."[28]

Beyond, the pamphlets, Mark Fakkema also started an NACS newsletter. First printed in the fall of 1948, The National Association of Christian Schools Newsletter came out at various times for several years. Fakkema used this publication to make the case repeatedly for Christian education and report the growth of new schools across the nation. Each newsletter always painted a dire picture of public education while also sharing stories of new schools popping up all over the map. For example, in describing the sacrifices made to start a school in the Los Angeles area, Fakkema mentioned a teacher who turned down a more lucrative position in a public school and also told the story of a local pastor who "sold his wrist watch, sold his car, and surrendered the title of his house" to raise money for a new Christian school in the neighborhood.[29] Fakkema also commented on news of the day to advance his agenda. He strongly criticized the 1948 Supreme

---

28. Fakkema, "Popular Objections," 2–3.
29. Fakkema, "Spirit of Self-Sacrifice," 2.

Court case, *McCollum v. Board of Education* and expressed fears about the United Nations and Communism.

Armed with an abundance of printed propaganda produced out of the NACS headquarters in Chicago, Fakkema also pushed Christian education by tirelessly traveling the nation, speaking in churches and parent meetings. While banging the drum for his cause, he also provided practical guidance for fledgling schools based on his long NUCS experience. *United Evangelical Action* reported in December 1947, that Fakkema would begin an extensive trip in the west to speak for the NACS and work with new schools.[30] Over the next few months, Fakkema would address crowds in Kansas City, Lincoln, Denver, Phoenix, Los Angeles, Portland, and Seattle to name just a few.[31] A typical example of his message appeared in a 1948 *United Evangelical Action* article that related Fakkema's visit to a parent group in Portland, Oregon. Using his uncompromising style, Fakkema posed the question: "Is it better to take the public school curriculum, strip it of its godless, evolution based ideals and then interject Christian values or is it preferred to draw up an entire new curriculum which placed God in the center of all knowledge and truth that molds students into a reflection of the living God?" To the NACS leader, an obvious answer came in the form of new schools with new curriculum designed to instill Christian principles in the students.[32] Another example came from a group of parents from Kansas City who attended the 1947 NAE conference for the purpose of hearing Mark Fakkema speak. They reported back that the NACS leader spoke not only about the grave need for Christian schools, but also gave specific guidelines for starting a school. One commented that Fakkema helped parents to see that this undertaking, which seemed impossible to some, could certainly become reality. Fakkema's fiery rhetoric obviously made an impact on the Kansas City parents because their report ended with this quote, "So we are looking to God to enable us to provide Christian Schooling for our little ones, lest Satan get his poison into their minds, which would hinder their usefulness in the Lord's service, and possibly wreck their lives and their souls for eternity."[33] In summing up the first year of the NACS, Fakkema reported that his speaking engagements and conferences logged him 12,000 miles in seventeen states and Canada over a period of fifteen weeks. He also had seventy-five specific appointments with parent groups interested in starting schools.[34]

30. United Evangelical Action, "Christian Day School Survey," 20.

31. United Evangelical Action, "Fakkema in West," 16.

32. Eyres, "How It Is Done," 7–8.

33. Kansas City Christian Schools, "Christian Day School Bulletin," 1–3.

34. Fakkema, *First NACS Anniversary,* 1.

Another important component of Mark Fakkema's work to promote the cause of Christian education focused upon teachers. He recognized from his NUCS days the critical need to attract good instructors to the new schools. Duplicating the structure of the National Union, Fakkema set up a placement service for teachers in 1948 to connect individuals desiring to work in Christian education with the schools. The only requirement involved the prospective teacher agreeing to sign the NACS doctrinal statement. By registering with the service, teachers could get their names on the NACS nationwide mailing list and receive inquiries.[35] At a 1949 NAE Board meeting, Dr. Enock Dyrness, an NACS board member, reported steady interest and growth of this placement service.[36] The next year Fakkema proudly claimed, "Despite the general shortage of teachers in this country, we have no such shortage in our agency."[37] In 1952, Fakkema reported that the service had 150 teachers on the waiting list seeking positions in Christian schools. "There are so many teachers in the public schools," he explained, "who find out that they are not allowed to have a Christian testimony and turn to the Christian school field."[38]

However, the NACS board recognized the greatest need among teachers in the young schools lay in the area of training in the field of Christian education. Early on, the board sought to develop a course in the philosophy of Christian education for teachers since most of them graduated from state universities. Again capitalizing upon the work already done by the NUCS, Fakkema noted in the first edition of *The National Association of Christian Schools Newsletter* that, "In cooperation with other Christian school agencies, the NACS will at the earliest possible date seek to solve our Christian school teacher training problem."[39] In 1947, the National Union published *Course of Study for Christian Schools*, which Fakkema had co-authored. As they had done with other NUCS publications, the NACS leadership encouraged all teachers to read this book and adopt its philosophies into their classrooms. *Course of Study for Christian Schools* covered a wide variety of important topics which included the philosophy of Christian education, general objectives for a school followed by an implementation of these objectives down into specific subject areas.[40]

35. Simpson, "Development of the National Organization," 183–84.
36. Dyrness, "Report of the Commission," 1.
37. Fakkema, "Report of the National Association," 50.
38. Fakkema, "Report of the National Association," 14.
39. Fakkema, "What God Hath Wrought," 2.
40. Educational Committee, *Course of Study.*

This book proved quite helpful in assisting teachers, but the NACS board encouraged Mark Fakkema to go further and develop a course in the philosophy of Christian education. In the summer of 1949, *The National Association of Christian Schools Newsletter* extended an invitation to all teachers to attend a workshop in Christian education. Wheaton College, Biola College in California, and the Friends Conference Grounds in Portland, Oregon all hosted this workshop entitled "The Philosophy of Christian School Activity." Touted as a college level course, it consisted of thirty-two one hour sessions all taught by Fakkema over a period of approximately ten days. The main subjects of study covered such questions as: what is a God-centered philosophy?, what is Christian school discipline and instruction in the light of a God-centered philosophy?, on a God-centered basis, how should various school studies be taught?, and how can and should those of different evangelical faiths cooperate in the same Christian school program?[41] The next summer, in 1950, a second course entitled, "The Philosophy of Christian School Teaching" was offered. This particular course contained more specifics for the classroom teacher with topics in methodology and biblical integration of particular subjects. Wheaton again hosted a summer class along with colleges in Los Angeles, Seattle and Winona Lake, Indiana.[42]

These summer workshops eventually produced a set of three books which served for years as the basis of these ongoing summer courses. Fakkema published *Book One—Christian Philosophy* in 1952 and *Book Two—Moral Discipline,* and *Book Three—Christian Teaching* in succeeding years. For the next few decades, these summer courses became a mainstay in the Christian school movement going beyond the original topics and enlisting the help of numerous Christian school educators. With its consistent message, these summer courses proved vital to the growth and stability of the movement into the twenty-first century. These courses not only assisted teachers currently employed in Christian schools but also served as a means of teacher recruitment. Dottie Hiatt attended Taylor University in the early 1950s and expected to teach in a public school having been taught that Christian schools produced a substandard education. In the summer of 1955, Hiatt attended one of Fakkema's summer courses at Winona Lake, Indiana, which greatly influenced her. "After hearing Fakkema speak," she said, "I decided to look for a position in a Christian school. Eventually, I got a job at Wheaton Christian Grammar School and taught there for the next thirty-nine years."[43]

41. Fakkema, "Christian School Workshops," 1–2.

42. Fakkema, "Christian Education Needs a Christian Philosophy," 1–2.

43. Dottie Hiatt was a teacher at the Wheaton Christian Grammar School from

One final way that the NACS assisted teachers came in the form of a professional publication. *The Christian Teacher* debuted on November 1, 1950. With a subscription rate of one dollar per year, this monthly journal started as simply a single sheet front and back designed primarily for Christian schoolteachers and board members. Again, Mark Fakkema wrote most of the articles and in the inaugural issue he described its purpose as providing practical and thought provoking pieces geared toward teachers and board members so as to enhance their roles in Christian schools.[44] While *The Christian Teacher* did indeed serve as another means of instilling the Christian philosophy of education, at the same time Fakkema also used this periodical to comment on a wide variety of issues. Examples include an article on reading curriculum but also one questioning whether Santa Claus should be in a Christian home or school. He would describe the details involved in starting a school but also comment on the dire need for Christian schools as a tool for the restoration of American democracy. Other topics included the dangers of the United Nations, socialism in public education, the negative effects of Halloween, and the death of John Dewey.[45] *The Christian Teacher* did provide practical tips for Christian school educators, but, Fakkema obviously also utilized this publication as to advance his cause.

While promoting the cause of Christian education consumed much of the early years of the National Association of Christian Schools, the issue of textbooks cannot be overlooked. Concerns about the need for Christian textbooks frequently appear in early NAE and NACS writings. In a 1948 NAE board meeting, Mark Fakkema proclaimed a great need for Christian textbooks as "even now the enemy is prostituting our own youth for the eventual realization of his God-dishonoring, Church-destroying purposes." Calling the state of public school textbooks "appalling," he claimed these books were anti-American and Communistic. Fakkema then requested NAE board members to assist by directing the NACS to private foundations willing to subsidize a textbook program because, "Our great textbook program is far beyond the meager resources of any arm of the NAE."[46] A year later at another NAE board meeting, Dr. Dyrness reported that the NACS board had

---

1961 to 2000. Dottie Hiatt, interview with the author, September 25, 2009, Wheaton, IL.

44. Fakkema, "Trimming Our Lamps," 1.

45. See Fakkema, "How Well Does America Read?"; "Shall We Invite Santa?"; "Prerequisites for Starting"; "Without the Christian Religion"; "Modern Revolutionary War"; "Socializing Our Public Schools"; "Shall We Celebrate Halloween?"; "John Dewey is Dead."

46. Fakkema, "Supplement," 2.

sponsored a fund for the publication of suitable textbooks and they expected to see some Christian texts in the coming year.[47]

In 1949, Mark Fakkema prepared a paper for distribution among NACS members entitled *Christian Textbooks, Why, How, and What*. He declared that a Christian school furnished with non-Christian texts to be a house divided against itself. He also addressed more practical matters relating a report given to the NAE board in which he explained that the NACS had taken steps "to launch a gigantic counter offensive" which included a textbook program to "raise a standard against the enemy." From there Fakkema called for individuals who are "blessed with the grace of giving" to each contribute one thousand dollars for a fund to publish Christian textbooks.[48] Specifically calling for the publication of a set of Christian based readers for grades one through eight, Fakkema proposed that a fund of $10,000 would be needed to properly start this venture. Detailed guidelines for the writing of such books concluded the paper.[49]

However, despite the extensive rhetoric and careful planning, the NACS failed to deliver any significant Christian textbooks in its first five years, despite the clear sense of need that seemed apparent in their meetings. The reasons for this failure remain unclear but some unpublished doctoral dissertations provide some speculation. Frances Simpson, who wrote in 1955 and had the opportunity to interview Mark Fakkema, asserted that he felt that the higher priority at the time lay in the formulation of a clear educational philosophy that would serve as the foundation of textbooks to be produced later.[50] A report from the 1950 NAE convention confirms this as Fakkema reported on the delay of textbook work due to concerns arising about a consistent philosophy to undergird these materials.[51] Warren Sten Benson, writing in 1972, postulated that even though the movement saw remarkable growth during the first five years, the market remained small, thereby making the books cost prohibitive to produce.[52] With the availability of textbooks from the NUCS, early NACS schools could rely upon this curriculum in the absence of anything from the National Association. In addition, Fakkema, while loudly advocating for textbooks, most likely found traveling the country to start new schools a more important priority.

47. Dyrness, "Report of the Commission," 2.

48. Fakkema, "Supplement," 4.

49. Fakkema, "Statement of Policy," 6.

50. Simpson, "Development of the National Organization," 182.

51. Fakkema, "Report of the National Association," 48–49.

52. Benson, "History of the National Association," 73.

Fakkema's statement in his 1955 interview with Simpson about the need for a clear educational philosophy for the movement reflected a genuine concern. As soon as the NACS started functioning, the NAE Commission on Education also directed that a subcommittee begin work on the writing of a philosophy of Christian education. In early 1949, this subcommittee on the Philosophy of Christian Education, chaired by Frank Gaebelein, began work on this document. The Commission reported to the NAE board in April that, "The report, when released, will be such as to command the respect of the educational world, and we are confident that it will make an outstanding contribution to the cause of Christian education."[53] In June, the NAE board met again and Dr. Leslie Marston of the subcommittee requested that Dr. Gaebelein be given the first $500 in royalties from this report that would eventually become a book. He made this request in light of the fact that Gaebelein wrote most of the document and had devoted several months exclusively to this work. Marston also stated the intention of the committee to get a non-evangelical publisher to issue this volume, "to assure a reading from a non-evangelical public."[54] At the 1950 NAE convention at Indianapolis, Dr. Enock Dyrness enthusiastically reported on the completion of Gaebelein's work. He reiterated their desire for this work to appeal to the "average Christian uninitiated in educational terminology." Oxford University Press agreed to publish the work in early 1951.[55]

Dr. Gaebelein's book, *Christian Education in a Democracy*, became the definitive philosophical work for all Christian school educators and has endured as a classic to the present. He opened by plainly stating that education in America had departed from God and religious teaching. In his preface, Gaebelein lamented the destruction of the previous world war, but expressed more concern about the destruction of men's minds. Referring to education, Gaebelein cited secularism as a reason for this threat of destruction and used an analogy of recent events to make his point, "The paganism of Germany was not a sudden thing. For over a half a century God and religion have been gradually disappearing from the schools in Germany. Education has become secular. A generation has arisen which acknowledges no God and no longer regards those basic moral sanctions which are the safeguard of national and international harmony and decency. That is why the churches of Germany are empty and the nation has turned its face toward the darkness in the wake of Adolf Hitler."[56]

---

53. Dyrness, "Report of the Commission," 1.
54. Marston, "Report on the Committee," 2.
55. Dyrness, "Report of the Commission," 47–48.
56. Gaebelein, *Christian Education in a Democracy*, 7.

Dr. Gaebelein acknowledged however, that the secular nature of the schools merely reflected the sad fact that American culture in general had turned secular. He further stated that the trend toward secularism came inevitably from the nation's democratic principles, which demanded no favoritism for any religious group in order to protect religious freedom for all. If a democracy seemed bound to turn secular, then at the start Gaebelein was led to ask why there existed a need for "Christian education in a democracy." Gaebelein felt that this inevitable trend would have disastrous consequences for America as he deemed religion and moral values to be a critical component of a child's education and critical for the future of the nation. The nation's founding principles could not sanction state-supported religious education, and yet a democratic nation's very survival depended on proper religious training of the young.[57]

From there, the second question of his book asked how Christian education in a democracy should most effectively be implemented. He called upon believers to strengthen all Christian institutions, not just private Christian schools, in order to bring biblical values back into society. Gaebelein called his book a "manifesto" and laid out the "unmistakable" challenge this way, "Effective religious education may indeed be impossible in the public schools. But it is just as possible as it ever was in the home, the Church, and in church directed agencies. Therefore, home, Church and their allies must answer the challenge. For only through the rebirth of family religion, the return of the Sunday school to vital Christianity, the extension of weekday instruction under church control, the presence of Christian teachers in public education, the promotion of Christian independent schools—day and boarding, elementary, secondary, and collegiate—is there any hope of stemming the rising tide of secularism in America today."[58]

Beyond being a "call to arms" *Christian Education in a Democracy* also strived to clearly set forth the philosophical foundations of the Christian school movement. He defined Christian education at home and church and also described at length the non-negotiable characteristics of a Christian school. He spent an entire chapter on the critical role of teachers and even chided Christian colleges and schools for the substandard salaries of their instructors. In his final chapter, "The Unfinished Business of Christian Education," Gaebelein reminded Christians about the dangers of the atomic age and Communism and stated that the only real solution for America lay in the return of Christ himself. However, in the meantime, Gaebelein explained that Christian education needed not only to transform America, but also to go beyond national borders and become a missionary enterprise for the salvation of the entire world.[59]

Over the next few years, the philosophy of Christian education became more clearly defined through Mark Fakkema's summer workshops and the publication of Gaebelein's second book, *The Pattern of God's Truth.* Fakkema's course, "Christian Philosophy and Its Educational Implications," addressed several important philosophical components of the movement. He clearly differentiated between an education focused on God, "theocentric," and one focused on man. This course taught that God was the basis of all truth and that everything in the universe reflected the "great original God." Fakkema taught that man had been created as an image-bearer of the great God and had been intended to show forth God's glory in all things. However, the fall in the Garden of Eden caused the image-bearer to die, but could be restored with salvation through Jesus Christ. Hence, Fakkema taught that the true purpose of Christian education would be to help the child, born as a flawed image, to grow spiritually so that a renewed image of God could be seen in their lives. Earthly rewards from a good education would be viewed as secondary to this highest goal meaning that moral training would be placed higher than academics.[60]

This basic premise of trying to build the image of God in children would have notable curriculum implications. Fakkema criticized curricula that featured book-centered, child-centered, or state-centered approaches because they did not recognize the authority of God. Instead, he proposed what called a much more comprehensive approach that not only taught the horizontal relationship of facts, but also included the teaching of the subject matter on the basis of a vertical relationship to God. This would require biblical integration of each particular subject.[61]

Gaebelein's 1954 work, *The Pattern of God's Truth,* addressed in detail how biblical integration worked in a Christian school. It started with the teacher, who must be trained in not only their academic discipline, but also in the Bible. With a strong foundation in Scripture, the teacher would easily be able to interpret and apply biblical principles to any subject of study. In mathematics, God's existence can be proven by the intricate sense of order and structure that appears in all of the specific disciplines. Science as well illustrates the power of a Supreme higher level being due to its precision, regularity, and complexity. Literature concerns itself with the human character and the manifestation of that character in human action. The Bible,

---

59. Gaebelein, *Christian Education in a Democracy,* 61, 206, 296.
60. Fakkema, *Christian Philosophy,* 1–6.
61. Fakkema, *How to Educate Children Mentally,* 7–8.

which is also a piece of literature, albeit divine, also illustrates human character and its relationship to a holy God. Teachers of literature in a Christian school can use the Bible as a standard whereby to judge human actions, both positive and negative, revealed in all forms of literature. History can be portrayed as "his story" revealing God's plan for the world and mankind. Stressing scholastic excellence, for Gaebelein meant that the subject matter would not be avoided or watered down; it would simply be interpreted from a biblical standpoint.[62]

Beyond academics, Gaebelein also described how biblical integration could even be applied to extra-curricular activities. Critical of some Christian educators of his day, Gaebelein disagreed with those who felt that athletics had no place in the Christian school. On the contrary, Gaebelein valued sports highly explaining it this way, "The place of athletics is a vital one. It is more a question of method; especially in sports, the manner in which they are conducted is all important. Team-play, the heart of which is self-restraint and self-sacrifice; the moral courage that is good sportsmanship—these can be learned on playing fields in such a way that they become lasting character traits to the glory to God."[63]

By understanding man's fallen state and God's exalted position, Fakkema and Gaebelein put together a philosophy that they felt made Christian education compelling for parents. Teaching children to respect God's truth and see it in every activity and discipline would cause them to "think and live Christianly." This education would place a premium on a godly lifestyle but also on scholarship by pointing to the effectiveness of the intellect of Augustine, Luther, Calvin, Edwards, and Wesley for the kingdom of God.[64]

At the 1951 NAE convention, Mark Fakkema gave an extensive progress report on the work of the NACS. Enthusiastically he stated, "We say without fear of contradiction that for at least the past hundred years there has never been a year of Christian school activity which is equal in scope and intensity to that of the past year." Approximately one hundred new schools started in the past twelve months, and Fakkema boasted that well over a thousand pastors now received NACS materials. Selling his propaganda pamphlets for a penny a piece, he noted that the office sold $1,432.33 worth of NACS materials. He also pointed out that the teacher placement service had one hundred on their waiting list and thirty-seven schools seeking teachers. Fakkema again commented on the need for Christian textbooks and encyclopedias and reviewed the NACS plans for improving these

62. Gaebelein, *Pattern of God's Truth*, 55–69.

63. Gaebelein, *Pattern of God's Truth*, 89–91.

64. Gaebelein, *Pattern of God's Truth*, 104–5.

materials. He also discussed the increased interest in his summer workshops for teachers, and he concluded his report by discussing a newly established legal counsel service for Christian schools.

In four years, Mark Fakkema, Frank Gaebelein, and the National Association of Christian Schools managed to move the Christian school movement from a small conglomeration of Dutch Reformed schools to an organized, more inclusive national organization. Fakkema's vast experience with the National Union of Christian Schools provided a readymade organizational structure of parent associations along with promotional materials and textbooks. As an extreme and uncompromising propagandist, Fakkema created awareness and a sense of urgency among parent groups and churches all over the map resulting in more and more Christian schools. With these same tactics, Fakkema also brought teachers into the fold convincing them of their need to sacrifice for the cause of Christian education. Gaebelein's Stony Brook model, with its broader theological appeal than the NUCS, served as the philosophical cornerstone of the movement manifested in *Christian Education in a Democracy* and clearly influenced the newer Christian schools such as the one at Wheaton. With an organizational structure now in place and a clearly defined philosophy, the leaders of the young National Association of Christian Schools faced the second half of the twentieth century with full confidence in Mark Fakkema's 1947 proclamation, "the Christian day school is a substitute for the public school."[65]

65. Fakkema, "Christian Day School," 37.

Chapter 7

"Christian Schools are America's Only Hope"

I n 1950, a correspondent for *The New York Times* published an article reporting that "a new type of Protestant Christian day school that provides
studies comparable to those in public schools and adds instruction in the
principles of Christianity has made its appearance in the United States and
Canada in gradually increasing numbers." The article estimated some two
hundred of these schools had been founded in the previous year, by evangelicals with no previous experience in education. The *Times* explained this
trend as a response by parents to recent controversies over the teaching of
religion in public schools.[1]

Controversy had indeed led to the birth of these alternative schools
and during the post war years, many additional issues arose which served
as catalysts for the appearance of more schools. Dr. Frank Gaebelein's *Christian Education in a Democracy* clearly reflected how serious issues of the
late 1940s had created a dire need for Christian schools. At one point he
pleaded, "Nothing less than the destruction of our western way of life, if
not of civilization as a whole, is around a corner which may be turned, not
a generation or two hence, but in this age."[2] In the context of the times,
with its heavy emphasis on secularism, Gaebelein saw a clear need for independent Christian education, repeatedly referring to it as a "missionary
enterprise."[3] Likewise, Mark Fakkema constantly pointed to events of the
day which confirmed to him the vast departure of America from its Christian origins. These disturbing events often caused him to draw stark battle

1. Sheldon, "Protestants," 53.

2. Gaebelein, *Christian Education in a Democracy*, 7.

3. Gaebelein, *Christian Education in a Democracy*, 296.

lines in the realm of education. For example, in his 1951 report to the NAE, he boldly stated, "Conscientious Christians are beginning to realize that the issue of being for or against the Christian school is basically the issue of being for or against Christ."[4]

At the same time, with the specter of Communism looming, the early Cold War years created an atmosphere that led to increased interest in religious matters marked by revival supported by conservative politicians, businessmen and many religious leaders. Studies on this period described the Cold War as "one of the world's great religious wars." The defeat of Nazi Germany enhanced the role of the U.S. as a defender of Christian values and revitalized the image of American exceptionalism. Most Americans at the time viewed the Cold War as not only an economic or military struggle, but also as a spiritual conflict with the U.S. standing on the side of righteousness.[5] Since the Soviet Union was closely identified with atheism and most Americans considered themselves religious, belief in God came to symbolize the difference between totalitarianism and democracy.[6]

Numerous examples from religious leaders of the day also confirm this surge of spirituality that was often tied to Cold War anxieties. In 1949, two days after President Truman disclosed the loss of America's nuclear monopoly, a young evangelist in Los Angeles spoke preached that the city would be one of the first targets of a Soviet nuclear attack based not upon the presence of industrial or military targets, but because of their rampant sin, which included a large number of communists. He concluded in dramatic fashion by saying, "God is giving us a desperate choice, a choice of revival or judgment. There is no alternative! The world is divided into two camps! On the one side we see Communism, which has declared war against God, against Christ, against the Bible, and against all religion! Unless the Western world has an old fashioned revival, we cannot last!" This relatively unknown pastor, Billy Graham, eventually preached to over 350,000 over the next few weeks. In later sermons he referred to Communism as the "Antichrist," that had infiltrated the minds of the young, and as "being masterminded by Satan himself."[7] Beyond fundamentalists like Graham, more liberal wings of the Protestant church also acknowledged a revival. The Federal Council of Churches issued a statement at this time reporting a major shift in attitudes toward Christianity. Noting that the nation had drifted slowly away from religion in previous decades, the FCC now proclaimed, "At the present time

4. Fakkema, "Report of the National Association," 51.

5. Kirby, *Religion and the Cold War*, 1–6.

6. Delfattore, *Fourth R*, 68.

7. Whitefield, *Culture of the Cold War*, 77–81; Silk, *Spiritual Politics*, 54–69.

all the signs—the cheap and the reverent, the serious and the trivial—lead to only one conclusion. Americans are going back to God."[8]

As a result, churches and church leaders stood high in popular esteem. In a study in the early 1950s, participants were asked to rate five institutions for trustworthiness—radio, newspapers, schools, government, and churches. Churches came in first place by a wide margin.[9] An additional study between the years 1942 and 1947 revealed attitudes toward religious leaders. Asked about which group "did the most good for the country," in 1942, the top three listed in order were government officials, businessmen, and religious leaders. By 1947, religious leaders had climbed to first place.[10]

Politicians joined in the religious anti-Communism crusade as well. In 1950, Edward Martin took the Senate floor to argue for a peacetime draft by saying, "America must move forward with the atomic bomb in one hand and the cross in the other." That same year, John Foster Dulles wrote that nuclear weapons could be rattled at the Russians, but what America lacked, he asserted, was "a righteous and dynamic faith."[11] Democrats such as Adlai Stevenson stated, "Organized communism seeks to dethrone God from his central place in the Universe. It attempts to uproot everywhere it goes the gentle and restraining influences of the religion of peace and love."[12] Perceiving the tension of the day and recognizing the appeal to voters, government officials had no issues during this era with an open commitment to God.

The religious aspect of this era was so significant that the U.S. government actually promoted Christianity, believing it to be vital to winning the war with the Communists. Believing that communism was an evil philosophy that could undermine democracy, many felt that a religious faith would be one of the most "potent arrows in the quiver of domestic security." Business leaders and government officials adopted a policy of religious revival in the name of national security and societal well-being. Beyond the achievements of adding "under God" to the pledge of allegiance or putting "In God We Trust" on the currency, many other actions were taken to create what historians have called, America's "Spiritual-Industrial Complex." Examples would include the previously mentioned initiatives of the National Education Association to promote the teaching of spiritual values in public schools and national faith drives such as the Freedom Train of 1945 and the Religion in American Life (RIAL) campaign of 1949. The RIAL campaign

8. Goldman, *Crucial Decade*, 43.

9. Perrett, *Dream of Greatness*, 390; Whitefield, *Culture of the Cold War*, 127.

10. Silk, *Spiritual Politics*, 95.

11. Whitefield, *Culture of the Cold War*, 87.

12. Silk, *Spiritual Politics*, 87.

sponsored scores of public service announcements geared toward reminding citizens of the importance of religious institutions in our nation and to call upon every American to participate actively in the church or synagogue of their choice. President Truman endorsed RIAL in a live address by saying, "Each one of us can do our part by a renewed devotion to his religion." Presidents Truman and Eisenhower both spoke of the U.S. as a Christian nation and drew upon spiritual themes of a crusade against communism as not only a rational course of action, but an absolutely essential one.[13] As a result, a partnership of sorts developed between religious groups and the U.S. government during the early Cold War.

Notably, this relationship grew despite the constitutional directives concerning church and state. Evangelicals became more politically active and eagerly joined with government officials in promoting the notion that religion and American nationalism were not only synonymous, but that Judeo-Christian teachings constituted an indispensable component of the redeemer nation against the evils of totalitarianism.[14] Official government sanctioned proclamations of prayer in American history occurred sporadically until the Civil War but waned in the decades afterward. However, they became more regular during the Truman administration and in 1952, an official National Day of Prayer was legislated by Congress.[15]

In her study of the U.S. military during this time, Lori Lyn Bogle noted how the armed forces promoted religious teachings heavily as part of an overall government commitment to intertwining patriotism and morality. In times of great tension internationally and at home, political leaders have often resorted to a type of "civil religion," to strengthen the nation. As Bogle states, "When government leaders (especially those in the military) perceived that the national character and will lacked the resolve they believed was essential to national defense, they used civil-religious imagery to improve the character of the American people and to foster greater national unity."[16]

Statistics do suggest a clear upsurge in religious activity in the post-war years. An overall increase in church membership shows significant growth in the 1940s. In 1932, church membership stood at just over 60 million and by 1942 this number rose to 68.5 million. However, by 1952, the number of church members shot up to 88.6 million. In addition, the amount of charitable giving to religious organizations also shows important increases in this decade. Statistics list the total amount of giving to religious causes in 1932 at

13. Herzog, *Spiritual-Industrial Complex*, 6, 8–9.
14. Schafer, "Cold War State," 19–50.
15. Gunn, *Spiritual Weapons*, 50–52.
16. Bogle, *Pentagon's Battle*, 10.

$579 million and by 1942 this number increased to $736 million. However, ten years later in 1952, this amount of giving skyrocketed to almost $2.4 billion.[17] Predictably, funds for construction of new churches rose dramatically. In 1945, the amount spent on building churches stood at $26 million. In 1946, the number rose to $76 million, in 1948 it went to $251 million and in 1950, the amount soared to $409 million.[18]

The religious fervor of the Cold War years brings to light important facts about this time period that should not be overlooked. The notable increase in interest toward religion in the U.S. during the forties provided a larger and more receptive audience to Christian school advocates. At the same time, starting Christian schools carried great expense, and while exact figures on these young educational enterprises do not exist, the substantial amount of money given toward religious causes during the forties indicates that evangelical Christians now possessed the means to build these new schools.

In his famous 1946 "Iron Curtain" speech, Winston Churchill proclaimed that the battle lines left over from World War II included a "fight to preserve Anglo-American Christian civilization from Soviet takeover."[19] This attitude reflects the conservative, reactionary, and religious tone during this time that provided an ideal setting for the messages of the early Christian school leaders. Hence, while the leaders of the National Association of Christian Schools diligently worked to create an internal structure for this new organization, they also utilized the concerns of the day and benefitted from a renewed interest in religious activity that strengthened their resolve and helped cultivate a desire for this alternative education in the minds of evangelicals nationwide. Building an association of schools could not by itself account for this nascent movement. Religious revivals and post war anxieties, felt throughout the evangelical world, fanned the flames of this cause and created fertile ground for the establishment of tiny independent Christian day schools.

While most Protestants relished the unofficial relationship with the U.S. government, the conservatives who sponsored Christian schools felt a real uneasiness during this period about encroaching governmental power. Reflecting long held suspicions of the government, Dr. William Ward Ayer, speaking at the first NAE convention in 1942, stated that, "As America advances further into some form of 'statism,' let us not be deceived into believing that religion will escape. Governmental regimentation and classification

---

17. Burke, "Religion," 900, 914.

18. Silk, *Spiritual Politics*, 38.

19. Edwards, "God Has Chosen Us," 83.

of religion has ever been deadly to its free expression and growth. It has always tended to make the Church the inferior handmaiden of the state. Our government is becoming increasingly paternalistic and feels that it should direct the activities of all phases of our national life."[20] At a 1949 NAE board meeting, the "Annual Report of the Committee on Christian Liberty" contained an extensive list of concerns about legislation in Washington that "staggers the imagination." Examples included Senate bill S-174, calling for the establishment of the Fair Employment Practices Commission. Because the bill dictated parameters for hiring so as to remove racial discrimination, the committee surmised that this bill "would open the way for large numbers of bureaucrats and investigators to pry into one's personal business." The report concluded, "If this bill passes you can anticipate the arrival of that day when the government will tell you with whom you must work, with whom your children must attend school, whom you must hire. The police-state is near at hand if this bill passes."[21]

Naturally, these trepidations about growing federal power extended into education. In 1945, *United Evangelical Action* reported concerns about proposed bills for federal aid to education because "they manifest what is feared may be a trend on the part of the federal government to assume control over state and city schools."[22] Mark Fakkema also complained about the dominance of the federal government. He criticized the *McCollum* decision because it allowed the government to "black out all religious teaching in regular school time."[23] In another 1948 newsletter, he commented on a Virginia court case that centered on the rights of parents to educate their children at home based upon their religious convictions. The Virginia courts required all children to be educated by state certified instructors. Fakkema sharply criticized this case by pointing out that under the guise of quality education, the state simply demanded compulsory public school attendance and thereby denied the rights of parents to educate their children. Fakkema called upon Christian schools to have standards superior to the minimum public school standards so as to avoid governmental scrutiny.[24]

In 1950, Reverend Earl E. Zetterholm, a pastor and Christian school educator from Seattle, argued in *The National Association of Christian Schools Newsletter* that nowhere in Scripture could it be found that education existed as a function of the state and hence, from a biblical perspective, education

20. Ayer, "Evangelical Christianity Endangered," 42–43.
21. Fowler, "Annual Report of the Committee" 4.
22. "Bill Proposes Federal Aid," 10.
23. Fakkema, "Educational Significance," 1.
24. Fakkema, "Legal Rumblings," 2.

should only be established outside the sovereign sphere of the government. He concluded, "Christian parents must take back the authority they have given to the state in order that they might fulfill their divinely-ordained task of 'training their children in the way they should go.' The only possible way of doing this is for Christian parents to inaugurate an extension of the Christian home by the formation of a Christian school."[25]

A century had certainly changed the attitude of these Protestants toward public education. In the days of Horace Mann, the new common schools exercised power to uphold the position of white Protestant Christians. The influx of immigrants only served to strengthen the bond between the public schools and the Protestant majority as they utilized the schools to instill and maintain the values they perceived to be core principles of the American republic. The boldness of Father John Hughes to suggest in the 1840s that the Catholics start their own schools seemed appalling and treasonous to most Protestants. However, as the nineteenth century concluded, the public schools extended into the secondary level and curriculum changed to reflect the needs of a changing society. Religious teaching and Bible reading waned significantly by the turn of the century. Hence, as Dr. Frank Gaebelein suggested in *Christian Education in a Democracy,* the schools necessarily became more secular as the result of a democratic system that had to be neutral in religious matters.[26] So, in 1944 Mark Fakkema responded to the changing relationship of governmental power and religion by writing, "Our children are our children. To feed them at the public intellectual crib should be more offensive to us than to see our children fed and clothed at public expense. Hasn't our country gone already too far on the road to Statism? Whatever we surrender to the State let it not be our own flesh and blood. He who educates his child molds his future destiny. To surrender our children to a religionless preparation for life is to surrender them to a religionless life."[27] Despite government support of the Christian faith in the Cold War, by 1950 Fakkema proclaimed that the "burning educational issue of the day" involved the question of government control. Reflecting once again his uncompromising approach, he stated plainly, "Does the child belong to the parents or to the State?"[28] By the 1940s, evangelical Protestants would have to admit a hundred years later that perhaps Father Hughes did not seem so audacious and unpatriotic after all.

25. Zetterholm, "Function of the State," 1–2.
26. Gaebelein, *Christian Education in a Democracy,* 23.
27. Fakkema, *Plea for Christian Education,* 22.
28. Fakkema, "Socializing Our Public Schools," 1.

Even though Christian school leaders would agree with the Catholic notion of establishing separate schools, the expansion of the Roman Church had also long posed a threat to Protestant power in America and hence, Christian school leaders continued to use this as another reason to promote their own schools. As noted earlier, the growing number of Catholic immigrants in the nineteenth and early twentieth century served as a major reason for strong Protestant support of the first public schools. The 1925 court case *Pierce v. Society of Sisters*, discussed in chapter four, tested an Oregon law, spearheaded by the Ku Klux Klan, which banned all private schools, as a way to target Catholic education. After World War II, America emerged triumphant, but felt a renewed challenge from the Catholics with some Protestant leaders fearful of the pope trying to assert a level of supremacy. Maintaining Protestant power would be key to preserving democracy.[29] Beyond Christian school leaders, liberals with Ivy League credentials, like Paul Blanshard, criticized Catholicism for impeding social progress with its spirit of intolerance and separatist institutions.[30] He saw the Church as a direct threat to America and pushed for a resistance movement. Blanchard clarified the nature of this resistance by saying, "This movement would offer no support to those who would curtail the rights of the Catholic Church as a *religious institution*. Its sole purpose should be to resist the anti-democratic social policies of the hierarchy."[31] However it would be two specific events in this decade, a court case and a bill for federal aid to education, that would most enflame evangelical Protestants against the Church of Rome and heighten their sense of urgency to establish separate schools.

According to one historian, the 1947 Supreme Court case, *Everson v. Board of Education of Ewing Township*, stands as the first major case arising under the establishment clause of the First Amendment.[32] The dispute involved a New Jersey law that allowed school districts to pay for transporting students to and from "any schoolhouse." In the township of Ewing, the schools applied this law to provide bus transportation beyond public schools to students attending private Catholic schools. At the time, this same practice took place in sixteen other states and the District of Columbia. Eventually, a court challenge to this statute arose claiming that this law violated the establishment clause in that public school services supported a religious institution. By a slim margin of five to four, the court upheld the

29. Hamburger, *Separation of Church and State*, 450–51; Gleason, *Speaking of Diversity*, 211–12.

30. Blanshard, *American Freedom*, 303–5.

31. Hutchison, *Religious Pluralism in America*, 206–7.

32. Cook, "Present Legal Situation," 25.

law's constitutionality. An opinion by Justice Hugo Black maintained that the "wall of separation" had not been breached in this case because the New Jersey law constituted a reasonable means of promoting the general welfare, not a particular religion. The law had a secular purpose to provide benefits to all students regardless of their religious affiliation. Black went on to observe that the government spent taxes to protect parochial schools against fire and crime and hence, providing bus service was analogous. Black concluded by saying that the First Amendment, "requires the state to be neutral in its relations with groups of religious believers and non-believers; it does not require the state to be their adversary."[33] While Black's remarks seem to make the government more sympathetic to religion, Protestants saw this case as a clear win for Catholics that could lead to them possibly receiving even more governmental support.

The *Everson* decision caused much derision from many sources. Liberal law professors published numerous articles opposing the decision because, according to one scholar, "it weakened American democracy." The American Unitarian Association staged an elaborate tribute to Thomas Jefferson's notion of "the wall of separation" and broadcast it on radio.[34] *The Washington Post* stated that Justice Black gave, "lip service to the principles of religious freedom," but actually undermined the concept of church and state. Justice Black received many sharply critical letters from Baptist pastors, such as Charles R. Bell from Alabama who claimed that Catholics were, "crushing our religious freedom."[35]

Another event of the decade which heightened evangelical fears about Catholicism revolved around the Federal Aid to Education Bill. The issue of federal aid to education had been raised frequently in Congress since the 1870s, but consistently failed to pass, no matter how strong the case could be made for the importance of such funds to strengthen the nation's schools. During World War II, the issue resurfaced when the army discovered illiteracy among a large number of its draftees. After the war, concerns focused upon the glaring inequities that existed among the America's school districts especially in the South. A perception also surfaced in the post-war years that schools in the United States possessed major problems with overcrowding, low pay for teachers, and racial inequality. The National Education Association, partnering with National Association for the Advancement of Colored People, felt the post-war years provided an opportunity to lobby Congress for a new federal education bill. With the support of President

33. Dierenfield, *Battle Over School Prayer*, 46–50.

34. McGreevy, *Catholicism and American Freedom*, 183–84.

35. Hamburger, *Separation of Church and State*, 464–65.

Harry Truman and the influential Senator Robert Taft, optimism over a new federal aid to education bill abounded in 1946.[36]

However, a myriad of issues surrounding federal aid to education arose and chief among these was the question of whether or not money should go to Catholic parochial schools. At one time, Catholic school leaders would have eschewed any public monies, but by the mid-1940s after benefitting from New Deal programs, the federal school lunch program, and the GI bill, they now sought federal funding and even lobbied for such support. A Supreme Court decision from 1930 allowed Louisiana schools to pay for textbooks and school lunches, so they reasoned that federal monies should not be any different from local district funding.[37]

Public school officials ardently opposed such measures believing that giving federal money to Catholic schools constituted a violation of the separation of church and state. A 1938 article in *The Nation's Schools* claimed financial support of religious schools would destroy one of the nation's most important integrating forces, the idea of a "common school." As a result, the piece predicted that, by offering aid to religious schools, the state would, "finance permanent divisions among its citizens but it would do little to promote harmony among them."[38] By the forties, more criticism appeared. In 1945, A New York City educator, V. T. Thayer, in a stinging indictment entitled, "Bondage Through Education," wrote, "Unless Catholics, or any group that professes an exclusive monopoly upon truth, accept some restriction upon the application of their beliefs in practice, the future is dark indeed. The way of intolerance and absolutism is the way of war and bloodshed and, ultimately, the identification of right with might."[39] In 1947, a study published in *The Christian Science Monitor* argued that giving aid to Catholic schools would only open the door for other religious groups to ask for assistance and would eventually deplete public school funds. In addition, by helping parochial schools, the government would be accentuating divisions among students rather than fulfilling the long established public school responsibility to provide unity and a common set of American values for all children.[40] One of the most notable concerns came from James Bryant Conant, president of Harvard University, who in a much publicized 1952 address said, "To my mind, our schools should serve all creeds. The greater the proportion of our youth who attend independent schools, the greater

36. Ravitch, *Troubled Crusade*, 5–26.
37. McGreevy, *Catholicism and American Freedom*, 183.
38. Burke, "Should the State Help Support?," 29–30.
39. Thayer, "Bondage through Education," 52.
40. Nettleton, "First Amendment Defense," 13.

the threat to our democratic unity. Therefore, to use taxpayers' money to assist such a move is, for me, to suggest that American society use its own hands to destroy itself."[41]

The *Everson v. Board of Education* case further complicated the plans for federal aid to education. Protestant groups and public school leaders, alarmed by the fact that the case upheld public funds to Catholic schools, amplified their opposition to any bill that might further build up parochial education. Catholics hoped that the *Everson* case could possibly lead to more aid than just bus service, to include such things as nonreligious textbooks and health services. As the controversy stirred, New York Archbishop Francis Spellman proclaimed in 1949 the presence of a new religious bigotry. He pronounced, "We must oppose any bill that fails to guarantee at least non-religious textbooks, bus rides and health services for all the children of all Americans." As the debate over a federal bill to aid education continued in the late 1940s, it only served to arouse more anti-Catholic sentiment. Although many factors ultimately doomed federal aid to education until the late 1950s, the issues associated with religion, most notably aid to Catholic schools, rank among the most significant.[42]

Perceiving the growth of Catholic power as a threat to their attempts to restore a Protestant Christian America, conservative Christians in the NAE and the NACS joined with public schools in staunch opposition to any governmental support of the Catholic Church and its schools. NAE leader Dr. Harold Ockenga sounded the alarm in 1945 by declaring that the Roman Catholic hierarchy "is now reaching out for control of the government of the United States." Ockenga further stated that the political activity of Catholic leaders could be viewed as dangerous and could involve "a change in American culture almost as fundamental as that of Joseph Stalin."[43]

Reporting on specific federal aid to education bills, *United Evangelical Action* in 1945 conveyed great concern over the fact that the Roman Catholic Church had exerted pressure on Congressional leaders to get money for their schools.[44] In a 1946 article in *United Evangelical Action,* Mark Fakkema exclaimed, "The Catholic school system as is increasingly becoming apparent is Rome's chief weapon for winning America for Catholicism. Reliable sources contend that Rome with its well-integrated and unified educational system from the kindergarten to the university, enrolling some two and one-half

41. Conant, *My Several Lives,* 665–70; McGreevy, *Catholicism and American Freedom,* 187.

42. Ravitch, *Troubled Crusade,* 26–41.

43. Ockenga, "Boston Minister Gives Views," 9.

44. United Evangelical Action, "Bill Proposes Federal Aid," 10.

million students, will succeed in its effort to get a strangle hold on the religious as well as political life of America unless the evangelical churches unite on a Christian educational program of their own."[45] The criticism continued in 1947 from Dr. James DeForest Murch, editor of *United Evangelical Action*. Portraying a crisis situation, Murch called upon all Protestants to take action to stop the encroachment of the Roman Catholic Church. He asserted that almost every state of the union had been infiltrated by Catholic lobbyists who sought to initiate legislation providing for public funds for their schools. Murch concluded the future of the nation to be in danger as Catholics threatened American law and freedom.[46]

In a 1948 report to the NAE board, the Committee on Christian Liberty expressed deep concerns over the fact that the Catholic Church had employed eight priests and appropriated $500,000 to lobby Congress on the aid to education bill. The committee recommended immediate communication with Congressional leaders outlining their firm opposition to any federal aid to parochial schools. Further, the committee requested that contact be made with officials of the National Education Association to receive counsel on how to best oppose the efforts of the Catholic Church with this bill.[47] Though NAE leaders would not consider themselves to be friends of the National Education Association, they nevertheless pragmatically sought their support against a common foe.

Of course, Protestant fears of the Catholic Church have deep roots in American history and these concerns had often manifested themselves in the realm of education. With the Supreme Court condoning the use public funds to parochial schools in the *Everson* case and with Congress considering a federal aid to education bill that included Catholic schools, panic abounded throughout Protestant America in the 1940s. Attaching themselves to this anxiety, Christian education leaders used these events to bolster their cause. Interestingly, the pathway of separate schools started by the Catholics in nineteenth century served as justification and as a blueprint for the Christian schools of the twentieth century. However, Christian school leaders drew a clear distinction. While they certainly supported the notion of private education, individuals such as Fakkema and Gaebelein would not favor Catholic schools as they espoused a dangerous philosophy that sanctioned control of education by an undemocratic top down papal hierarchy. As patriotic citizens and as guardians of the nation's Protestant

45. Fakkema, "Christian Schools," 3–5.
46. Murch, "State Aid Menace," 12.
47. Taylor, *Report from the Committee*, 5–6.

heritage, they could support parochial Catholic schools no more than they could the "godless" public schools.

Historian Philip Hamburger provides additional insight into Protestant fears of Catholicism in his work, *Separation of Church and State*. In describing the evolution of this concept that came to be regarded as a constitutional right, he explains how evangelical Christians had no problem with separation of church and state in the nineteenth and early twentieth centuries. During these decades, Protestants controlled such institutions as the public schools and used this belief to stifle Catholic power. Church and state became to be viewed as an important component of Americanism and an essential part of their liberty. However, when the notion of separation of church and state began to extend to all forms of religion, such as in the previously mentioned *McCollum* case, evangelicals complained loudly and bemoaned such actions as leading to the destruction of the nation. Over time, later Supreme Court cases would cause many evangelicals and Christian school leaders to realize that they faced a far greater threat from secularism than Catholicism.[48]

Beyond worries about Catholicism, those establishing the new Christian day schools in the 1940s also became engulfed in the widespread Cold War fears of the day. Frequent references to Communist infiltration of the nation's schools appear in many publications and addresses of NAE and NACS leaders. The issue of school textbooks often garnered much attention. Charges that socialistic and communistic ideals permeated many of the public school texts could be heard in many quarters. Controversy arose over the social studies textbooks of Harold Rugg which faced charges of being anti-American. More than five million students in five thousand school districts had utilized at least one book in his fourteen volume series by 1940. The series, entitled *Man and His Changing Society,* seemed get the most criticism about a ninth grade text *Citizenship and Civic Affairs* due to its claims that the "American Spirit" evolved from individualism to cooperation. The book seemed to imply that free enterprise could no longer be considered a foundational American ideal.[49]

Predictably, evangelicals and Christian school leaders also commented on the perceived "atheistic and communistic" textbooks. In the 1948 first year anniversary NACS report, Mark Fakkema devoted several paragraphs to this issue. He criticized the National Education Association for "foisting a subversive textbook upon an unsuspecting public." He claimed anti-democratic principles penetrated social studies books that praised radicals

48. Hamburger, *Separation of Church and State*, 477; Ivers, *To Build a Wall*, 82.

49. Spring, *American School*, 351; Hartman, *Education and the Cold War*, 43.

like Thomas Paine while ignoring American heroes who possessed Christian virtues. Without giving any specifics, Fakkema simply declared the present status of American textbooks to be appalling and said, "Some of the books are so 'red' and so 'hot' that we are not permitted by our informants to divulge that which we would like to make public."[50] Fakkema not only borrowed McCarthyite arguments, but also employed his methods by citing evidence he could not disclose while also feeding the growing paranoia.

Fakkema continued his crusade against the public schools' "communist" textbooks in later NACS publications. In a 1949 newsletter, he stated, "God willing, for every God-denying school that the Communists have opened we will open a hundred God-honoring schools. For every socialist inspired textbook that now disgraces our educational system, we will publish a hundred Christian textbooks. In every subversive endeavor of the enemy we will match philosophy with philosophy, passion with passion, sacrifice with sacrifice!"[51] Several months later, a resolution from NAE leaders expressed more concern about textbooks containing "seriously contaminated un-American doctrine" and praised the work of the House Un-American Affairs Committee for its commitment to examine these books.[52] In a 1952 edition of *The Christian Teacher*, Fakkema noted that due to the educational leadership of the nation, many textbooks "have turned against the American way of life and are seeking to establish a new social order." He quoted an official from the 1952 annual meeting of the Daughters of the American Revolution who stated that in a survey of more than 450 of the most widely used high school social science textbooks, every one of them encouraged socialist thinking in the students.[53]

Fears about anti-American textbooks revealed only a portion of widespread Cold War concerns about education. Following World War II charges arose that the schools had become infiltrated with Communists. The Life Adjustment movement, already facing much negative publicity, received even more challenges. In seeking to provide a less academic curriculum in order to meet the needs of the majority who would not attend college, Life Adjustment advocates appeared to be harming scholastic standards and thereby limiting America's technological competition with the Soviet Union.[54]

50. Fakkema, "Supplement," 7.
51. Fakkema, "Axe Lies at the Root," 2.
52. Fowler, "Annual Report," 4.
53. Fakkema, "Textbooks Without God," 1.
54. Spring, *American School*, 390–91.

The Christian school movement, with its extreme conservatism, easily fit into to the chorus of Cold War critics by adding a religious element to the discussion. Without specifically mentioning the Christian school movement by name, historian Diane Ravitch noted that many extremist organizations tapped into a right wing paranoia that roiled the country in the post war years by exploiting fears that a "vast and sinister conspiracy had subverted American education and had turned it against not only traditional education but against American ideals." These groups published books, pamphlets, and magazines, asserting, among other things, that "public schools were failing to teach the fundamentals, failing to discipline children, wasting money on fads and frills, and espousing progressive education, which promoted collectivism, godlessness, and juvenile delinquency."[55] In an article for *Phi Delta Kappan*, Robert Skaife, Field Secretary of the National Defense Commission of the NEA, pointed out several extreme groups, with patriotic and/or politico-economic motives, who actively sought to subvert the positive strides made by progressive education. The most common charge leveled centered on the fact that the schools had indoctrinated students against the American system toward socialism. Reminding readers that schools remained locally controlled and possessed a responsibility to educate all citizens whether they are going to college or not, Skaife called these critics, "sincere, but unintelligent, sincere, but often unethical."[56]

Along with Cold War uneasiness, fears about the role of the newly created United Nations also aroused indignation among evangelicals and in the field of education, the United Nations Educational, Scientific, and Cultural Organization (UNESCO) drew much attention. A 1945 London conference of educators from forty-four nations led to the creation of this organization. Among those involved included NEA president F.L. Schlagle. From the beginning, the conference reinforced the notion that UNESCO would promote the democratic tradition of education so that all nations of the world would adopt the belief that education should be offered to all children and not just an aristocratic few. They drew up a constitution declaring not only democratic ideals, but also a commitment to "the unrestricted pursuit of objective truth, and in the free exchange of ideas and knowledge, and are agreed to and determined to develop and to increase the means of communication between their peoples."[57]

Phi Delta Kappan published several articles on the merits of UNESCO throughout the late forties. In 1946, an article explained the serious need

55. Ravitch, *Troubled Crusade*, 70.
56. Skaife, "Sound and the Fury," 357–62.
57. "UNESCO," 102.

for such an organization during the global recovery from World War II. By providing the most basic educational supplies to impoverished countries, UNESCO could serve as an agency to strengthen education in every nation and hence lead to better understanding and cooperation across the world.[58] George Kabat, the chief of the European Educational Relations Section of the U.S. Office of Education, commented several months later about the need for UNESCO in *Phi Delta Kappan*. Stating that the primary purpose of UNESCO focused upon improving international understanding, he called for a re-examination of the nation's elementary and secondary public school curriculum. Kabat described current curriculum as too provincial and pushed for materials with more international studies. By providing American children with more ideas about foreign cultures, UNESCO could fulfill the United Nations mandate to promote world peace through appreciation and understanding of the world's diversity.[59] Over the next three years, UNESCO developed an extensive program in thirty-one nations led by an executive board of international educators. Projects included the improvement of educational facilities and standards in war ravaged nations, exchange of teachers, and the creation of curriculum standards to promote mutual understanding. A budget of almost $7 million from the contributions of fifteen nations supported UNESCO in 1947.[60]

This post war idealism of the United Nations, which included organizations such as UNESCO, aroused sharp criticism from the evangelical community. In a 1947 editorial appearing in *Moody Monthly*, Dr. Wilbur Smith, a Moody Bible Institute faculty member, called UNESCO a program for world education without God. He expressed concern about the "secret" selection of Dr. Julian Huxley, a renowned atheist, as the first director-general of this organization. Smith went on to lament the noticeable exclusion of religion and God in the UNESCO educational program and speculated that this development signaled the end times and the coming of the anti-Christ.[61] A few months later in an article entitled "We're Footing the Bill for Atheism," Smith again blasted UNESCO, expressing outrage over the fact that $3 million of their $7 million budget came from the United States.[62]

The Sunday School Times called UNESCO a "dangerous movement" and cited concerns over their goals of a "one world culture" which could not align

58. Kabat, "UNESCO and Its Implications," 11–14.
59. Kabat, "Public Schools and UNESCO," 106–8.
60. "UNESCO and You," 62–65.
61. Smith, "Program for World Education," 532.
62. Smith, "We're Footing the Bill," 747.

itself with any one particular set of religious beliefs.[63] As part of the textbook debate, Dr. Wilbur M. Smith in 1947 criticized Kabat's ideas in regard to the provincial nature of American elementary and secondary curriculum, and related his concerns about a recent meeting of the National Education Association and its plans to adopt so-called "world textbooks." Smith charged that these texts would weaken loyalty to America by promoting a worldwide tolerance of all systems of government under the guise of eliminating "national bias." In terms of religion, he blasted these books for their inclusion of various world religions by saying, "In these world textbooks are we in America going to allow the pantheism of India, the Buddhism of the far east, Confucian teachings from China, and the fatalistic views of modernism to level our religious thinking and give us an eclectic conglomeration in which the idea of the God of Abraham, Isaac and Jacob, the God and Father of Jesus Christ our Lord, the Eternal One and the Creator, will be blotted out in a mist created by the fumes arising from these man-made and wholly inadequate, and often vicious and cruel systems of religion?"[64]

Due to its educational emphasis, UNESCO could not escape the scrutiny of Christian school leaders. In a 1948 report to the NAE Board of Administration, Mark Fakkema took the occasion to describe the grim state of a world that appeared to have atheistic domination on the horizon. He criticized the liberal Federal Council of Churches for promoting ecumenical religious beliefs that would only weaken the power of traditional Protestant Christianity. From there, Fakkema mentioned the "Godless position of world education crystallized in the recently organized world movement known as UNESCO."[65] In *The Christian Teacher*, Fakkema continued his assault on UNESCO. In 1951 he proclaimed, "We are in a revolutionary war. The issue at stake is not the overthrow of some earthly potentate. The revolutionary slogan is: Dethrone the King of kings; down with the Lord of lords. Great gains are claimed by the revolutionists. A war strategy meeting was held of the world council. I refer to a meeting of the United Nations Scientific Cultural Organization (UNESCO—the school board of the world)." Fakkema pleaded for Christian schools by saying, "Our duty is plain. It is dictated by God as well as by present situations and future omens. Christian children must not be trained in Christ-ignoring schools. While it is still legal—and by way of perpetuating its legality—the "remnant" must establish their own schools, cost what it may."[66]

63. Gordon, "UNESCO," 673–74.

64. Smith, *Increasing Peril*, 35–36.

65. Fakkema, "Supplement," 7.

66. Fakkema, "Modern Revolutionary War," 1.

The new evangelicals of the post war years shared several common characteristics. Trying to restore their image damaged from the 1920s, these Christians appealed to a broader base while also firmly planting themselves in the conservative right. New evangelicals became more politically active, supporting wider movements that were anti-Communist, anti-United Nations and anti-New Deal.[67] Outspoken concerns of Christian school leaders about governmental power, Communism, and UNESCO all indicate Fakkema and others to be in step with contemporary evangelicalism which played well to parents seeking educational alternatives for their children.

At the same time, the concerns of Christian school leaders about the power of the federal government, Communism, the Roman Catholic Church, and world domination of the United Nations also corresponded with the evangelical belief in premillennialism. As noted previously, fundamentalists possessed an obsession with prophecy and frequently pointed to contemporary events as signs of the anti-Christ, the destruction of the world, or the return of Christ as foretold in the Scriptures. In the 1940s, references to a one-world government under the spell of the anti-Christ seemed to be apparent with organizations like the United Nations and UNESCO, which to many evangelicals, indicated a push toward placing the education of all children under a single, religionless philosophy. With the atomic bomb ending World War II, conservative Christians such as the previously mentioned Dr. Wilbur Smith, continued the tradition of seeing apocalyptic signs in the events of the day. Smith, and many others, pointed to II Peter 3:10 which portrayed the destruction of the earth by fire in which "all will be laid bare," as clear indication of impending nuclear holocaust.[68] Holding to the beliefs about the rapture of the saved, the eventual defeat of Satan at the battle of Armageddon, and the thousand year reign of Christ, Christian school leaders saw their institutions as not only places of refuge for children, but also places to train soldiers for the cause of Christ to redeem America and the world. As Sutton says, "Religious leaders of this time sensed that despite their fears of centralized control, the only way to deal with the developing totalitarian state in the United States was to centralize fundamentalist efforts—to fight fire with fire."[69]

The decade of the 1940s proved to be the most significant era for the growth of the Christian school movement to date. Many factors came together simultaneously to move Christian education from a small conglomeration of Dutch Reformed Schools in the upper Midwest to an expanding

67. Stevens, *God-Fearing and Free*, 66.
68. Boyer, *When Time Shall Be No More*, 115–22.
69. Sutton, "Was FDR the Antichrist?," 1070–71.

assembly of evangelical Protestant schools embracing a variety of denominations across the nation. Dynamics both within the Protestant community and the outside world fused together to bring about the birth and subsequent stability of the National Association of Christian Schools.

From within American Protestantism, fundamentalism rebounded and re-emerged as "evangelicalism," a more unified and broad based conservative Christianity. Through the vision of individuals such as J. Elwin Wright and Harold Ockenga, the National Association of Evangelicals laid a foundation for the future growth of the religious right. As Patrick Allitt explained, "The work of these men, plus the later work of Billy Graham, took the hard edge off of fundamentalism. It shifted the balance of power among American religious groups. They showed mainstream Protestants that evangelicalism and fundamentalism, far from being dead and forgotten, were more powerful, more up to date and more influential than at any time in the twentieth century and that they would continue to play an important role in national life."[70] The fundamentalists had retreated during the 1930s and formed their own subculture and networks consisting of "shelter belts" as historian Joel Carpenter has noted.[71] This proved to be critical to their revival of the 1940s. Although almost imperceptible, the presence of new Christian based elementary and secondary schools across the nation along with the newly organized National Association of Christian Schools, served as one of these "shelter belts" and as another of their networks that would unify evangelicalism in the decades ahead.

Protestant evangelicals faced many threats during this decade that shook their world. Even though the vast majority of Protestant leaders still firmly supported public education as a means of upholding their values, widespread concerns did exist about the nation and the world. Court cases, expanding governmental power, fears of communism, the Catholic Church and the United Nations fed into fears about a loss of community and family values. In a world careening out of their reach, evangelical Protestants in the 1940s found themselves desperately desiring more control, seeking more unity within their ranks, and passionately longing to restore a mythical "Christian America."

For a tiny, but growing minority of conservative Protestants, individuals such as Mark Fakkema and Frank Gaebelein offered a solution that corresponded to their hopes and fears. Private Christian schools, with their commitment to traditional Protestant biblical principles, parental control, community-based autonomy, and a commitment to restore a

---

70. Allitt, *Religion in America*, 13–15.

71. Carpenter, *Revive Us Again*, 3.

Christian America provided a wishful panacea. Within the context of the 1940s, Fakkema, Gaebelein, and many conservative pastors and college professors capitalized on the spirit of the times to launch this movement. Their frequent and often exaggerated chants about the decline of religious values in the nation's public schools painted them as hopelessly tainted and irreparable. Disregarding the efforts of the public schools to adapt to a rapidly changing American society, as well as their efforts to keep religious values as a part of their curriculum, Christian school leaders, characteristic of the earlier fundamentalists, painted the picture in a simplistic, black and white, good and evil scenario. Individuals such as Fakkema and Gaebelein used the anxieties of this era to create a sense of doom which they anticipated would compel all committed Protestants to flee the poison of public education and protect their children in Christian schools. At the 1946 NAE convention, the Commission on Christian Educational Institutions issued this ominous warning, "Unless the Protestants of this land awake to the paganizing influence and philosophy of most American education they have no reason to believe that historic Protestant Christianity will have the ascendancy in this nation fifty years from now."[72]

Beyond fear tactics, Christian leaders also made sure that their movement reflected a patriotic American spirit. The theme of a connection between Christianity and America resonated loudly from the NAE and the NACS. In a 1947 edition of *United Evangelical Action,* an article entitled "Jesus Christ and the American Tradition" proclaimed, "We sincerely believe that the true American tradition gives Jesus Christ first place."[73] Dr. Gaebelein argued in several of his writings that private schools served as a bulwark of democracy. If the nation had been founded upon freedom of religion, then parents should have the right to educate their according to their religious convictions.[74] Fakkema wrote that without the Christian religion, democracy would be imperiled. He claimed that as the nation secularized, the need for more governmental power would arise since atheism and agnosticism would produce a citizenry bereft of morals. So, in a decade of war, growing secularism, conservative politics, and uncertainty about the future in an atomic world, a tiny, but growing number of conservative evangelicals looked toward this new type of education believing that being for or against the Christian school was indeed the same as being for or against Christ."[75] Mark Fakkema concluded that, "If

72. Paine, "Report of the Commission," 4.

73. Boyle, "Jesus Christ," 3–4.

74. Gaebelein, "Christian Education," 6–8.

75. Fakkema, "Report of the National Association," 51.

a citizen is not ruled by Christian convictions from within, he must be governed by a control tower from without." Hence, he predictably asserted Christian schools to be America's only hope.[76]

76. Fakkema, "Without the Christian Religion," 1.

Chapter 8

"What God Hath Wrought"

I n 1952, the National Association of Christian Schools celebrated its fifth anniversary and on this occasion published an extensive report for the NAE authored by Mark Fakkema. His opening statement proclaimed that, "It is but proper that we call attention to what God hath wrought in this short period."[1] This document contained a brief description of the historical antecedents of the movement as well as statistics designed to illustrate sharp growth. Fakkema pointed out that in 1920 private religious schools constituted only 7.5 percent of the total student population. By 1937, that percentage increased to 9.5 percent and by 1948, the percentage shot up to 11.5 percent. Focusing specifically on the growth of evangelical Christian schools, he noted that a distinct difference existed between Catholic and non-Catholic institutions. While both types of schools grew in the years between 1937 and 1948, Protestant Christian schools posted much more significant gains. Whereas Catholic schools saw an enrollment increase of 7 percent between 1937 and 1948, non-Catholic schools showed a 60 percent enrollment boost during the same time period. Specific numbers from 1952 showed a total of 1,734 Christian schools nationwide. This number consisted of schools in the NUCS and the NACS as well as Lutheran and Mennonite institutions. The report listed by name eighty-three schools directly affiliated with the NACS in twenty-four states. California boasted the largest number with twenty-one schools. Fakkema claimed that the formation of the NACS did not initiate this movement but rather arose in response to the needs of this phenomenal upsurge in private Christian education.[2]

1. Fakkema, "Historical Antecedents," 1–4.
2. Fakkema, "Developments," 4–5, 12.

The NACS report also described the wide variety of services developed by the association since its inception. Promotion remained a key element in the NACS with many pamphlets and books listed in the report for assisting member schools in a variety of areas from student recruitment to operational policies. Fakkema also chronicled his travels, specifically mentioning the summer of 1951 in which he delivered three hundred addresses in six different states all designed to stir interest or give practical advice. He speculated that over the past five years, more than five hundred localities had either opened Christian schools or taken steps toward that end. The report went on to express gratitude toward the many donors who assisted them toward maintaining their $15,000 annual budget. This section concluded with a listing of the NACS board members and among the names were Dr. Enock Dyrness of Wheaton College and Dr. Frank Gaebelein of Long Island, New York.[3]

This rather detailed report ended with a lengthy discourse on the philosophy of Christian education. Mark Fakkema again emphasized the importance of a consistent philosophy for this young movement. Citing the turmoil and moral confusion of the day, he called for an educational philosophy grounded in Christian principles so as to prepare young people for a life of service to God. Complimenting Gaebelein's ideas in *Christian Education in a Democracy,* Fakkema again distinguished the Christian school as being God-centered as opposed to the man-centered ideology of public education. In his typical polemic style, Fakkema ended this fifth anniversary report in this way, "For teaching to be true, it—according to God's Word—must seek 'the glory of God.' Since neither the philosophy of secularized instruction, nor the teaching that is based upon it, is to the glory of God, we are forced to the conclusion that the instruction of a secularized school is not true. In the interest of truth, God-fearing parents, living in a state in which state instruction and religion are divorced, are compelled to provide for their children a private school whose teaching and philosophy is 'to the glory of God' which they are doing and that with acceleration."[4]

Fakkema's report possessed a clear agenda. In his goal of showing what he called "significant" growth of Christian schools, he also sought to imply decline in the popularity of Catholic schools. While Christian schools had indeed increased faster than their Catholic counterparts, the report neglected to mention the fact that the Catholic schools were already very widespread and established, hence these institutions would not reflect as much growth in terms of sheer numbers. Christian schools did indeed number 1,734, but

3. Fakkema, "NACS Program of Action," 6–14.
4. Fakkema, "Need of a Christian Philosophy," 14–17.

only eighty-three belonged to the now five year old NACS. Total enrollment in NUCS and NACS schools stood at approximately 17,000 students. Catholic schools, by contrast, in 1952, still numbered 10,778 nationwide with a total student enrollment at just over three million.[5] The NACS could indeed point to growth, but the movement still paled in significance to other private schools in the overall landscape of American education.

Nevertheless, Fakkema continued to travel tirelessly and more schools joined the fold each year. Gaebelein's *Christian Education in a Democracy* received widespread circulation, further cementing his philosophy among conservative Christians. *The New York Times* claimed at this time that more Protestant and Roman Catholic children received a religious based education than at any other time in the history of America by citing a number of statistics including an increase of Protestant school enrollment of 61 percent from the past fifteen years since 1937. This number reflected the greatest increase in sectarian institutions such as Lutheran and Mennonite schools, but the article also mentioned the NACS and its interdenominational evangelical schools.[6] Although unnoticeable in mainstream educational circles in 1952, Fakkema and Gaebelein had managed to sell a product to a conservative Christian market, albeit still quite tiny and still rather primitive. Examining what "God hath wrought" in 1952 reveals a smattering of tiny schools spread across the nation with similar characteristics. Although barely perceptible, they nevertheless represent the origins and the future of the Christian school movement destined to become a significant part of the religious right of late twentieth century.

Many of the schools listed on the fifth anniversary report did not survive to the present, but a few still exist and with limited archives, they provide some sketchy details of life in these fledgling institutions. Examples of such survivors include the already mentioned Wheaton Christian Grammar School (1942), Vineland Christian School of Vineland, New Jersey (1946), Wilmington Christian School of Wilmington, California (1946), Old Paths Christian School (known today as Phoenix Preparatory Christian School) of Phoenix Arizona (1947), Riverside Christian Day School of Riverside, California (1948), Plumstead Christian School of Plumsteadville, Pennsylvania (1948), Delaware County Christian School of Newtown Square, Pennsylvania (1950), and Lincoln Christian School of Lincoln, Nebraska (1951).

Each of these schools organized in a similar fashion, using the model promoted by Mark Fakkema, of establishing parent societies that have their roots in the Dutch Reformed schools of the NUCS. These societies consisted

5. National Center for Education Statistics, "Enrollment and Instructional Staff."
6. "Peak is Attained," 8.

of a group of parents, usually from a few churches in the same community, who came together with a common interest in starting a Christian school. Eventually, these societies selected a board of directors to oversee the operation of the school through a principal and faculty. This model reflected the conviction of those who felt that the biblical responsibility of the education of their children lay with parents, not the state.[7] The Wheaton Society for Christian Instruction consisted of several Wheaton College professors. Their archives from 1941 reveal that this group of parents possessed a desire to provide an education that included instruction in the Bible, with no specific negative comments about the public schools.[8] The society that established Wilmington Christian School consisted initially of a board from The First Assembly of God Church of Wilmington.[9] However, in the case of most of these schools, the records indicate these parent societies came from a group of "concerned" or "visionary" parents.[10]

Following the Stony Brook School curriculum model, these schools committed to teaching all of the standard subjects found in public schools with additional instruction in the Bible. In the articles of incorporation of Vineland Christian School, it clearly stated that the school would provide, "instruction in all subjects normally taught in public and private schools." However the document went on to say that the subjects must be taught in "accord with the Word of God."[11] As stated previously, Wheaton Christian Grammar School made similar claims with its charter from the state of Illinois saying the object of the formation of this entity is, "to provide elementary education in common school subjects including instruction in the Word of God."[12] Hence, most Christian schools taught all the normal subjects along with Bible.

Since the NACS failed to provide biblically based textbooks in the early years, many of these schools used public school texts and materials. At the same time they also integrated biblical truths by utilizing textbooks long employed by the NUCS. This process of teaching with interwoven biblical concepts most notably appeared in history books and supplemental readers to go along with public school materials used by these schools. Two previously mentioned books, *Christian Interpretation of American History* and *Sketches*

7. Sheldon, "Protestants Hail New Type Schools," 53.

8. Tucker, *Wheaton Christian Grammar School*, 21.

9. Wilmington Christian, "History."

10. Jones, "Lincoln Christian School," 1; Delaware County Christian, "History."

11. Vineland Christian, "Certificate of Incorporation."

12. Wheaton Society, "Certificate of Incorporation."

from Church History, both published by the NUCS in the 1920s, received widespread usage by many Christian schools for several decades.

Christian Interpretation of American History, first published in 1928, provides numerous examples of a subject with an explicit religious interpretation. In a chapter on the age of exploration and colonization, a more conventional discussion of the reasons for European exploration appears, but at the same time, this book notes how God providentially directed Christopher Columbus to discover the southern part of the New World for Spain leaving open North America for later colonization by the English. This led the author to conclude that, "Columbus's trips were confined to the southern part of the new world, with the result that the Northern Hemisphere was open to Protestants. Shortly after the discovery of America the Protestant Reformation started in Europe. God in His infinite wisdom provided a home for them when life became intolerable in Catholic lands of Europe. He provided a home in a land where liberty of thought and speech were to become national principles."[13] English domination of colonial America also led the author of this text to state, "History here again shows clearly that God intended ours to be an English civilization, Protestant in religion and democratic in government." A chapter on the Civil War analyzed the conflict from the standpoint of sin and its consequences. In discussing Lincoln's comment in the Gettysburg address about all men being created equal, the author summarized the era in this way, "Certainly if our nation had adhered consistently to the principles professed from the beginning, the test would never have been necessary and we would have been pleasing to God. Therein chiefly lay our sin; we departed from the purposes of God. The Lord's aims will prevail, however, and He had this nation pass through the purifying fire of a war to recall us to those purposes. We shall miss the point if we regard slavery as a sin of the South alone. It was a national sin, and the war a punishment for the North as well as the South. The federal constitution recognized and protected the institution, federal laws, such as the fugitive slave law, strengthened it. Time after time the Federal Congress surrendered principle to compromise."[14]

The text concluded with remarks about the moral decay of America in the 1920s, which it blamed on liberalism and secularization of the society. However, it ended on an optimistic note by characterizing the growth of an independent Christian school system as a "bright hope for the future" that would defend the Christian religion and uphold the faith of their fathers.[15]

13. Heyns and Roelofs, *Christian Interpretation*, 67, 104.
14. Heyns and Roelofs, *Christian Interpretation*, 135.
15. Heyns and Roelofs, *Christian Interpretation*, 169–70.

Sketches from Church History, A Supplemental Reader for History Classes in Christian Schools, also enjoyed widespread popularity for many years. This book provided information highlighting the history of the Christian church and its leaders so as to supplement public school history texts which neglected to cover such information. Much attention focused upon the early church and its leaders as well as the Protestant Reformation. The author blasted the Medieval Roman church by stating, "There was great pomp and outward show in abundance but all worship was empty and without content. The ritual was mere formality; the preaching sounding brass; the priests, selfish seekers of worldly pleasures and gross sensualities; the people utterly ignorant and hopelessly lost in superstition." On the other hand the book referred to Martin Luther as a "star of the first magnitude in the Kingdom of God."[16]

In a discussion of America, the text describes the Protestant church as being divided neatly into two camps, the Modernists, referred to as "worshippers of the goddess of Science," and the Fundamentalists, who "refuse to accept the dictates of science if they contradict the teachings of God's Word." At the same time, expressions of concern appear in the book over those contemporary church-goers who placed human reasoning above the authority of the Bible. "These men glory in the theories of evolution and deny and ignore the truths of revelation; they undermine the cornerstones of faith."[17]

These textbooks provide a glimpse of the type of teaching found in the early Christian schools. The fundamentalist impulse of American trusteeship appears often as the books point to the mythic image of a nation founded upon Protestant Christianity. Much lament about the decline of America due to secularism often surfaces resulting in clearly drawn battle lines between science and God's Word or liberalism and conservative values. Anti-Catholic biases also permeate the books. In addition, these materials portray the providential hand of God as a cornerstone of all the events of history. Students also received a clear message about the importance of Christian schools in terms of "upholding the faith of their fathers." Hence, early textbooks of history in many Christian schools served the purpose of framing the world in a God focused plan carried out by bold Protestants. In sum, these texts outlined the grave challenges to America's Protestant Christian heritage by portraying the nation as turning away from God by pursuing secularism, science, and Catholicism.[18]

16. Bennick, *Sketches from Church History*, 96, 121.

17. Bennick, *Sketches from Church History*, 198.

18. Heyns and Roelofs, *Christian Interpretation*, 169–70.

These early schools also possessed humble beginnings in terms of facilities and enrollment. Wheaton Christian Grammar School opened at Wheaton Bible church serving grades 1–6 with a total of fifteen students. Due to zoning issues, the school moved three times in the first month and eventually purchased a house in town to hold classes starting in the fall of 1943.[19] The house needed much repair and several parents worked nights to enclose the front porch, which would eventually provide space for a kindergarten class. Four years later, the school purchased another house next door to provide for increased enrollment. WCGS received donations of old playground equipment, an old piano, and Wheaton College donated used desks and textbooks. To raise money for the school, they leased some of the unused rooms in the houses to boarders and also leased space for a barbershop and for music lessons. In 1947, WCGS graduated its first eighth grade class of eight students. Barbara Bedell, an eighth grade student in 1950, commented on conditions in this new school. Her class had a total of twelve students as compared to thirty-five per section at the local public school. Her classroom in one of the houses crammed desks in a tiny front room in order to accommodate both seventh and eighth grades. They played in a small front yard and on rainy days, they used the gym at Wheaton College.[20]

Other schools faced similar accommodations and numbers. Vineland Christian School first met in an old church annex and served seventeen students in grades 2–6.[21] Riverside Christian Day School met in a two story house in downtown Riverside, California to teach twenty-eight students in its first year.[22] Plumstead Christian School met in a Mennonite chapel in 1948 serving twenty-three students in grades 1–10.[23] Lincoln Christian School held its inaugural year of classes in the basement of a Presbyterian Church and outfitted the class with books and desks purchased at an auction from a nearby Lutheran School. Starting three days late, the school enrolled thirteen students in grades K–4.[24] Delaware County Christian School also met in a church basement with a larger student body of fifty-eight students in grades K–5.[25] Phoenix Christian Preparatory School started from the ministry of Ezra Weed and his family who started a small Christian elementary school in 1912. However, real growth and credibility came with the

19. Knowles, "Wheaton Christian Grammar School," 13–16.

20. Tucker, *Wheaton Christian Grammar School*, 22–28.

21. Cumberland Christian, "History."

22. Riverside Christian, "School History."

23. Plumstead Christian, "History."

24. Jones, "Lincoln Christian School," 1.

25. Delaware County Christian, "History."

establishment of a high school in 1949.[26] Despite these lowly beginnings, each of these schools went on to purchase land and build more appropriate facilities in the following years.

With no public funding and relying exclusively on tuition and financial gifts, all Christian schools of this era predictably struggled with finances. Meager budgets and low teacher salaries created constant challenges. With a monthly tuition of $8 per month per child, the only full-time teacher at WCGS, Miss Mary Ross, received a salary described as just under half of the average for public school teachers.[27] Marilyn Himmel, who taught at WCGS for forty-one years starting in the early 1950s, initially received an annual salary of $2,250. Since the school could only afford a part time janitor, she performed some of the cleaning services herself.[28] The founders of Delaware County Christian School established their parent society in 1949 with only $44.87 in their treasury. Eventually, when they opened their doors in 1950, they operated the entire year on a budget of $6,907.[29] With such financial restrictions, many schools received assistance from local churches and parents in the form of donated labor for building projects and legal assistance.

These schools also encountered a myriad of problems and in the case of Lincoln Christian School (LCS), had to fight for credibility. With an enrollment of thirteen students and one teacher meeting in the basement of Faith Orthodox Presbyterian Church, the school opened in the fall of 1951. However only a few days later, a city administrator arrived at the new school to inform their teacher that their school did not possess the approval of the state. Although initially left alone, local public educators reported LCS to state officials during the school's second year and soon several men from the Nebraska state office of education came and inspected the operation. A teacher from the school remarked later that one of the state officials thought LCS was a correctional institution, while another rejected the school's claims to be non-sectarian. Weeks later, a report arrived from the state superintendent with several demands. LCS would need to develop a more cumulative record system, update their playground, expand their library and take all schoolrooms out of the basement and locate them on the first floor of the church. This created great hardship for the new school, but ultimately, proved beneficial because these expectations moved school leaders to start building a permanent facility.[30]

26. Phoenix Christian, "About."

27. Tucker, *Wheaton Christian Grammar School*, 27–28.

28. Marilyn Himmel was a teacher at the Wheaton Christian Grammar School from 1955 to 1996. Marilyn Himmel, interview with the author, September 25, 2009, Wheaton, IL.

29. Delaware County Christian, "History."

30. Jones, "Lincoln Christian School," 3–4.

With tiny enrollments, underpaid teachers, crowded campuses, very limited resources, and often lacking community acceptance, these early Christian schools did not appear to be institutions capable of restoring a Christian America much less providing a quality education for their pupils. However, the parents and educators remained vigilant in their commitment. Stories abound about sacrifices made for this cause. Parents took out second mortgages to pay tuition. Teachers worked for decades at substandard salaries. Families often did maintenance on school facilities. A student at WCGS from this era, Ruth Johnson, remembered how much her parents sacrificed to pay for tuition. Her father, a contractor, commuted to his job for years so the family could live in Wheaton and his daughter could attend WCGS. Ruth stated that her blue-collar dad often remarked that he saw an education at WCGS as a need, not just a want.[31]

Compared to public and Catholic education, these first Christian schools lacked much, but still possessed an appeal to this small segment of evangelical Christianity. This came in part due to the great anxiety of evangelicals in the post-World War II years with specific concerns about the family, loss of community, and lack of control in their local and national spheres. These autonomous schools reflected populist tendencies of twentieth-century parents, offering these individuals a renewed sense of power and the ability to teach their children the values of their faith. Beneath the sweeping proclamations of Mark Fakkema and today's religious right, this phenomenon rested upon individuals in local communities who sacrificed to establish these schools based upon their own convictions. In a rapidly changing world, these institutions reflected a search for control and community among conservative fundamentalist believers. These Christian schools were established and maintained by local families resulting in a small bureaucracy allowing parents to take control of their lives and the lives of their children from a perceived anonymous, elitist, and secular world. The Christian school, according to Susan Rose, author of the previously mentioned *Keeping Them Out of the Hands of Satan: Evangelical Schooling in America*, became part of a coherent network of the institutions of church, home, and school that allowed evangelicals to "exercise greater control over the definition and transmission of their values and norms." Hence, she describes the founding of these small schools in this way, "Caught in a world whose complexity tends to render people impotent, evangelicals have chosen to delimit their world in order to gain control of it."[32]

---

31. Ruth Johnson was a student at the Wheaton Christian Grammar School from 1951 to 1959. Ruth Johnson, interview with the author, September 24, 2009, Wheaton, IL.

32. Rose, *Keeping Them Out*, 3–10.

Conclusion

The National Association of Christian Schools continued with steady growth into the late 1950s. Almost by default, the NACS board had given complete authority to Executive Director Mark Fakkema during the years of 1941 to 1958. However, by the late 1950s, the board had grown concerned about Fakkema's financial dependence for the organization upon close friends. Hence, the NACS possessed a weak financial foundation. In addition, the NACS board had grown weary of Fakkema's dogmatic approach of "us versus them" in establishing Christian schools. The struggles with the NACS board led to his eventual resignation in 1960.[1] Dr. John Blanchard took over the leadership of the NACS in 1961. Blanchard succeeded in improving the financial status of the organization as well as develop close ties with several independent regional Christian school associations. Today's largest nationwide group, the Association of Christian Schools International, was officially formed in 1978 and remains the dominant Christian School organization both nationally and internationally.

Dr. Frank Gaebelein remained the headmaster of Stony Brook School for forty-one years until 1963. After his passing in 1983, his daughter wrote that his long-term commitment to Stony Brook that came from his belief that a forthright Christian testimony and academic excellence could go hand in hand.[2] He embodied the idea of the "new evangelical" of the National Association of Evangelicals by demonstrating "an adherence to orthodoxy while showing an interest in the sociological problems of the day." His support of the Billy Graham Crusade in 1957 at Madison Square Garden brought criticism

1. Benson, "History of the National Association," 111–12.
2. Hull, "Frank Gaebelein," 17.

from narrower fundamentalist circles.[3] He was later active in the Civil Rights rallies of the 1960s. Eventually, he would go on to be a regular contributor to *Christianity Today* until his death. Gaebelein's model of Christian schools being an academically rigorous, well rounded education, embracing athletics and fine arts while also stressing involvement in current sociological issues still resonates in the Christian school movement.

With the origin of the Christian school movement nearing the century mark, it's reactionary nature remains evident. Corresponding to the growth of evangelical Christianity in the 1930s and 40s, Christian schools grew as a parental reaction against modernity with its godless science, religious pluralism and changing social mores. These schools came from a parent backlash against public education, feminism, social protest movements and fears about the disintegration of the family.[4] James Carper and Thomas Hunt described Christian schools as a form of dissent tied to concerns of evangelical Christians about "higher criticism of the Bible, Darwinism, growing cultural and religious pluralism, and the fundamentalist-modernist controversy that fractured many Protestant denominations."[5]

The writings of Mark Fakkema and Frank Gaebelein do indeed reveal this tendency with their constant criticism of public education, rising state control, secularism, declining morals, evolution, and the Roman Catholic Church. Early Christian school leaders also often spoke with a sense of urgency and doom calling for America to return to its Christian roots, a mission which could be accomplished in part by establishing these schools. Myriad examples can be seen and a good case in point appears in Gaebelein's preface for *Christian Education in a Democracy*, which states, "Today we see the spectacle of a drowned civilization, a culture which, originally owing much to Christianity, has now been thoroughly inundated by the deluge of secularism. In short, western civilization is on the way to an almost complete de-Christianization."[6]

However, to call this movement a response to events confined in the early twentieth century would be shallow as these reactionary tendencies have deeper roots in America's past. By 1952, Christian day schools, although quite small, had come into being after decades of controversy and concerns reaching back into the nation's history over the role of Protestant Christianity in American society.

3. Lockerbie, *Way They Should Go*, 103.

4. Rose, *Keeping Them Out*, x–xi.

5 Carper and Hunt, *Dissenting Tradition*, 201.

6. Gaebelein, *Christian Education in a Democracy*, 4.

Protestant dreams for America and corresponding concerns about power and influence go back to colonial days. From the Puritan concept of a "City on a Hill" Anglo Protestants carried a vision for a future of the New World. This concept conceived of the United States as "the redeemer nation entrusted with a millennial destiny."[7] Patrick Allitt argued that American Christians possess a long tradition of believing that "their republic would only prosper if it was inhabited by virtuous Christian citizens."[8] Many American Christians possess a long held belief that God anointed the United States as his chosen nation and people.[9] Finally, religious historian Diana Eck suggests that the narrative of a Christian America has always had a hold on the collective imagination of Americans. This narrative moves through each chapter in American history and in turn, is deeply embedded in our consciousness.[10]

With this deeply embedded belief, later evangelicals would interpret the nation's beginnings as a Christian event that established a foundation for America's future.[11] However, over time, they came to believe that this dream diminished due to multiple causes. Consequently, evangelicals in the twentieth century sought to restore the rapidly eroding foundation of their nation. Education naturally became a chief means to achieve their hope.

The nineteenth century produced the first serious threats. Increased immigration brought more variety to the country and the most disconcerting menace emerged in the form of Roman Catholicism. The Common School movement of the 1830s sought to deal with the changing demographics of the citizenry by attempting to set up a common belief system, which included Bible reading in the classroom, into all of the nation's school children. At that time, conservative Protestants played instrumental roles in the creation of the new public schools seeing them as a means of instilling their version of American values into the next generation and maintaining their cultural power. However, more hazards arose from increased ethnic and spiritual diversity resulting in diminished Bible reading in the public schools. The Catholic Church grew stronger and decided to establish its own private school system causing more of an uproar for the Protestant majority in charge of the public schools. By the end of the 1800s, conservative Protestants who had once dreamed of a godly nation, now looked back longingly at a mythic past of a Christian America.

7. Tyack and Hansot, *Managers of Virtue*, 19.

8. Allitt, *Religion in America*, 6.

9. Hughes, *Christian America and the Kingdom*, 18.

10. Eck, *New Religious America*, 42.

11. Meacham, *American Gospel*, 84.

Into the twentieth century, Protestant power and influence in education and society at large received near fatal assaults. Darwin's theory of evolution, overturning conventional Biblical beliefs, frightened conservative Christians and immediately emerged as a major antagonist in their fight for the future of America. In addition, new educational theories, most notably the progressive ideas of John Dewey, further eroded the Christian hold on public schools. Numerous Christian historians virtually vilify Dewey for his insistence upon child-centered education that suggested a denial of original sin and the marginalization of religion in education.[12] Fractures from within the Christian community in the form of liberal theology and expanding Catholicism further weakened traditional Protestant power. All of this would have devastating effects in the new century and would lead conservative Christians to the harsh realization that Protestantism in the twentieth century no longer set the moral agenda for the nation.[13]

In the midst of so much progressive change, the fundamentalists of the 1920s set in place many critical components of the future Christian school movement. George Marsden's ideas about fundamentalism's separatist tendencies and commitment to building a Christian civilization explains the context whereby conservative Protestants might resort to creating their own schools. "Faced by a culture with a myriad of competing ideals," he explained, "and having little power to influence that culture, they reacted by creating their own equivalent of the urban ghetto. An overview of fundamentalism reveals them building a subculture with institutions, mores, and social connections that would eventually provide acceptable alternatives to the dominant cultural ethos."[14]

In 1920, a forerunner of this subculture appeared with the establishment of the National Union of Christian Schools, which sprouted from Calvinist Dutch Reformed schools in the upper Midwest that first appeared in the late 1800s. The NUCS provided an organizational framework for parent controlled Christian day schools still utilized today. Along with this, the Stony Brook School of Long Island, New York founded in 1922, went beyond the narrow Reformed theology of the NUCS and established a model of building pan-evangelical institutions by appealing to a broader Protestant base. This inclusiveness became a significant foundation stone for the growth of the Christian school movement in later decades.

The twenties also produced two individuals of invaluable worth to the rise of Christian schools. Mark Fakkema and Dr. Frank Gaebelein emerged

---

12. Anthony and Benson, *Exploring the History*, 344.

13. Hammond, "Protestant Twentieth Century," 285.

14. Marsden, *Fundamentalism and American Culture*, 6–7, 124, 204.

as the two leading "Founding Fathers" of the movement. Fakkema rose to prominence through his involvement in the NUCS and became the face of the movement through his highly visible promotion efforts spanning the entire nation, which accelerated with his appointment to the position of executive director of the National Association of Christian Schools in 1947. Fakkema served as the movement's chief propagandist by his far-reaching travels, speeches, and extensive writings. Previous research portrays Fakkema as possessing a "near saintly" reputation, considered by his co-workers as indispensable to the origins of the movement because he was "indefatigable in his pursuit of the goal of inspiring parents to establish and support Christian day schools."[15] Gaebelein did not have the initial notoriety of Fakkema having quietly served as the headmaster of the Stony Brook School for twenty-five years before the formation of the NACS. However, he soon surfaced as the movement's most creative thinker and articulate apologist.[16] His books, *Christian Education in a Democracy* and *The Pattern of God's Truth,* established the philosophical groundwork of the entire movement. When published, Oxford University Press proclaimed his first work to be an "epochal volume" that stated "cogently and graphically the nature of education which is basically and intrinsically Christian."[17] Gaebelein's books, articles and Stony Brook experiences proved immensely useful in transcending denominational differences among Protestants and thereby galvanizing the struggling movement.

The 1940s became a pivotal decade resulting in the most visible growth of Christian schools and the birth of a true national association. Critical factors included the rebirth of conservative Christianity in America with the formation of The National Association of Evangelicals. This organization served a prominent role in bringing unity and credibility to conservative Protestants as they moved away from the negative image of fundamentalism and replaced it with a more appealing, albeit still traditional view of the faith known as evangelicalism. As an affiliate member of the NAE, the newly formed National Association of Christian Schools gained much traction by the energy of surging evangelical Christianity. The NACS joined with the NAE as they both sought to regain cultural power and influence.

In addition, this decade also created an atmosphere conducive to the growth of a separate Christian school system. Leaders of the Christian school movement seamlessly joined in the cacophony of conservative criticism

---

15. McLeod, "Rise of Catholic and Evangelical Schools," 36; Benson, "History of the National Association," 25.

16. Benson, "History of the National Association," 43.

17. Benson, "History of the National Association," 46.

toward public education during this era by adding charges of atheism and secularism to the debate. Concerns over federal aid to education and the growing power of the Catholic Church provided another avenue for NACS leaders to call for the formation of Christian schools. Cold War fears, which included concerns about Communism in education, gave Christian school leaders even more ammunition to assault public schools. The Cold War battle against "godless communism" caused a notable upsurge in religious activity tied to nationalism which also assisted the Christian school cause.[18] Reacting to well-intentioned attempts to promote worldwide peace through organizations such as UNESCO, conservative Christian leaders portrayed this as yet another example of permeating atheism in public education and another step toward a one-world government. After decades of diminishing influence in education, the 1940s provided the right blend of anxiety and re- ligious revival to produce fertile ground for a small, but determined group of Christian educators devoted to launching a decidedly spiritual educational alternative to public schools. Although still almost insignificant numerically in America's educational landscape, seeds were nonetheless planted which would expand and become a vital cornerstone of the religious right of the late twentieth and early twenty-first centuries.

The reactionary nature of Christian schools has also brought about frequent charges of racism. The previous mentioned work of Nevin and Bills, *The Schools That Fear Built: Segregationist Academies in the South,* implied that these schools arose in the South as a result of school inte- gration.[19] Paul Parsons, a Kansas journalist, made similar claims in his 1987 book *Inside America's Christian Schools* which stressed the desire of parents to change a perceived pagan society from the bottom up. Parsons stated that during the turbulent 1960s parents sought out private educa- tion, which included Christian schools, to avoid racial integration and as a result, these schools have been tainted, along with all Southern private schools, as "White Flight Academies."[20]

This conclusion is sadly true to some degree during the era of Civil Rights, but these authors neglect to consider the actual origins of these schools in the years that predate the major conflicts over racial integration in America. Studies of racist academies have also neglected to note that the first Christian schools of the 1940s started in the northeast, upper Mid- west and California and hence did not emerge in the more racially charged environment of the South. Going further, Dr. Jack Layman produced a

18. Gregory, "Course of Religion," 222.

19. Nevin and Bills, *Schools That Fear Built.*

20. Parsons, *Inside America's Christian Schools,* 113–16.

study on the growing number of black Christian educational institutions and stated that Christian schools in general have long struggled to attract minority students. This book asserts that Christian schools from the beginning have possessed a homogeneous constituency coming primarily from a sponsoring congregation and nearby churches holding similar doctrinal positions while black churches have remained separate.[21] Layman puts it this way, "To this day black churches are separated socially and, in most cases, organizationally from white churches. This lack of social contact would have hindered black participation in the Christian schools with or without Southern traditions of separation or segregation."[22] Historian Neal Devins also noted that while Christian schools did see growth in the South during the Civil Rights struggles, the movement really reflects a larger pattern of conservative rebellion against trends in public education. During the time of desegregation the courts of the nation also suppressed prayer, Bible reading, and even the most indirect symbolic indications of respect for religion in the public schools.[23]

Although very little commentary about racial issues exist among early Christian school leaders, Frank Gaebelein did express concerns to his school board about the lack of black students at Stony Brook in the early 1940s. Even though Stony Brook had already enrolled several Asian students, they did strive to break the color barrier by admitting their first African American student in 1955.[24] In 1950 *The Sunday School Times* reported on the opening of several new Christian schools and among the names given they listed the Free Methodist Colored Day School of Shreveport, Louisiana. Serving grades 1 through 8 with an enrollment of fifty-seven students, the presence of such a school dispels the image of Christian schools being exclusively white in this era.[25] In the midst of the civil rights struggles of the 1960s, the NACS refused to admit schools into the association that made race a condition for the admission of students.[26] The number of Christian schools in the 1950s and 60s did increase faster than in the 1940s, and racism no doubt played a part which again reveals the reactionary spirit of Christian schools. However, attempts to make racism a root cause neglects the deeper origin of the movement and reflects a simplistic

---

21. Nordin and Turner, "More Than Segregation," 392.

22. Layman, *Black Flight*, 30–33.

23. Devins, *Public Values, Private Schools*, 144–45.

24. Lockerbie, *Way They Should Go*, 97–98.

25. Bell, "Saving Children," 499–503.

26. Benson, "History of the National Association," 173.

view of a very diverse educational phenomenon by attempting to lump all Christian schools in with the "White Flight" academies.

Christian schools continued to grow unabated into the latter half of the twentieth century due to more concerns about public education and American society in general. Court rulings in the 1960s in regard to school prayer along with anxiety about the drug culture, declining test scores, perceptions of a lack of discipline, and school violence all continued to simply confirm to evangelical parents of the late twentieth-century Mark Fakkema's long standing claims about public education. Christian schools became a more viable alternative with a more prosperous economy in the 1980s and 1990s giving their constituents the means to build more and more of these institutions. Into the twenty-first century, state of the art facilities and extra-curricular programs further established the credibility of Christian schools. Although they have always branded public education in a negative light, Christian schools of today mimic many characteristics of public schools in order to gain cultural acceptance and maintain their prestige in educational circles.

To further understand the birth of the Christian school phenomenon, it must be remembered that education has always taken on the role of being the process whereby a society transmits itself to the next generation thereby making the school a cultural furnace where a particular image of human nature, the world, and a way of life can be forged and passed on.[27] Because of this role, education has always been a source of conflict and being established as a mechanism for acculturation and nationalism also causes problems with groups that possess dissenting viewpoints. Hence, if parents want to raise their children according to their own belief system and the educational institutions begin to promote values contrary to the convictions of the parents, opposition naturally arises.[28] With a deeply held personal faith and a desire for more power in their homes, communities, and nation, Protestant evangelical parents and teachers made the necessary sacrifices to launch a separate Christian school system in the years 1920 to 1952. In the grand tradition of American Protestantism, the birth of the Christian school movement in middle of the twentieth century distinctly reflected their long held vision of a "Christian America."

America's evolving diversity not only served as the chief catalyst for the movement, but also revealed the paradoxical characteristics of the Christian school movement. Christian leaders constantly criticized the fact that cultural and spiritual diversity threatened the heritage of the nation, while also enjoying the same freedoms that would allow them to be different and

27. Randall, "Religious Schools in America," 71–72.
28. Rury, *Education and Social Change*, 17.

establish their own separate school system. Another contradiction in the movement can be found in Hamburger's previously mentioned thesis about separation of church and state. While evangelicals upheld this notion as a right when used to keep Catholics at bay in terms of public funding, they also fumed when the same principle was used to remove their sectarian beliefs from public education.[29] In addition, with every Catholic charge that public education was effectively Protestant education, public school leaders found it necessary to weaken the religious element of the schools. This led to a final contradiction best described by B. Edward McClellan, "By the mid-twentieth century the public school had become so devoid of religious content that even many Protestant groups who had been its strongest defenders now turned against it, finding themselves in the end closer to the Catholic position on religion and morality than to the non-sectarianism that their forebears had done so much to create."[30] While contradictions appear to exist, they are nevertheless consistent with the thesis of this work: the Christian school movement, responding to a century of change and adversity, emerged in the twentieth century as a means for evangelical Christians to reclaim their loss of power within the nation, their communities, and their homes in an increasingly complex American society.

With this pluralistic identity emerging in America, education responded and inevitably moved toward secularization, as Dr. Gaebelein predicted. Public education had evolved as a system of schooling serving the needs of a widely diverse population. Questions about the establishment of religion in the nation's schools became clarified through important laws and court cases. However, for a small number of conservative Protestants, this new image of America signaled a threat to their commitment to a good society. Hence, by the late 1940s, Mark Fakkema would sadly conclude that his nation "has now passed the fertile valley of American Christian culture and has entered the arid regions of un-Christian pagan ideology" leading him to defiantly pronounce that, "the only course left for us as Christians is to establish and support private Christian schools, cost what it may."[31] Believing themselves to be guardians of the culture since the earliest days of the Republic, these evangelicals sought and continue to seek a return to Christian ideals for America. This could be accomplished from the bottom up through these small schools focused on restoring and reinforcing their spiritual values.

---

29. Hamburger, *Separation of Church and State*, 477.

30. McClellan, *Moral Education in America*, 45.

31. Fakkema, "Educational Significance," 1.

As a result, Christian schools found their place in the religious right that surfaced in late twentieth-century America. One need look no further than the current political discourse to hear frequent commentary about the role of evangelical Christians in the nation. Much attention has indeed centered on evangelical opposition to such things as gay marriage or to their power as a voting bloc reflecting a re-emerged subculture. While the most visible components of this resurgence can be seen in politics, Christian media, and mega churches, the religious right in twenty-first century also contains an extensive network of thousands of Christian schools that are autonomous, conservative, thriving and almost invisible. Despite their widespread footprint, they have notably retained a very consistent fundamentalist theology.

Protestant Christian schools occupied a tiny piece of American education in 1952 and remain very small to this day in the midst of our nation's massive educational system. Yet growth continues. According to the Association of Christian Schools International (ACSI), the modern day equivalent of the National Association of Christian Schools, their organization currently boasts of some 22,000 schools worldwide.[32] Christian Schools International (CSI), the organization originally known as the National Union of Christian Schools, claims to currently serve approximately five hundred schools in North America.[33] Notably, Catholic schools have reported a drop of over 500,000 students and have closed some 1,750 schools since 2000.[34]

Frank Gaebelein once called the Christian school movement, "a minority of a minority."[35] This remains true, but starting from the concerns of a "devoted few" which grew into their "mighty army," these Christian school parents and educators can now observe "what God hath wrought" by the number of Protestant Christian elementary and secondary educational institutions spread across the land. Despite the even greater level of ethnic and religious diversity in twenty-first century America, they remain completely devoted in their quest to protect and advance their values in their homes, their communities, and their nation. This unobtrusive component of today's religious right continues to respond to the growing secularity of American culture with scores of teachers and children in small Christian schools pledging allegiance to America with Bibles in their backpacks. After decades of discouragement marked by secularism, Roman Catholics, and John Dewey, Christian schools remain intact. Today, with the battle continuing to

32. Simmons, *Worth It*, xii.

33. Christian Schools International, "About CSI."

34. Matheson, "48 Catholic Schools."

35. Gaebelein, "Christian Education," 8.

rage on—with issues arising from the LGBQT agenda, religious liberty, and the political left—the descendants of Mark Fakkema and Frank Gaebelein faithfully continue undaunted, believing that the blurred and faded image of a Christian America is still obtainable.

Works Cited

Allitt, Patrick. *Religion in America Since 1945: A History.* New York: Columbia, 2003.

Anthony, Michael J., and Warren S. Benson. *Exploring the History and Philosophy of Christian Education: Principles for the Twenty-First Century.* New York: Kregel Academic and Professional, 2003.

Ayer, William Ward. "Evangelical Christianity Endangered by its Fragmentized Condition." In *Evangelical Action! A Report of the Organization of the National Association of Evangelicals for United Action,* 42–43. Boston: United Action, 1942.

Balmer, Randall. "The Age of Militancy." In *Religion in American Life: A Short History,* edited by Jon Butler, et al., 57–69. New York: Oxford University Press, 2003.

Bankston, Carl, and Stephen J. Caldas. *Public Education—America's Civil Religion.* New York: Teachers College, 2009.

Beggs, David W., and R. Bruce McQuigg. *America's Schools and Churches: Partners in Conflict.* Bloomington: Indiana University Press, 1965.

Bell, Ralph R. "Saving Children Through the Christian Day School." *Sunday School Times,* June 25, 1950, 499–503.

Bennick, Bernard John. *Sketches from Church History: A Supplemental Reader for History Classes in Christian Schools.* Grand Rapids: Eerdmans, 1926.

Benson, Warren Sten. "A History of the National Association of Christian Schools During the Period of 1947–1972." PhD diss., Loyola University, 1975.

Bloch, Ruth. *Visionary Republic: Millenial Themes in American Thought.* Cambridge: Harvard University Press, 1985.

Bogle, Lori Lyn. *The Pentagon's Battle for the American Mind: The Early Cold War.* College Station: Texas A&M University Press, 2004.

Boodin, J. E. "Education for Democracy." *School and Society,* June 22, 1918, 724–31.

Bowers, C. A. *The Progressive Educator and the Depression: The Radical Years.* New York: Random House, 1969.

Boyer, Paul. *When Time Shall Be No More: Prophecy Belief in Modern American Culture.* Cambridge: Harvard University Press, 1992.

Boyle, Samuel E. "Jesus Christ and the American Tradition." *United Evangelical Action,* September 15, 1947, 3–4.

Brubaker, John S. "Why Force Religious Education?" *Nation's Schools* 35.5 (1945) 23–24.

Burke, Arvid J. "Should the State Help Support Sectarian Schools?" *Nation's Schools*, 1938, 29–30.

Burke, Colin B. "Religion." In *Historical Statistics of the United States from Earliest Times to the Present*, edited by Susan B. Carter, 900–14. Cambridge: Cambridge University Press, 2006.

Burns, Hobert W., and Charles J. Brauner. *Philosophy of Education*. New York: Ronald, 1962.

Button, Warren, and Eugene F. Provenzo. *History of Education and Culture in America*. Englewood Cliffs: Prentice Hall, 1988.

Carpenter, Joel A. "Fundamentalist Institutions and the Rise of Evangelical Protestantism, 1929–1942." In *Fundamentalism and Evangelicalism*, edited by Martin Marty, 62–75. New York: K. G. Saur, 1993.

———. *Revive Us Again: The Re-Awakening of American Fundamentalism*. New York: Oxford University Press, 1997.

Carper, James C. "The Christian Day School." In *Religious Schooling in America*. Birmingham: Religious Education, 1984.

Carper, James C., and Thomas C. Hunt. *The Dissenting Tradition in American Education*. New York: Peter Lang, 2007.

Carter, Susan B., ed. *Historical Statistics of the United States: Earliest Times to the Present*. Cambridge, MA: Cambridge University Press, 2006.

Cartlidge, A. Ray. "The Battle of Champaign." *United Evangelical Action*, August 15, 1945, 3–4.

Christian Schools International. "About CSI." https://www.csionline.org/about.

Church, Robert L., and Michael W. Sedlak. *Education in the United States: An Interpretive History*. New York: Free Press, 1976.

Collins, Kenneth J. *The Evangelical Moment: The Promise of an American Religion*. Grand Rapids: Baker Academic, 2005.

Conant, James Bryant. *My Several Lives: Memoirs of a Social Inventor*. New York: Harper and Row, 1970.

Cook, David M. "The Present Legal Situation." In *America's Schools and Churches: Partners in Conflict*, edited by David W. Beggs and R. Bruce McQuigg, 24–38. Bloomington: Indiana University Press, 1965.

Cooke, Robert L. "What is Wrong with American Education?" *The Sunday School Times*, June 22, 1941, 459–61.

Council for American Private Education. "Private School Statistics at a Glance." http://www.capenet.org/facts.html.

Counts, George S. "Dare the School Build a New Social Order?" *Progressive Education* 9.4 (1932) 9–14.

Cremin, Lawrence A. *American Education: The Colonial Experience, 1607–1783*. New York: Harper and Row, 1970.

———. *American Education: The Metropolitan Experience, 1876–1980*. New York: Harper and Row, 1988.

———. *The Transformation of the School: Progressivism in American Education, 1876–1957*. New York: Alfred A. Knopf, 1969.

Culver, Raymond B. *Horace Mann and Religion in the Massachusetts Public Schools*. New York: Arno, 1969.

Cumberland Christian School. "History." http://www.cccrusader.org/history.cfm.

Davis, William F. "Public Policy, Religion, and Education in the United States." In *Religion and Schooling in Contemporary America: Confronting Our Cultural Pluralism*, edited by Thomas C. Carper and James C. Hunt, 181–96. New York: Garland, 1997.

Davison, Hunter James. *Culture Wars: The Struggle to Define America.* New York: Basic, 1991.

Delaware County Christian School. "History." https://www.dccs.org/page.cfm?p=889.

Delfattore, Joan. *The Fourth R: Conflicts Over Religion in America's Public Schools.* New Haven: Yale University Press, 2004.

Devins, Neal. *Public Values, Private Schools.* London: Falmer, 1989.

Dewey, John. *The School and Society.* Chicago: University of Chicago Press, 1899.

Dierenfield, Bruce J. *The Battle Over School Prayer: How Engel v. Vitale Changed America.* Lawrence: University of Kansas Press, 2007.

Duncan, M. H. "American Education Needs a Standard." *Moody Monthly* 41.10 (1941) 569–70, 587.

———. "The Bible in Life and Education." *Moody Monthly* 42.10 (1946) 425, 438–39.

———. "Something is Missing in our Schools." *Moody Monthly* 46.7 (1947) 673–74.

Dyrness, Enock C. "Report of the Commission on Education." In *Minutes of the Meeting of the Board of Administration, National Association of Evangelicals*, edited by the National Association of Evangelicals, 1. Chicago: National Association of Evangelicals, 1949.

———. "Report of the Resolutions Committee." In *Advance From Omaha!: A Report of the Fifth Annual Convention of the National Association of Evangelicals*, edited by the National Association of Evangelicals, 35–36. Chicago: National Association of Evangelicals, 1947.

Eck, Diana L. *A New Religious America: How a "Christian Country" Has Become the World's Most Religiously Diverse Nation.* San Francisco: Harper Collins, 2001.

"Editorial." *Catholic Sentinel*, June 4, 1925, 5.

Educational Committee of the National Union of Christian Schools. *Course of Study for Christian Schools.* Grand Rapids: Eerdmans, 1947.

Edwards, Mark. "'God Has Chosen Us': Re-Membering Christian Realism, Rescuing Christendom, and the Conquest of Responsibilities During the Cold War." *Diplomatic History* 23 (2009) 67–94.

Elias, John L. *A History of Christian Education: Protestant, Catholic, and Orthodox Perspectives.* Malabar: Krieger, 2002.

Eyres, Lawrence. "How it is Done in the Pacific Northwest." *United Evangelical Action*, July 1, 1948, 7–8.

Fakkema, Mark. "The Axe Lies at the Root of the Tree of the True American Way of Life." In *National Association of Christian Schools Newsletter*, edited by the National Union of Christian Schools, 1–2. Chicago: National Union of Christian Schools, 1949.

———. "The Case for the Christian Day School." *United Evangelical Action*, June 15, 1954, 7.

———. "The Christian Day School: Its Place in our Christian Program." In *Advance From Omaha!: A Report of the Fifth Annual Convention of the National Association of Evangelicals*, edited by the National Association of Evangelicals, 1–5. Chicago: National Association of Evangelicals, 1947.

———. "Christian Education Needs a Christian Philosophy." In *National Association of Christian Schools Newsletter*, edited by the National Union of Christian Schools, 1–2. Chicago: National Union of Christian Schools, 1950.

———. "Christian School Promotion Activity." In *Christian School Annual, Year 1946: Christian School Expansion*, edited by the Executive Committee, 50–53. Chicago: National Union of Christian Schools, 1946.

———. "Christian School Statistics." In *Christian School Annual, 1942*, edited by the National Union of Christian Schools, 42–43. Chicago: National Union of Christian Schools, 1942.

———. "Christian School Workshops." In *National Association of Christian Schools Newsletter*, edited by the National Union of Christian Schools, 1–2. Chicago: National Union of Christian Schools, 1949.

———. "Christian Schools for Such a Time as This." *United Evangelical Action*, January 15, 1946, 3–5.

———. *Christian Schools or a Pagan Nation—What Shall it Be?* Chicago: National Association of Christian Schools, 1948.

———. "Closing of Schools." In *Christian Home and School*, edited by the National Union of Christian Schools, 8–12. Chicago: National Union of Christian Schools, 1933.

———. "Developments in the Past Five Years." In *Evangelical Christian School Movement—Christian School Survey 1952*, edited by Mark Fakkema, 4–5, 12. Chicago: National Association of Christian Schools, 1952.

———. "The Educational Significance of the Supreme Court Decision." In *National Association of Christian Schools Newsletter*, edited by the National Union of Christian Schools, 1. Chicago: National Union of Christian Schools, 1948.

———. *First NACS Anniversary—For Such a Time as This.* Chicago: National Association of Christian Schools, 1948.

———. "Historical Antecedents." In *Evangelical Christian School Movement—Christian School Survey 1952*, edited by Mark Fakkema, 1–4. Chicago: National Association of Christian Schools, 1952.

———. "How Well Does America Read?" *The Christian Teacher* 12 (1951) 1–2.

———. Interview by Frances Simpson. Wheaton, IL. April 16, 1954.

———. Interview by Warren Sten Benson. Blue Island, IL. June 24, 1974.

———. "John Dewey is Dead." *Christian Teacher* 22 (1952) 1–2.

———. "Legal Rumblings—Private Instruction Placed on a Par with Public Instruction." *National Association of Christian Schools Newsletter* (1948) 1–2.

———. "The Modern Revolutionary War." *Christian Teacher* 5 (1951) 1–2.

———. "NACS Program of Action." In *Evangelical Christian School Movement—Christian School Survey 1952*, edited by Mark Fakkema, 6–14. Chicago: National Association of Christian Schools, 1952.

———. "The National Association of Christian Schools." In *United—"Cooperation Without Compromise!" A Report of the Sixth Annual Convention of the National Association of Evangelicals*, edited by the National Association of Evangelicals, 15. Chicago: National Association of Evangelicals, 1948.

———. "Need of a Christian Philosophy." In *Evangelical Christian School Movement—Christian School Survey 1952*, edited by Mark Fakkema, 14–17. Chicago: National Association of Christian Schools, 1952.

———. *A Plea for Christian Education.* Chicago: National Union of Christian Schools, 1944.

————. *Popular Objections to the Christian School.* Chicago: National Association of Christian Schools, 1948.

————. "The Prerequisites for Starting a Christian School." *Christian Teacher* 4 (1951) 1–2.

————. "Report of the National Association of Christian Schools." In *Minutes of the Executive Committee,* edited by the National Association of Evangelicals, 14. Chicago: National Association of Evangelicals, 1952.

————. "Report of the National Association of Christian Schools, NACS in Action." In *Evangelicals Move Forward for Christ: A Report on the Eighth Annual Convention of the National Association of Evangelicals,* edited by the Executive Committee of the National Association of Evangelicals, 48–51. Chicago: National Association of Evangelicals, 1950.

————. *Report to the Promotion Committee.* Grand Rapids, MI: National Union of Christian Schools, 1947.

————. *The Result of a High Court Decision.* Chicago: National Association of Christian Schools, 1963.

————. "Shall the Church Build Its Own Schools?" *United Evangelical Action,* October 1, 1945, 3–4, 20.

————. "Shall We Celebrate Halloween?" *Christian Teacher* 23 (1952) 1–2.

————. "Shall We Invite Santa into Our Home and Into the Christian School?" *Christian Teacher* 2 (1950) 1–2.

————. "Socializing Our Public Schools." *Christian Teacher* 13 (1951) 1–2.

————. "A Spirit of Self-Sacrifice in Evidence." *National Association of Christian Schools Newsletter,* edited by the National Union of Christian Schools, 1–2. Chicago: National Union of Christian Schools, 1948.

————. "Statement of Income and Expense." In *Minutes of the Meeting of the Board of Administration,* edited by the National Association of Evangelicals, 6. Denver: National Association of Evangelicals, 1948.

————. "Statement of Policy." In *Christian Textbooks: Why, How, What,* edited by the National Association of Evangelicals, 6. Chicago: National Association of Evangelicals, 1949.

————. "A Supplement to the Printed Anniversary Report Intended for the NAE Board of Administration." In *Minutes of the Meeting of the Board of Administration,* edited by the National Association of Evangelicals, 2. Chicago: National Association of Evangelicals, 1948.

————. *A Survey of the Free Christian Schools in America.* Grand Rapids, MI: National Union of Christian Schools, 1922.

————. "Textbooks Without God." *Christian Teacher* (1952) 1–2.

————. "Trimming Our Lamps." *Christian Teacher* (1950) 1–2.

————. "What God Hath Wrought." *The National Association of Christian Schools Newsletter,* edited by the National Union of Christian Schools, 1–2. Chicago: National Union of Christian Schools, 1948.

————. "Without the Christian Religion We Can Have No True Democracy." *Christian Teacher* 3 (1951) 1–2.

Fakkema, Mark, et al. *Round Table Discussion: The Need for Private Christian Day Schools for the Children of the Christian Parents of America.* Chicago: National Union of Christian Schools, 1942.

"Fourth R at Stony Brook School." *Christian Science Monitor,* September 7, 1929, 9.

Fowler, Frederick C. "Annual Report of the Committee on Christian Liberty." In In *Minutes of the Meeting of the Executive Committee of the National Association of Evangelicals*, edited by the National Association of Evangelicals, 4. Chicago: National Association of Evangelicals, 1949.

Friend, George C. "Shall We Educate Teenagers Without Christ?" *United Evangelical Action*, February 1, 1947, 3–4.

Fuller, David Otis. "Letter to the Temporary Committee for United Action Among Evangelicals." Personal Letter. Grand Rapids, March 23, 1942.

Gaebelein, Frank E. *The Christian, the Arts, and Truth: Regaining the Vision of Greatness.* Portland, OR: Multnomah, 1985.

———. "Christian Education and the Independent School." *United Evangelical Action*, Decermber 1, 1949, 6–9.

———. *Christian Education in a Democracy.* New York: Oxford University Press, 1951.

———. *The Pattern of God's Truth: The Integration of Faith and Learning.* Colorado Springs: Association of Christian Schools International, 1954.

Gangel, Kenneth O., and Warren S. Benson. *Christian Education: Its History and Philosophy.* Chicago: Moody, 1983.

Garrison, J. Gorham. "The Role of the Public Schools in the Development of Moral and Spiritual Values." In *Proceedings of 86th Annual Meeting*, edited by the National Education Association, 169–71. Washington, DC: National Education Association, 1948.

Garson, Robert A. "Political Fundamentalism and Popular Democracy in the 1920s." In *Fundamentalism and Evangelicalism*, edited by Martin Marty, 103–32. New York: K. G. Saur, 1993.

Gleason, Philip. *Speaking of Diversity: Language and Ethnicity in Twentieth-Century America.* Baltimore: Johns Hopkins University Press, 1992.

Goldman, Eric F. *The Crucial Decade—And After: America, 1945–1960.* New York: Alfred A. Knopf, 1966.

Gordon, Ernest. "'UNESCO,' A Dangerous Movement." *Sunday School Times*, July 12, 1947, 673–74.

Greenawalt, Kent. *Does God Belong in Public Schools?* Princeton: Princeton University Press, 2005.

Gregory, Ross. "Religion." In *Cold War America, 1946–1990*, by Ross Gregory, 32–38. New York: Facts on File, 2003.

Gunn, T. Jeremy. *Spiritual Weapons: The Cold War and the Forging of an American National Religion.* Westport: Praeger, 2009.

Gutek, Gerald L. *Historical and Philosophical Foundations of Education: A Biographical Introduction.* New Jersey: Merrill Prentice-Hall, 2001.

Hamburger, Philip. *Separation of Church and State.* Cambridge: Harvard University Press, 2002.

Hammond, Phillip E. "In Search of a Protestant Twentieth Century: American Religion and Power Since 1900." *Review of Religious Research* 24.4 (1983) 281–94.

Handy, Robert T. *A Christian America: Protestant Hopes and Historical Realities.* New York: Oxford University Press, 1971.

Hartman, Andrew. *Education and the Cold War: The Battle for the American School.* New York: Palgrave Macmillan, 2008.

Harvard Committee. *General Education in a Free Society: Report of the Harvard Committee.* Cambridge, MA: Harvard University Press, 1945.

Hassard, John R. G. *Life of John Hughes: First Archbishop of New York.* New York: Arno, 1969.

Haverhouse, William. "A Plea for a God Centered Education." *United Evangelical Action,* February 15, 1943, 4.

Hayes, William. *Horace Mann's Vision of the Public Schools.* Lanham: Rowman and Litchfield Education, 2006.

Henry, Carl F. H. "The Harvard Report." *United Evangelical Action,* April 1, 1947, 15.

Herzog, Jonathan P. *The Spiritual-Industrial Complex: America's Religious Battle Against Communism in the Early Cold War.* Oxford: Oxford University Press, 2011.

Heyns, Garrett, and Garritt Roelofs. *Christian Interpretation of American History.* Chicago: National Union of Christian Schools, 1928.

Hill, Henry H. "Report of the Educational Policies Commission." In *Proceedings of 90th Annual Meeting,* edited by the National Education Association, 141–44. Washington, DC: National Education Association, 1952.

Holsinger, M. Paul. "The Oregon School Controversy, 1922–1925." *Pacific Historical Review* (1968).

Hughes, Richard T. *Christian America and the Kingdom of God.* Chicago: University of Illinois Press, 2009.

Hull, Gretchen Gaebelein. "Frank Gaebelein: Character Before Career." *Christianity Today,* September 21, 1984, 14–18.

Humphrey, Heman. "The Bible in Common Schools." In *The Lectures Delivered Before the American Institute of Instruction, 1843,* by Heman Humphrey. Boston: William D. Ticknor, 1844.

Hutchinson, William. "Diversity and the Pluralist Ideal." In *Perspectives on American Religion and Culture,* by William Hutchinson, 34–47. Malden, MA: Blackwell, 1999.

———. *Religious Pluralism in America: The Contentious History of a Founding Ideal.* New Haven: Yale University Press, 2003.

"Increased Need for Christian Education." *Sunday School Times,* April 19, 1947, 402–3.

Ivers, Gregg. *To Build a Wall: American Jews and Separation of Church and State.* Charlottesville: University of Virginia Press, 1995.

Jones, Melvin. "Lincoln Christian School . . . In the Beginning." *Lincoln Christian School Messenger* (1991) 1–4.

Kabat, George J. "The Public Schools and UNESCO." *Phi Delta Kappan* 28.3 (1946) 106–8.

———. "UNESCO and Its Implications." *Phi Delta Kappan* 28.1 (1946) 11–14.

Kaestle, Carl F. *Pillars of the Republic: Common Schools and American Society.* New York: Hill and Wang, 1983.

Kansas City Christian Schools. "Christian Day School Bulletin." *Christian Day School Bulletin* (1948) 1–3.

Keinel, Paul A. "The Forces Behind the Christian School Movement." *Christian School Comment* 1.3 (1977).

———. *A History of Christian Education.* Colorado Springs: Association of Christian Schools International, 1998.

Kirby, Dianne. *Religion and the Cold War.* London: Palgrave Macmillan, 2003.

Knowles, Earl K. "The Wheaton Christian Grammar School." MA thesis, Wheaton College, 1957.

Kraushaar, Otto F. *American Non-Public Schools: Patterns of Diversity.* Baltimore: Johns Hopkins University Press, 1972.

Kuiper, Henry. "From the First Union to the Second." In *Christian Home and School,* edited by the National Union of Christian Schools, 16–18. Chicago: National Union of Christian Schools, 1954.

———. "The National Union Begins to Function." In *Christian Home and School,* edited by the National Union of Christian Schools, 16–18. Chicago: National Union of Christian Schools, 1954.

———. "A National Union of Christian Schools is Born." In *Christian Home and School,* edited by the National Union of Christian Schools, 2–3. Chicago: National Union of Christian Schools, 1954.

Kuizma, Dorr. "Michigan's Attitude Towards the Union." *Christian School,* November 1926, 243.

Lambert, Frank. *The Founding Fathers and the Place of Religion in America.* Princeton: Princeton University Press, 2003.

Layman, Jack. *Black Flight: The Emerging Black Christian Schools.* Columbia: Columbia International University, 1994.

Lazerson, Marvin. "Understanding American Catholic Educational History." *History of Education Quarterly* (1977) 297–315.

Lockerbie, D. Bruce. *The Way They Should Go.* New York: Oxford University Press, 1972.

Marsden, George M. *Fundamentalism and American Culture: The Shaping of Twentieth-Century Evangelicalism, 1870–1925.* Oxford: Oxford University Press, 1980.

Marston, Leslie R. "Evangelical Christianity in a Pagan Age." In *Program of the Fourth Annual Convention of the National Association of Evangelicals,* edited by the National Association of Evangelicals, 19–26. Chicago: National Association of Evangelicals, 1946.

———. "Report on the Committee on a Christian Philosophy of Education." In *Minutes of the Meeting of the Executive Committee of the National Association of Evangelicals,* edited by the National Association of Evangelicals, 2. Chicago: National Association of Evangelicals, 1949.

Marty, Martin E. *The Noise of the Conflict, 1919–1941.* Vol. 2 of *Modern American Religion.* Chicago: University of Chicago Press, 1991.

———. *Righteous Empire: The Protestant Experience in America.* New York: Dial, 1970.

Matheson, Kathy. "48 Catholic Schools in Philly to Close, Reorganize." *Deseret News,* January 6, 2012. https://www.deseretnews.com/article/700213090/48-Catholic-schools-in-Philly-to-close-reorganize.html.

May, Henry F. *The Divided Heart: Essays on Protestantism and the Enlightenment in America.* New York: Oxford University Press, 1991.

McClellan, B. Edward. *Moral Education in America: Schools and the Shaping of Character From Colonial Times to the Present.* New York: Teachers College Press, 1999.

McGreevy, John T. *Catholicism and American Freedom: A History.* New York: Norton and Co., 2003.

McLaughlin, Raymond. *A History of State Legislation Affecting Private Elementary and Secondary Schools in the United States, 1870–1925.* Washington, DC: Catholic University of America Press, 1946.

McLeod, Philip Donald. "The Rise of Catholic and Evangelical Christian Schools in the Nineteenth and Twentieth Centuries." PhD diss., Marquette University, 1993.

McLoughlin, William G. *Revivals, Awakenings, and Reform: An Essay on Religion and Social Change in America, 1607–1977*. Chicago: University of Chicago Press, 1978.

McQuilkin, Robert C. "How Can We Have Moral Education Without God?" *Sunday School Times*, June 5, 1948, 497–99.

Meacham, Jon. *American Gospel: God, the Founding Fathers, and the Making of a Nation*. New York: Random House, 2006.

Messerli, Jonathan. *Horace Mann: A Biography*. New York: Alfred A. Knopf, 1972.

Michaelsen, Robert. "A Case Study in Church–State Relations, Cincinnati, 1869–1870." In *Church History*, by Robert Michaelsen, 201–17. Colorado Springs, CO: Association of Christian Schools International, 1969.

———. *Piety in the Public School: Trends and Issues in the Relationship Between Religion and the Public School in the United States*. London: Macmillan Company, 1970.

Minnich, Harvey C., ed. *Old Favorites From the McGuffey Readers*. New York: American Book Co., 1936.

Mondale, Sarah, and Sarah B. Patton. *School: The Story of American Public Education*. Boston: Beacon, 2001.

Moore, R. Laurence. "Bible Reading and Nonsectarian Schooling: The Failure of Religious Instruction in Nineteenth-Century Public Education." *Journal of American History* 86.4 (2000).

———. *Religious Outsiders and the Making of Americans*. New York: Oxford University Press, 1986.

Mosley, James G. *A Cultural History of Religion in America*. Westport: Greenwood, 1981.

Murch, James DeForest. "The State Aid Menace." *United Evangelical Action*, March 15, 1947, 12.

Nasaw, David. *Schooled to Order—A Social History of Public Schooling in the United States*. New York: Oxford University Press, 1979.

National Association of Christian Schools. *Constitution of the National Association of Christian Schools*. Chicago: National Association of Christian Schools, 1949.

———. "Evangelical Christian School Movement." In *Christian School Survey*, 9. Chicago: National Association of Christian Schools, 1952.

National Association of Evangelicals. "Christian Education Report." *United Evangelical Action*, May 15, 1948, 21.

———. "Report of Committee on Policy and Fields of Endeavor." In *United We Stand: A Report of the Constitutional Convention of the National Association of Evangelicals*, edited by the Committee on Policy and Fields of Endeavor, 34–38. Boston: National Association of Evangelicals, 1943.

———. "Resolutions." In *Evangelicals Move Forward for Christ: A Report of the Eighth Annual Convention of the National Association of Evangelicals*, edited by the National Association of Evangelicals, 11. Chicago: National Association of Evangelicals, 1950.

———. "Roster of Delegates at the St. Louis Conference." In *Evangelical Action! A Report of the Organization of the National Association of Evangelicals for United Action*, edited by the National Association of Evangelicals, 92–100. Boston: United Action, 1942.

———. "What Next?" In *Evangelical Action! A Report of the Organization of the National Association of Evangelicals for United Action*, edited by the National Association of Evangelicals, 129. Boston: United Action, 1942.

National Center for Education Statistics. "Enrollment and Instructional Staff in Catholic Elementary and Secondary Schools by Level, 1919–1920 through 2009–2010." https://www.nces.ed.gov/programs/digest/d17/tables/dt17_205.70.asp.

National Education Association. *Research Bulletin*. Washington, DC: National Education Association, 1949.

National Union of Christian Schools. "Proceedings of Annual Business Meeting." In *Proceedings of Annual Business Meeting*, 34–35. Grand Rapids, MI: National Union of Christian Schools, 1946.

———. "Proceedings of the Board of Directors." In *Proceedings of the Board of Directors*, 141–44. Grand Rapids: National Union of Christian Schools, 1947.

Nettleton, Tully. "First Amendment Defense Mapped; Cost of Sectarian Aid Spotlighted." *Christian Science Monitor*, April 14, 1948, 13.

Nevin, David, and Robert E. Bills. *The Schools That Fear Built: Segregationist Academies of the South*. Washington, DC: Acropolis, 1976.

Nordin, Virginia Davis, and William Lloyd Turner. "More Than Segregation Academies: The Growing Protestant Fundamentalist Schools." *Phi Delta Kappan* 62.3 (1980) 392.

Ockenga, Harold J. "America Pay Attention or Beware!" In *Emergency Sermons for the Nation*, by Harold J. Ockenga, 48–55. Boston: John W. Shaeffer and Co., 1939.

———. "Boston Minister Gives Views on Roman Catholic Aims." *The Christian Science Monitor*, May 4, 1945, 9.

———. "Christ for America." *United Evangelical Action*, May 4, 1943, 3–5.

———. "Christ for America." In *United We Stand: A Report of the Constitutional Convention of the National Association of Evangelicals*, edited by the National Association of Evangelicals, 9–16. Boston: National Association of Evangelicals, 1943.

———. "The Unvoiced Multitudes." In *Evangelical Action! A Report of the Organization of the National Association of Evangelicals for United Action*, edited by the National Association of Evangelicals, 19–39. Boston: United Action, 1942.

Paine, Stephen W. "Report of the Commission of Christian Educational Institutions." In *Program of the Fourth Annual Convention of the National Association of Evangelicals*, edited by the National Association of Evangelicals, 57–59. Chicago: National Association of Evangelicals, 1946.

———. "Report of the Commission on Christian Educational Institutions." In *Onward From Omaha! A Report of the Fifth Annual Convention of the National Association of Evangelicals*, edited by the Executive Committee of the National Association of Evangelicals, 7. Chicago: National Association of Evangelicals, 1947.

———. "Report of the Commission on Christian Educational Institutions." In *Progress at Minneapolis: The Report of the Fourth Annual Convention of the National Association of Evangelicals*, edited by the Executive Committee of the National Association of Evangelicals, 55–57. Chicago: National Association of Evangelicals, 1946.

———. "Report of the Policy Committee." In *Evangelical Action! A Report of the Organization of the National Association of Evangelicals for United Action,* edited by the Executive Committee of the National Association of Evangelicals, 101–15. Boston: United Action, 1942.

Parsons, Paul F. *Inside America's Christian Schools*. Macon: Mercer University Press, 1987.

"Peak is Attained in Church Schools." *New York Times*, May 2, 1952, 8.

Perko, F. Michael. "Catholics and Their Schools from a Culturist Perspective." *New Catholic World* (1987) 124–29.

Perrett, Geoffrey. *A Dream of Greatness: The American People, 1945–1963*. New York: Coward, McCann, and Geoghegan, 1979.

Phoenix Christian Preparatory School. "About." http://www.phoenixchristian.org/about.

"The Pierce Case." *Catholic Sentinel*, June 4, 1925, 1.

Plumstead Christian School. "History." http://www.plumsteadchristian.org/about_history.php.

Postma, Richard. "School Board." In *Christian Home and School*, edited by the National Union of Christian Schools, 7. Chicago: National Union of Christian Schools, 1932.

Provenzo, Eugene F. *Religious Fundamentalism and American Education: The Battle for the Public Schools*. Albany: State University of New York Press, 1990.

Pulliam, John D., and James J. Van Patten. *History of Education in America*. Upper Saddle River: Merrill Prentice Hall, 2003.

Randall, E. Vance. "Religious Schools in America." In *Religion and Schooling in Contemporary America: Confronting our Cultural Pluralism*, edited by Thomas C. Carper and James C. Hunt, 83–105. New York: Garland, 1997.

Rausch, David A. *Arno Gaebelein, 1861–1945: Irenic Fundamentalist and Scholar*. New York: Edwin Mellen, 1983.

Ravitch, Diane. *The Troubled Crusade: American Education, 1945–1980*. New York: Basic, 1983.

"The Real Issue." *Catholic Sentinel*, August 10, 1922, 4.

Reed, James E., and Ronnie Prevost. *A History of Christian Education*. New York: Broadman and Holman, 1993.

"Religious Instruction in Co-operation with the Public Schools." *School Review* 12.4 (1926) 170–74.

"Religious Instruction in Public School." *The Educational Review* 21.3 (1923) 170–72.

"Religious Instruction and Public Education." *School and Society* 2.5 (1916).

Riverside Christian Day School. "School History." https://wcss.org/about-us/history.

Rose, Susan. *Keeping Them Out of the Hands of Satan: Evangelical Schooling in America*. New York: Routledge, Chapman, and Hall, 1988.

Rury, John L. *Education and Social Change: Contours in the History of American Schooling*. New York: Routledge, 2008.

Rushdoony, Rousas J. *Intellectual Schizophrenia: Culture, Crisis, and Education*. Philadelphia: Presbyterian and Reformed, 1961.

Sandeen, Ernest R. *The Origins of Fundamentalism*. Philadelphia: Fortress, 1968.

Schafer, Axel R. "The Cold War State and the Resurgence of Evangelicalism: A Study of the Public Funding of Religion Since 1945." *Radical History Review* (2007) 19–49.

Selke, George A. "Education for Moral and Spiritual Values." In *Proceedings of 88th Annual Meeting*, edited by the National Education Association, 172–73. Washington, DC: National Education Association, 1950.

Sheldon, Preston King. "Protestants Hail New Type Schools." *New York Times*, January 15, 1950, 53.

Silk, Mark. *Spiritual Politics: Religion and America Since World War II*. New York: Simon and Schuster, 1988.

Simmons, Brian S. *Worth It: The 15,000-Hour Decision*. Colorado Springs: Purposeful Design, 2011.

Simpson, Frances. "The Development of the National Organization of Christian Schools." PhD diss., Southwestern Baptist Theological Seminary, 1955.

Sisson, Edward O. "Teaching Religion in Public Schools is Playing with Fire." *The Nation's Schools*, June 1945, 43–44.

Skaife, Robert A. "The Sound and the Fury." *Phi Delta Kappan* 34.9 (1953) 357–62.

Smith, Christian. *Christian America? What Evangelicals Really Want*. Berkeley: University of California Press, 2000.

Smith, Wilbur M. *The Increasing Peril of Permitting the Dissemination of Atheistic Doctrines on the Part of Some Agencies of the United States Government*. Chicago: Van Kampen, 1947.

———. "A Program for World Education—Without God." *Moody Monthly* 47.8 (1947) 532.

———. "We're Footing the Bill for Atheism." *Moody Monthly* 47.11 (1947) 747.

Spring, Joel. *The American School: From Puritans to No Child Left Behind*. Boston: McGraw Hill, 2008.

"Statistics on Non-Public Secondary Schools." In *Biennial Survey of Education, 1946–48*, 6–7. Washington, DC: US Office of Education, 1948.

Stevens, Jason W. *God-Fearing and Free: A Spiritual History of America's Cold War*. Cambridge: Harvard University Press, 2010.

"Suburb to Hail $80,000 School in 3 Day Jubilee." *Chicago Daily Tribune*, November 22, 1951, 6.

Sutton, Matthew Avery. "Was FDR the Antichrist? The Birth of Fundamentalist Antiliberalism in a Global Age." *Journal of American History* (2012) 1052–74.

Taylor, Clyde W. "NAE Celebrates 30 Years of Service." *Action* (1972) 8–9.

———. "Report from the Committee on Christian Liberty of the National Association of Evangelicals." In *Meeting of the Committee on Christian Liberty*, edited by the Executive Committee of the National Association of Evangelicals, 5–6. Washington, DC: National Association of Evangelicals, 1948.

Thayer, V. T. "Bondage Through Education." *Nation's Schools* 35.5 (1945) 51–52.

Tucker, Ramona Cramer. *Wheaton Christian Grammar School: Training and Nurturing Children for Godliness and Excellence*. Wheaton: Wheaton Christian Grammar School, 2006.

Tyack, David, and Elizabeth Hansot. *Managers of Virtue: Public School Leadership in America, 1820–1980*. New York: Basic, 1982.

Tyack, David, et al. "State Government and American Public Education: Exploring the 'Primeval Forest.'" *History of Education Quarterly* 26 (1986) 39–69.

"UNESCO." *Phi Delta Kappan* 27.4 (1945) 102.

"UNESCO and You." *Phi Delta Kappan* 29.2 (1947) 62–65.

United Evangelical Action. "Bill Proposes Federal Aid for Schools." *United Evangelical Action*, July 16, 1945, 10.

———. "Christian Day School Survey is Under Way." *United Evangelical Action*, December 15, 1947, 20.

———. "Fakkema in West for Christian Day Schools." *United Evangelical Action*, March 1, 1948, 16.

United States Department of the Interior. *Biennial Survey of Education, 1928–1930, Bulletin 1931*. Washington, DC: United States Department of the Interior, 1932.

Urban, Wayne J., and Jennings L. Wagoner, Jr. *American Education: A History*. New York: Routledge, 2009.

Van Bruggen, John. "At the Crossroads." In *Christian Home and School*, edited by the National Union of Christian Schools, 7. Chicago: National Union of Christian Schools, 1947.

Vander Ark, John A. *22 Landmark Years: Christian Schools International, 1943–65*. Grand Rapids: Baker, 1983.

————. "Tribute to an NUCS Founder." In *Christian Home and School*, edited by the National Union of Christian Schools, 6–10. Chicago: National Union of Christian Schools, 1970.

Vineland Christian School. "Certificate of Incorporation of the Christian School Association of Vineland, New Jersey." Official Document. Vineland. September 24, 1948.

Warren, Frank H. "Education Without Christ Public Enemy Number One." *United Evangelical Action*, July 1, 1946, 3–8.

Waterman, Leroy. "Without Religion Education is Incomplete." *Nation's Schools* 36.5 (1946) 53–54.

Watt, David Harrington. "The Private Hopes of American Fundamentalists and Evangelicals, 1925–1975." *Religion and Culture: A Journal of Interpretation* 22 (1991) 165–66.

Welter, Rush. *Popular Education and Democratic Thought in America*. New York: Columbia University Press, 1962.

Wheaton Christian Grammar School. "Prayer Letter." Wheaton, October 17, 1953.

Wheaton Society for Christian Instruction. *Announcing the Wheaton Christian Grammar School*. Wheaton: Wheaton Society for Christian Instruction, 1942.

Wheaton Society for Christian Instruction. "Certificate of Incorporation of The Wheaton Society for Christian Instruction." Official Document. December 2, 1942.

Whitefield, Stephen J. *The Culture of the Cold War*. Baltimore: Johns Hopkins University Press, 1991.

Wilhoit, Jim. *Christian Education and the Search for Meaning*. Grand Rapids: Baker, 1991.

Wilmington Christian School. "History of the School." http://www.wcscalif.org.

Wright, J. Elwin. "An Historical Statement of Events Leading Up to the National Conference at St. Louis." In *Evangelical Action! A Report of the Organization of the National Association of Evangelicals for United Action*, edited by the Executive Committee of the National Association of Evangelicals, 3–16. Boston: United Action, 1942.

————. "Report of the Promotional Director." In *United We Stand: A Report of the Constitutional Convention of the National Association of Evangelicals*, edited by the Executive Committee of the National Association of Evangelicals, 5–9. Boston: National Associaton of Evangelicals, 1943.

Wuthnow, Robert. *The Restructuring of American Religion: Society and Faith Since World War II*. Princeton: Princeton University Press, 1988.

Yocum, A. Duncan. "Report of the Committee on the Teaching of Democracy." In *Addresses and Proceedings of the National Education Association*, edited by the National Education Association, 505–10. Washington, DC: National Education Association, 1922.

Zetterholm, Earl E. "The Function of the State Is Such That It Should Not Educate." *National Association of Christian Schools Newsletter* (1950) 1–2.

.